Difference Matters

Second Edition

Difference Matters

COMMUNICATING SOCIAL IDENTITY

Second Edition

Brenda J. Allen

University of Colorado at Denver

Long Grove, Illinois

For information about this book, contact:
Waveland Press, Inc.
4180 IL Route 83, Suite 101
Long Grove, IL 60047-9580
(847) 634-0081
info@waveland.com
www.waveland.com

10-digit ISBN 1-57766-673-9
13-digit ISBN 978-1-57766-673-8

Printed in the United States of America

7 6 5 4

To my students,
who are also my teachers

Contents

Preface

Difference Matters: Communicating Social Identity describes and analyzes six categories of social identity that currently matter in the United States: gender, race, social class, ability, sexuality, and age. I explain how and why differences within and between those categories matter. Throughout the book, I stress how communication helps constitute social identity, and I explore relationships between social identity, discourse, and power dynamics. To illustrate impacts of social identity issues, I offer overviews of historical developments. I also focus on various contexts, with an emphasis on organizations because they are prime sites of social identity construction.

Difference Matters is appropriate for communication courses or training programs that cover any or all of the six social identity categories that I explore, and for any curricula that delve into topics such as diversity, multiculturalism, and intercultural communication. Because I highlight how humans enact difference within organizations, the book is especially appropriate for organizational communication courses at undergraduate and graduate levels. However, many other disciplines also can benefit from perspectives on communicating difference, including business administration, human resources management, organizational behavior, education, sociology, ethnic studies, gender studies, media studies, disability studies, industrial psychology, health behavioral sciences, political science, and social psychology.

While developing this text, I considered my experiences with students who struggled with learning about theories, and who wanted to cut to the chase to learn information and skills for their everyday lives. I also remembered that students tend to prefer texts that are comprehensive, but easy to understand, and that make connections to the real world. This book honors those concerns while also covering theoretical perspectives that matter to most instructors. I employ an interactive style and share stories from my life to clarify some of my points. I hope that the content and approach of this book meet the needs of students and instructors alike. To assist instructors and enhance students' learning, I have developed a Web site that contains ideas and resources for teaching difference matters: http://www.differencematters.info.

For this second edition of *Difference Matters*, I have updated statistics, incorporated recent research, and cited more examples of intersections of social identities. I also have provided new spotlights on media. In addition, I include tools throughout the text to help you to apply what you're learning.

Acknowledgments

This project was underway for several years, well before I realized that I should write a book on difference matters. During that time, many people offered invaluable inspiration, guidance, and support. Although I never can adequately express my gratitude, I wish to acknowledge their contributions.

Countless students (who also were/are my teachers) were fundamental to the first edition of this book. Among those, I especially recognize Heidi Burgett, Margarita Olivas, Karen Ashcraft, and Jennifer Simpson for exhibiting passion and commitment to learning and teaching difference matters. They also gave me invaluable feedback as the book project unfolded. In addition, research assistant Aaron Dimock located a wealth of literature that extended my scope of knowledge about social identity groups.

Many of my colleague-friends read and responded to portions of the manuscript and/or directed me to important information sources. Their input helped to deepen and strengthen the book. A million thanks to Patrice Buzzanell, Karen Tracy, George Cheney, Mark Orbe, Terry Rowden, Jim Barker, Jim Cohn, Dawn Braithwaite, Diane Grimes, Sally Thee, Omar Swartz, Phil Tompkins, Patrick Johnson, Deborah Burgess, Ralph Smith, Brett Anderson, Kurt Nordstrom, and Anna Spradlin.

A special thanks to Deborah Borisoff at New York University for extending the first invitation for me to present a guest talk about difference matters. I also am grateful to other departments and universities that invited me to present my work, including Arizona State University, Western Michigan University, the University of Utah, Wooster College, Colorado State University-Pueblo, Loyola Marymount University, Creighton University, the University of Texas-Austin, St. Edward's University, and my alma mater, Howard University.

Last in a long list of colleagues, but particularly pivotal to the completion of this project, Sonja K. Foss was instrumental from inception through publication of this book. I owe her a deep debt of gratitude.

When the publishers invited me to write a second edition, I was honored and humbled. I have been pleased with positive responses to the book, and gratified to have a second opportunity to delve into difference matters. I am extremely grateful to Ryann Dubiel and Julian Long for their research assistance for this second edition.Thanks also to Jennifer Blair, Seema Kapani, and Tre Wentling for invaluable insights.

I also greatly appreciate Jeni Ogilvie for providing fabulous editing expertise for both editions. This book is much better than it would have been without her wise and warm counsel.

Finally, thanks to my soul mate and life partner, Theodis Hall, for his steadfast support as well as his practical perspectives on difference matters.

Chapter 1

Difference and Other Important Matters

During a summer break, I exchanged pleasant e-mails with a student I had never met named Jason[1] who wanted to enroll in a critical thinking course I would be teaching in the fall. A few weeks into the class, while we were discussing how assumptions affect critical thinking, Jason confessed that when he first saw me, he was shocked that I'm black.[2] He had assumed I would be white. And, he questioned his reaction: "Does that mean I'm racist?" I assured him his response did not necessarily mean he was racist. After all, few minority professors were employed at the university. And, throughout Jason's education, none of his teachers had been black. Plus, we rarely see black women teachers or scholars on TV, in films, or in textbooks. (Have you?) So, Jason understandably was not prepared to encounter a black female college professor. His reaction to me was a good example of how we usually don't even realize we've assumed anything until something contradicts that assumption. Referring to points we had covered about critical thinking, the class and I concluded that Jason's assumption was logical.

I also assumed things about Jason. I figured he would be a young white male, based on his first name and the university's predominantly white, traditional college-aged student population. I would have been surprised if he had been a female, older, or any race except white. I hadn't even considered these subconscious expectations until Jason told me how he reacted to me.

This story implies several matters related to difference and communicating that this book addresses. First, we tend to expect certain types of people to be in certain roles. To see how this tendency works, slowly read the following list of roles, or better yet, have someone else read it to you. Notice the image that comes to your mind for each:

secretary
CEO
soldier
hair stylist
janitor
minister

welfare recipient
plastic surgeon
female impersonator
gang member
flight attendant
doctor

professional basketball player	gardener
hotel maid	special education student
manager	mail carrier
news anchor	chemist
elementary school teacher	hip-hop artist
interior decorator	nurse

For each of these, you probably pictured someone with a combination of social identities such as gender, race, social class, age, sexuality, religion, and ability status (with or without some type of disability). I think most people in the United States probably would see similar images for each role. Why do you think people might come up with comparable images?

We often expect certain individuals to play certain roles based on a relationship between context and expectations. Jason and I met one another in the late twentieth century at a predominantly white university in Colorado, where I was one of only three black women professors. I also was the first person of color on the faculty in the department where the course was offered. That context helped to shape Jason's expectations, and mine.

My story implies another point: when we interact with people, we often draw on what we expect and assume about the groups they represent to form our attitudes and to direct our behaviors. For instance, we might depend on ***stereotypes,*** oversimplified preconceptions and generalizations about members of social groups "that provide meaning and organize perceptions, inferences, and judgments about persons identified as belonging to a particular social category."[3] Jason might have assumed I was an affirmative action employee, a token hired only because I am black and female, not because I am qualified and competent. He might have expected me not to be intelligent or capable of being a professor. He also could have anticipated that I would be nurturing or aggressive. He might have unconsciously gotten these notions from a variety of sources (including the media, his family, peers, and teachers) that depict black women in stereotypical ways, for instance, as a Mammy/caretaker or as loud-mouthed and sassy.[4] Likewise, I could have drawn on negative media stereotypes of white male college students to conclude that Jason would not be a serious student. I could have presumed he was interested only in partying and doing the minimum amount of work. I might even have thought he would be prejudiced against me because I am black.

In addition to depending on insights from various sources to infer meaning about each other, Jason and I might have relied on our personal experiences with (similar) different persons. I could have reminded him of a black female coworker, or he may have resembled any number of smart, sincere white male students I have taught. We will explore these and related issues about expectations, including how and why we routinely rely on assumptions and stereotypes when we interact with others.

Another reason we might suppose that certain persons occupy particular roles (as well as the fact that certain types of persons actually *do* tend to occupy particular roles) stems from a complex history in the United States of systemic, socially reproduced inequities. For instance, the history of racial and gender discrimination in the United States helps explain the disproportionately low number of black women faculty in universities. We will explore many of these inequities as well as factors in history that help to create, maintain, challenge, and change them.

In addition to highlighting issues related to roles, social identity, and expectations, my story reveals a common misunderstanding of the meaning of "-isms" such as racism, sexism, heterosexism, ageism, ableism, and classism. Jason's concern about being racist illustrates a tendency to consider -isms simply as characteristics of a "bad person." As organizational communication scholar Jennifer Simpson observes, "This thinking, however, tends to keep the focus on -isms as individual behaviors that result from internally located meanings."[5] This attitude neglects larger, systemic forces that contribute to discrimination and prejudice. Throughout the book, we will delve into these and related issues.

My story also illustrates the value of critical thinking skills for reflecting on difference matters. Critical thinking helps you to "distinguish between fact and opinion; ask questions; make detailed observations; uncover assumptions and define their terms; and make assertions based on sound logic and solid evidence."[6] I encourage you to improve your critical thinking skills as we explore difference matters.

A final issue raised in the story is that people rarely talk openly about topics like race or racism in mixed racial groups. Is that true for you? Why or why not? In my experience, these topics often are difficult to discuss or even acknowledge in mixed company. They may arouse uncomfortable responses, such as anxiety, fear, shame, guilt, anger, frustration, hostility, or confusion. However, under the right circumstances, thinking and talking about these topics can enlighten and empower us. When we explore and express our thoughts, feelings, and experiences, we might understand ourselves, as well as others, better. We also might be more likely to enjoy effective, open communication with one another. Jason shared his concerns with me because he felt safe in our classroom. I took his question seriously, and I responded by referring to concepts we were studying in our critical thinking class. We had a productive discussion about assumptions, expectations, identity, and communication. That classroom moment marked a turning point in my career as a scholar.

Additional teaching/learning experiences with students, colleagues, friends, and family encouraged me to focus my teaching and research on social identity and interaction. Eventually, I gained enough information and confidence to write this book. I hope to offer insight that helps people of diverse social identities to communicate positively and productively within various contexts.

In this chapter, I set the stage for the rest of the book. I clarify why difference matters, after which I explain concepts that underpin the book. Then, I provide an overview of the rest of the book. To conclude, I will tell you a bit more about myself because I want you to have a sense of me as a real person.

First, though, let me explain the title of the book, beginning with the phrase, "Difference Matters."

Difference Matters

I got the idea for the book's title from a critically acclaimed book entitled *Race Matters.*[7] However, in addition to race, I discuss other categories of social identity. For our purposes, *difference*[8] refers to a characteristic of identity such as gender, race, or age. Although people frequently use the word "diversity" for such distinctions, I prefer "difference" because it aligns better with my focus. As sociologist Richard Jenkins explains: "the notion of identity simultaneously establishes two possible relations of comparison between persons or things: *similarity,* on the one hand, and *difference,* on the other."[9] He elaborates: "similarity and difference are the dynamic principles of identity, the heart of social life."[10] If we think about similarity and difference as labels on a continuum:

we might recognize that as we perceive differences between people, we also can see similarities. This perspective on identity also helps us avoid the tendency to separate things into *either/or* categories. I mean, is there anyone else in the world who is exactly the same as you, or who is totally different from you? So, our look at difference will consider how humans vary in gender, race, class, ability, sexuality, and age. Religion and nationality are also very important social identity categories. However, due to their broad scope and the space constraints of this text, I mention these identity categories throughout the text rather than in separate chapters.

As we consider each social identity category, we will investigate implications for members of dominant and nondominant groups. ***Dominant groups*** tend to have more economic and cultural power than ***nondominant groups,*** who tend to have less economic and cultural power. This perspective on identity deviates from how people tend to conceptualize difference by focusing only on the nondominant category. For instance, when you think of difference in terms of sexual orientation, what comes to your mind first, straight (heterosexual) or gay (homosexual)? I would be surprised if you said, "straight" or "heterosexual." What about race? If I said we were going to discuss difference and race, most people would think about blacks or people of color rather than whites or Caucasians. Why does this tend to happen? Usually, "different" refers to how an individual or a group varies from, or compares to, the unspoken norm of the dominant group. For example, gender often is defined by equating gender with femaleness/women, which can preclude thinking of males/men as gendered. Please understand that, in this book, "difference" refers simply to *ways that each of us can vary from one another.* We will delve into how we humans differ, and we will explore ways that those differences matter.

How do you define "matter"? As a verb, it means to be important, to be of consequence, to count, as in "Your opinion *matters* to me." As a noun, it means something of concern: "What's the *matter*?" Applying those two definitions of "matter," we will: (1) explore the idea that difference counts (it matters), and (2) examine a variety of important concerns or issues (matters) related to difference. As the title indicates, we will focus on relationships between social identity differences and communicating. Before I discuss the second part of the title (*Communicating Social Identity)*, I need to explain why difference matters enough for me to have written this book.

Why Difference Matters

Although people in the United States are alike in many ways, we need to think about how we differ, for several related reasons. First, U.S. society is changing. We are experiencing an increase in numbers of persons of color, elderly citizens, and people with disabilities. Perhaps you have heard some of the projections: by the year 2030, Hispanics, blacks, Asians, and other racial-ethnic minorities will account for one-third of the population. In addition, age will become more of a factor as baby boomers (people born between 1946 and 1964) like me become elders. For the first time in history, four different age generations comprise the workforce. This change can affect communication processes because members of each age cohort or group tend to have differing experiences, values, and interests.

As demographics change, some social identity groups and their allies have become more vocal about rights and recognition in the workforce and other sectors of society. For instance, in 1990, due in large part to social activists, Congress passed the Americans with Disabilities Act, which legislates equal access and employment opportunities for persons with disabilities. More recently, the Employment Non-Discrimination Act of 2007 (ENDA), seeks to protect employees from discrimination based on actual or perceived sexual orientation. Consequently, some organizations fear lawsuits or boycotts.

Changing demographics, increasing demands for equal access and opportunity, and fear of lawsuits or boycotts have made difference (usually called "diversity") a hot topic. Many types of organizations (from national and international corporations to government agencies to public and/or private universities) have responded with various strategies. To be competitive and to prevent charges of discrimination, organizations are striving to value diversity. Many of them are providing diversity training programs or workshops to help their members understand and address diversity issues to build stronger organizational communities. They also are implementing formal programs to hire, retain, mentor, and promote members of nondominant groups. Some organizations customize marketing and advertising to appeal to various groups, for example, by advertising products and services in Spanish as well as English. Institutions of higher education fund initiatives and programs to recruit and retain diverse faculty and students and to establish multicultural curricula. Many colleges and universities now require each student to take at least one course that concentrates on some aspect of "diversity." Have you experienced any of these?

These and other initiatives can yield important benefits. Potential rewards of valuing difference include increased creativity, productivity, and profitability; enhanced public relations; improved product and service quality; and higher job satisfaction.[11] If organizations deal effectively with difference and embrace it as a positive force rather than as something to be shunned or feared, they can optimize accomplishing their goals. For example, organizations may broaden their markets and increase profits when they seek and incorporate input from members of diverse groups.

Equally as important (if not more so), when we value differences, we can help to fulfill the United States credo of liberty and justice for all. And, we can enhance our lives. My life certainly is enriched because I enjoy relationships with many different types of family members, friends, students, and colleagues. If we take time and care to think and talk about difference, we might have productive and enjoyable interactions with one another across our differences. Unfortunately, however, numerous obstacles can block attempts to understand and value difference. These obstacles further reinforce the point that difference matters.

Obstacles to Valuing Difference

As I noted earlier, difference is a difficult, challenging topic. Efforts to address difference can arouse negative feelings from members of nondominant and dominant groups. Nondominant group members, such as women, persons of color, homosexuals, and persons with disabilities, as well as persons affiliated with certain religious groups or from particular ethnic backgrounds, may feel singled out during discussions about groups with which they identity. Students of color in predominantly white classrooms often feel pressured to represent "their" group when the class discusses race. Nondominant group members also may feel frustrated during diversity training sessions because members of dominant groups seem apathetic or hostile to them. They may appear to minimize concerns of nondominant groups, or accuse them of whining or being too sensitive.

At the same time, members of dominant groups, including men, white people, heterosexuals, and persons who do not have disabilities, may believe that nondominant group members are exaggerating. Because dominant group members may not have had similar experiences, they may downplay issues that matter to nondominant persons. Also, some dominant group members may resent the attention they think nondominant groups are receiving when the topic of diversity arises in the workplace.

Dominant group members may feel uncomfortable during diversity training or teaching sessions. Males sometimes feel like they are being attacked when the topic of "male domination" arises. White males may resent feeling blamed for the "sins of the father," such as blatant discrimination against blacks in early U.S. history: white male students have told me they were not guilty of those racist acts. Some people may not speak their true thoughts or feelings because they worry that others will perceive them to be sexist, racist, homophobic, or otherwise prejudiced against other groups. Dominant group members may feel threatened because they fear that including minorities means excluding majorities. For instance, some white people believe that initiatives like affirmative action give minority racial group members unfair advantages; they think that employers hire and promote minorities for their group-based identity rather than their individual qualifications, such as education and expertise. As people compete for jobs, changes such as downsizing, mergers, and layoffs help to compound these attitudes. As you will see, times of economic distress tend to heighten conflict between dominant and nondominant groups, with members of the dominant group often feeling more entitled.

Societal norms and tendencies also hinder efforts to deal with difference. Norms about political correctness[12] may block members of all groups from expressing themselves, as might fear of lawsuits or other reactions. Such obstacles can increase resentment. A strong norm in our society to appear objective and rational, rather than revealing our emotions, may further obstruct openness to engaging difference matters. Also, because society teaches us to "stick with" our own groups, some people might resist trying to understand or accept other groups due to fear that their group members might shun or criticize them. They may be concerned that someone from their in-group will accuse them of being inauthentic or not true to their roots.

Another norm in our society drives us to define ourselves in opposition to others, which may invite a chain reaction: "my sense of myself is built on my ability to distinguish myself from you; therefore I value the ways in which I am different from you; therefore I begin to devalue the traits that make you distinct from me."[13] This view of oneself and others can become self-perpetuating and hard to change. An individual may struggle with anticipated consequences of viewing "different" people in positive ways. She or he may feel a false need to surrender a positive sense of self in exchange for viewing an "other" more positively. For instance, a heterosexual man may feel that his manhood would be threatened if he responded favorably to a gay person or if he advocated gay rights.

I referred earlier to another tendency that can affect attitudes toward difference: Members of both nondominant and dominant groups may unconsciously connect "difference" with nondominant groups. They may view the social identity category as the defining and potentially constraining characteristic of members of nondominant groups. This attitude can divide groups and place undue responsibility for dealing with difference on one group more than another. For instance, a black male human resources director objected to allowing a white man to chair an employee diversity committee, based on the "principle" of assigning the position to someone who does not represent a minority group. He assumed that only a person of color should be in that role. The white man's qualifications and interest in the position did not seem to matter. When I presented a seminar on difference and communication as an invited guest of a communication department, only women attended; a white male professor was overheard saying to a white male colleague, "That's women's work." These examples illustrate the premise that difference is the domain only of nondominant groups and that members of nondominant groups should limit themselves to roles and issues related to their groups. This perspective also insinuates that members of nondominant groups are not qualified to do anything else. Furthermore, this mind-set can discourage majority group members from getting involved in difference matters because they might feel alienated and/or defensive.

Not only do attitudes about difference tend to focus on the nondominant "other," but they also tend to dichotomize and polarize social identity groups. That is, they often divide social identity groups into two, opposing categories. Reducing identities to two "opposites" simplifies complex constructions of social identity. Consequently, one is forced to identify oneself or someone else as "either/or." For instance, discourse about race often focuses on or implies blacks and whites. Denoting these racial groups as polar opposites may compel members of other categories to identify as either white or non-white, and to feel excluded or marginalized. A similar dynamic operates for sexuality (i.e., heterosexual or not).

Related to the tendency to categorize groups into polar opposites is the tendency to identify others and ourselves in limited, simplistic ways. We often fail to acknowledge that social identities are complex and multifaceted. We reduce a person to one or two identity labels, without considering the complex nature of everyone's identity. When I ask students to describe themselves only by listing three social identity groups they belong to, they feel frustrated. They know themselves to be *so* much more than three categories could ever portray. Yet, when we talk about this, they confess to perceiving other persons—especially those who seem "different"—in terms of only one or two facets of identity. Combined with the impulse and the expectation to align with one's "own" group, this tendency to see a person strictly as representing one or two social identity groups can diminish the possibility that the persons will try to get to know one another. These attitudes also can increase the likelihood of conflict between individuals from different groups.

Many people do not believe that difference deserves attention, and/or they view it as significant only in extreme cases. Some persons view difference as noteworthy only when an individual or a group commits blatant, overt acts of discrimination or hate, such as physical assault or murder, against a member of a nondominant group. Because we have made significant strides in dealing with various -isms, many people believe that U.S. society has overcome discrimination, despite evidence to the contrary. They do not understand that prejudice, discrimination, and stereotypes infuse our everyday interactions, often in subtle ways.

As I have explained, a complex set of barriers may prevent progress toward valuing differences between and among social identity groups.

Throughout the book, I employ several strategies for addressing these obstacles. I provide information and data from a variety of scholarly sources to disprove myths and clarify assumptions about difference matters. I also share examples of how to value and negotiate differences, and I recommend ways to deal with difficult situations. Because I understand that difference matters can be difficult, controversial, and sensitive, I speak with you in the first person, and sometimes I share my personal experiences. I acknowledge potential challenges that anyone might face, sometimes by confessing my own struggles. So, rather than take the typical approach of a textbook author who offers only rational, objective information, at times I reveal my emotions and thoughts to help you understand what I'm saying, and to model ways that you might process your thoughts and feelings.

To try to ease any concern you might have about negating your own identity because of the tendency to define self in opposition to others, I

Tool No. 1

Mindfulness

Become more mindful difference matters. What does being "mindful" mean? When you are mindful, you actively process information, you are open to new ideas and insights, and you are sensitive to context.[14] Also, mindfulness is "a heightened state of involvement and wakefulness or being in the present."[15] In other words, being mindful requires you to observe yourself in the process of thinking.[16] Put even more simply, being mindful means thinking about what you're thinking about. Becoming more mindful can help you become more sensitive to your environment, more open to new information, more conscious of how and what you perceive, and more aware of multiple perspectives for solving problems.[17]

To be more mindful about difference matters, notice and question how you categorize and characterize others. Try to notice when you are relying on stereotypes and prejudices about social identity groups. When you meet someone different than you, be aware of which social identity cues you highlight, and remember that each person embodies a complex set of social identities. Monitor your thoughts and feelings related to other people based on their gender, race, age, and so forth, *including people who belong to the same groups as you*. Cultivate curiosity about how you and others construct and perform social identities. Also pay attention to how you perceive that others are responding to you. Look for ways that you are guilty of *TUI (Thinking Under the Influence)* of dominant belief systems or stereotypes, and try to restructure your thoughts.

To *really* develop this tool, improve your critical thinking skills. Consider taking a course or referring to books or Web sites on critical thinking. Please see my Web site [www.differencematters.info] for links to critical thinking sites.

encourage you to define yourself in more complex ways. I invite you to reflect on how matters of difference affect and have affected your life, to become curious about how you became the person you are. I encourage you to recognize how multifaceted you are, because exploring yourself can help you to acknowledge and appreciate the complex identities of others.

To conclude, difference matters for a variety of reasons, including changing demographics, increasing demands for equality, and a related heightened interest in diversity. Although numerous obstacles might delay our progress toward valuing difference, the promise of benefits should motivate us to hurdle or remove those barriers. Now that I have explained why difference matters, next I introduce other matters that inform the remainder of the book, as implied in the second part of the title.

Communicating Social Identity

Communicating

Our study of difference (and similarity!) centers on communication. I use the verb form, *communicating*, to refer to the dynamic nature of processes that humans use to produce, interpret, and share meaning. These processes are complex, continuous, and contextual. And, they constitute our social reality.[18] To understand how communicating helps to create reality, we will explore factors related to how we communicate social identity. We will consider how various sources provide implicit and explicit messages about communication styles and norms of social identity groups and dominant beliefs (including stereotypes) related to social identity groups. We will focus on ***discourse,*** "systems of texts and talk that range from public to private and from naturally occurring to mediated forms."[19] We will investigate how discourse helped to construct social identity throughout the history of the United States. We also will review changing meanings of discourse related to social identity groups, and their impacts. For instance, varying meanings of femininity and masculinity have affected policy in medicine, law, and education. Throughout the book, we will explore ways that discourse "produces, maintains, and/or resists systems of power and inequality,"[20] especially as related to social identity. We will consider matters related to communicating social identity within and across a variety of contexts in the United States, where structural circumstances have varied widely across history.

We will study interactions between and among members of social identity groups in a variety of interpersonal, group, and institutional/organizational settings. I highlight organizations because we spend so much time within them, and because they play pivotal roles in difference matters. Although most persons might think about organizations as large, for-profit businesses such as corporations, I take a broader perspective that spans a wide range, including large corporations, government agencies and institutions, small businesses, nonprofit groups, sports franchises, hospitals, advocate/

activist groups, educational institutions, religious institutions, restaurants, social groups (sororities, fraternities), and so forth.

We spend most of our days dealing with organizations as customers, clients, constituents, consumers, congregants, coworkers, employees, patients, students, and representatives, to name several roles. Also, we learn much of what we know about social identities (ours and others') in organizational settings, such as school, church, health care facilities, and at work. Conflict and controversy related to social identity groups usually center on organizations: demands for and disputes about equal employment opportunity and access, education, health care, benefits, and media depictions all implicate various types of organizations. Matters of difference increasingly are apparent and important in organizations, because members of different social identity groups are likely to interact more frequently. Due to population projections, we are more likely now than ever to encounter differences in those settings. Furthermore, as nondominant members of social identity groups continue to gain access to roles they traditionally have not held, we are likely to encounter them/us in unexpected roles, as when Jason and I met.

We often identify ourselves based on organizational relationships and roles. For instance, I am a professor (at a university) and a volunteer (at an elementary school). As members of organizations perform their roles, they also make friends and enemies, gossip, indulge in romances, advance themselves professionally and personally, and endure a variety of conflicts. A final reason for highlighting organizations regards power dynamics, which I discuss in chapter 2. Power dynamics drive the communication processes that constitute organizations and societies, as different groups strive to serve their own interests and to control various resources.

In addition to organizations, I discuss media and their pivotal roles in communicating social identity. In each social identity chapter, I highlight a specific form of media and how it matters to that category.

Social Identity

Identity refers to an individual and/or a collective aspect of being. Sociologists Judith Howard and Ramira Alamilla observe that identity is based not only on responses to the question "Who am I?" but also on responses to the question "Who am I in relation to others?"[21] We will focus on *social identity,* aspects of a person's self-image derived from group-based categories. Most human beings divide their social worlds into groups, and categorize themselves into some of those groups. In addition, we become aware of other social groups to which we do not belong, and we compare ourselves to them. We often define ourselves in opposition to others: "I know who I am because I am not you."[22] Thus, ***social identity*** refers to "the ways in which individuals and collectivities are distinguished in their social relations with other individuals and collectivities."[23]

Social identity differs from personal identity, one's sense of self in terms of variables such as personality traits. For instance, a person may be characterized as "shy" or "outgoing." However, "a person's self actually consists of a personal identity and multiple social identities, each of which is linked to different social groups."[24] An individual can "belong" to numerous social identity groups. Some of my social identities are: professor, black, woman, wife, homeowner, U.S. citizen, heterosexual, baby boomer, middle-class, Steelers fan, executive coach, and volunteer. Although infinite possibilities exist for categories of social identity groups, I focus in this book on six that are especially significant in contemporary society: gender, race, social class, ability, sexuality, and age.

As we consider difference matters and social identity, two important ideas to remember are: (1) identity is relational and (2) human beings develop their social identities primarily through communicating.[25] This perspective represents the ***social constructionist*** school of thought, which contends that "self is socially constructed through various relational and linguistic processes."[26] In other words, "our identity arises out of interactions with other people and is based on language."[27] Let's look at how communicating helps to construct social identities.

From the time we are born (and even prior to birth, due to tests that determine a baby's sex or congenital defects), socially constructed categories of identity influence how others interact with us (and vice versa) and how we perceive ourselves. When a child is born, what do people usually want to know? Generally, they ask if "it" is a boy or a girl. Why is the sex of the child so important? Sex matters because it cues people on how to treat the baby. If the newborn is a girl, relatives and friends may buy her pink, frilly clothes and toys designated for girls. Her parent(s) or guardian(s) may decorate her room (if she's fortunate enough to have her own room) or sleep area in "feminine" colors and artifacts. These actions and others will help to "create a gendered world which the infant gradually encounters and takes for granted as her social consciousness dawns, and which structures the responses to her of others."[28]

And that's just the beginning. As she grows up, she will receive messages from multiple sources, including family members, teachers, peers, and the media about what girls are allowed and supposed to do (as contrasted with boys). This process is known as ***socialization,***

> the total set of experiences in which children become clear about norms and expectations and learn how to function as respected and accepted members of a culture . . . children are socialized at both conscious and unconscious levels to internalize the dominant values and norms of their culture, and in so doing, develop a sense of self.[29]

The same scenario applies for a male. He, too, will receive numerous messages, blatant and subtle, that will mold his self-perception. Simultaneously, both female and male children will learn about additional identity categories like race, ethnicity, class, ability, age, sexuality, and religion. What they learn may vary depending on their identity composites. For instance, a

Jewish boy in a working-class family probably will be socialized differently than a Latino Catholic in a middle-class family, even as they each may receive similar messages about being male. Meanwhile, an able-bodied Asian American boy probably will receive different messages than a white boy labeled as "developmentally challenged," even as all of these males receive comparable lessons about masculinity in general. These individuals also will learn communication styles particular to their groups, such as vocabulary, gestures, eye contact, and use of personal space.

As these children become indoctrinated into social identity groups, they will receive information about other groups, including contrasts between groups, and "rules" for interacting (or not) with members of other groups. They will learn stereotypes about groups, and they may accept these stereotypes as facts. They also will learn about hierarchies of identity. They may learn that being young is more desirable than being elderly, or that being heterosexual is preferable to being gay. These and other "lessons" about distinctions between and within groups will recur throughout their lives—and the lessons may contradict one another.

Due to socialization, children will accept social identity categories as real and natural. Yet, they are not. Persons in power across history have constructed categories and developed hierarchies based on group characteristics. In 1795, a German scientist named Johann Blumenbach[30] constructed a system of racial classification that arranged people according to geographical location and physical features. He also ranked the groups in hierarchical order, placing Caucasians in the most superior position.

Although scientists have since concluded that race is not related to capability, many societies in the world still adhere to various racial classification systems because the idea of race has become essentialized. ***Essentialism*** refers to assumptions that social differences stem from intrinsic, innate, human variations unrelated to social forces. For example, so-called racial groups are viewed as if they have an "ultimate essence that transcends historical and cultural boundaries."[31]

Thus, while we accept social identity groups as real and natural, we also perceive them as fixed (essentialized) and unchanging. However, these categories are not only artificial, but they also are subject to change. In different times and different places, categories we take for granted either did/do not exist or they were/are quite unlike the ones that we reference in the United States in the twenty-first century. Currently, the same person identified as black in the United States may be considered white in the Dominican Republic; in the nineteenth century choices for racial designations in the United States included gradations of enslaved blacks: mulattos were one-half black, quadroons were one-quarter black, and octoroons were one-eighth black.[32]

To develop these types of categories, human beings often refer to physical or physiological distinctions. It's logical to compartmentalize humans according to physical characteristics. If we did not have labels to distinguish groups of items that are similar, we would have to create and remember a separate "name" for everything and everyone. What a challenge that would be! Therefore, it makes sense that we use cues like skin color, facial features, body parts, and so forth to distinguish and group people.

However, problems can arise when people assign meaning to neutral descriptors. They may use categories not only to distinguish but also to discriminate and dominate. Categorizing can lead to in-group/out-group distinctions that may negatively affect intergroup interactions. For instance, ***social identity theory*** (SIT) describes humans' tendency to label self and others based on individual and group identity.[33] SIT contends that members of social identity groups constantly compare their group with others, and they try to show that their group is positively distinct. When an individual perceives someone else to be a member of an out-group, that person will tend to react more to perceived *group* characteristics than to the other person *as an individual.* Stereotypes and prejudice occur more frequently in this scenario. In contrast, stereotypes and prejudice are less likely when a communicator views another person as an individual, especially when both persons belong to the same social identity group(s).

As I noted earlier, individuals often use identity markers like skin color to develop hierarchies. Moreover, many people accept and reinforce such hierarchies as natural and normal. Organizational communication scholars Charles Conrad and Marshall Scott Poole explain: "As people *internalize* the values and assumptions of their societies they also internalize its class, race, gender, and ethnicity-based hierarchical relationships."[34] These perceptions facilitate the social construction of inequality, which results in favoritism and privilege for some groups and disadvantage for others. Thus, for instance, regardless of level of education and even with similar qualifications, men of all races in the United States generally earn higher salaries than women of all races, and whites earn more than members of other racial/ethnic groups.

One way to understand differences in status based on social identity is the concept of ***privilege.*** Sociologist Peggy McIntosh coined this term to refer to men's advantages in society, based on her experiences teaching women's studies.[35] McIntosh noticed that while men in her classes were willing to concede women's disadvantages, they were unaware of advantages they enjoyed simply because they were men. She later extended her analysis to encompass race, and she developed the concept of white privilege, which I discuss in chapter 4.

In case you're not familiar with this concept, one way to think about privilege is handedness. Are you right-handed or left-handed? Did you know that people used to consider being left-handed as deviant, sinister, and dangerous? I'm left-handed, and one of my elementary teachers tried to change me to being right-handed. Of course, Ma didn't allow that. In our society, being right-handed is the dominant expectation. Although neither of these is better than the other, we have structured society in favor of right-handed people (primarily because of numbers). And, right-handed people rarely are aware of the benefits they receive as they move around in a right-hand world. They enjoy the privilege of not knowing, until someone points it out. As a lefty, I often have awkward moments with tools, utensils, scissors, desks, and other things designed for right-handed people. And, people have told me, "Your handwriting looks good, for a lefty." We use our right hand to pledge allegiance to the flag, to shake hands when we meet someone, and to take oaths. Right-handed people can't avoid the benefits of being right-handed. We all inherited a system handedness that benefits some and disadvantages others.[36]

So, privilege tends to "make life easier; it is easier to get around, to get what one wants, and to be treated in an acceptable manner."[37] On the Public Broadcasting System's video *People Like Us*, which explores social class in the United States, a white male plumber describes how sales clerks tend to treat men in suits better than they respond to him when he wears his work clothes. Similarly, a working-class college student reported that he would change out of his work clothes before going to campus because he felt that faculty and staff treated him less favorably when he wore them.[38]

Privilege allows people to be oblivious to how their lives differ from others'. Members of privileged social identity groups often don't recognize their advantages. In fact, they may assume that others enjoy similar experiences to theirs. For instance, I never thought about my heterosexual privilege until a coworker friend told me she was a lesbian and began to describe the many challenges she has faced because of her sexual orientation. I just didn't know how privileged I was. Before I got married, I could easily discuss my [heterosexual] dates or romantic relationships during small talk at work. Now that I am married, I often discuss how my husband and I spent the weekend, our plans for vacations, and so forth. If I wanted to, I could put our wedding photo on my desk without thinking twice, especially since we're the same race and about the same age. Yet, persons who are not heterosexual may hesitate to engage in such activities because they fear verbal abuse, ostracism, being fired, or even physical assault. Even if none of these ever happened, some homosexuals live with the persistent perception that *these reactions might happen.*

This potential difference in perceiving the world related to social identity can inhibit interactions between privileged and nonprivileged persons. A person who is not privileged (or who does not feel privileged) may seem hypersensitive to an individual who is privileged. In contrast, the person who is privileged (or whom the other person perceives to be privileged) may seem hyper*insensitive.* Privileged individuals sometimes diminish, dismiss, or discount experiences of others who are not advantaged. If a privileged person witnesses or hears about an incident where someone demeans or humiliates a less privileged person, she or he may interpret the incident as an exception rather than the rule. That person also may accuse the less-privileged person of overreacting or misinterpreting the situation. When I assign my friend Anna Spradlin's article[39] on the challenges she faced as a lesbian passing as heterosexual at work, some students respond with comments such as, "She's making a big deal out of nothing," or "She shouldn't care what others [her students and colleagues] think." Of course, that's easy for them to say. Discussions about privilege among nondominant and dominant groups can be productive when each "side" tries to understand the other's perspectives and experiences.

To elaborate on the idea of privilege, most of us simultaneously occupy privileged and nonprivileged social identity groups. Although I may experience or anticipate discrimination based on my race, gender, and age, I also can reap benefits associated with being heterosexual, able-bodied, educated, and middle-class. I also enjoy the privilege of speaking English as my native language, and being able to read and write. We will consider the concept of privilege and its complexities as we study gender, race, class, ability, sexuality, and age. For now, I hope that you have a basic understanding of the concept of privilege (if it's new to you) and that you can see how privilege helps to construct and maintain inequalities.

Another consequence of internalizing dominant values and assumptions about social identity groups is that members of nondominant groups often help to perpetuate hierarchies because they believe that their group is inferior and that the dominant group is superior. Accepting these ideas and believing negative stereotypes about one's group is known as ***internalized oppression.***[40] When I was a little girl, my friends and I used to sing: "When you're white, you're right; when you're brown, stick around; but when you're black, oooh baby, get back, get back, get back." We had internalized a hierarchy of skin color, or *colorism.*[41] Sadly, this attitude persists: a dark-skinned black employee alleged that his light-skinned Black supervisor called him a "tar baby," "black monkey," and "jig-a-boo," and told him he needed to bleach his skin.[42]

To summarize, social identities emerge mainly from social interactions. We learn from a variety of sources about who we are and who we might become, mainly through interacting with others. We also learn about other groups. We learn communication styles and rules based on our membership in certain groups, and we communicate with other people based on how we have been socialized about ourselves and about them. As we interact, we are subject to biases and expectations about social identities that can affect what, how, when, why, and whether or not we communicate. And, most interactions occur within established normative contexts where members of groups tend to be more or less privileged than others.

About Me

Before I outline the remainder of the book, I want to tell you more about myself, to show how some of the points I've raised operate in my life, and to give you a better sense of who I am. As you read this abbreviated autobiography, notice how it exemplifies many of the issues I've mentioned, including the social construction of social identity, intersections of social identities, privilege, the role of context, and communication processes.

In the 1950s and 1960s, I grew up in Ohio in a small apartment in the Youngstown Metropolitan Housing Authority ("the projects") with my mother, my brother, and my sister. I was a toddler when my family moved into the projects after my father died. Residents of the projects comprised a well-known social identity group in Youngstown, and many of us are proud of having grown up in what we fondly call "Brick City." Since the projects were restricted to low-income families (most of whom were black), I was aware at an early age of being a member of a specific social economic class. Thanks to the Red Feather Agency (which the state government administered) and the city-funded community center, my friends and I enjoyed a variety of organized, year-round recreational activities (including arts and crafts, camp, drill team, variety shows, and sports). Although I was athletically inclined, I received subtle messages that discouraged me from pursuing my talents. Only a few sports activities in school were reserved for girls. And, because I was labeled as "smart," I learned that I shouldn't also aspire to be an athlete. In those days, people classified you as either one or the other. It seemed that you couldn't be both. I was tracked according to IQ, and placed in advanced classes in junior high and high school. I usually was the only black girl in those classes, along with one black boy and our white classmates. Because I was on the Honor Roll, I believed that I could go to college even though no one in my family had ever done so. However, I knew that my mother couldn't afford to send me. So, to prepare for life after high school graduation, I completed both college preparatory and secretarial skills courses. Those secretarial skills have come in handy throughout my life!

My mother instilled a strong work ethic in my siblings and me. She always worked hard for the money to take care of us, initially as a maid and eventually as a clerk for the U.S. Post Office. I believed without thinking about it that I would have to work all of my life. When I was a little girl, I wanted to be either a teacher or a nurse when I grew up. Based on messages from teachers and community members, those seemed the only options for a smart colored girl like me. From an early age, I worked at various jobs, on my own initiative. I earned money by babysitting, going to the store for elderly neighbors, or taking out their trash.

During high school, I worked for the federal government's Comprehensive Education and Training Agency, which assigned jobs and paid minimum wage to teenagers from low-income families. Fortunately, one of my jobs was to assist the guidance counselors at my school. Although I was a star pupil, neither the guidance counselors nor any of my teachers encouraged me or informed me about applying to colleges. Why do you think that happened? Fortunately, I paid attention to my white classmates as they discussed the SAT and the ACT, and I persuaded Ma to pay for me to take those tests. While filing materials in the guidance office, I came across information about scholarships and I applied for one of them. In a city-wide competition, I won a full scholarship (yessss!). I applied to and was accepted at Case Western Reserve University, the predominantly white university that Lillian Jones, "the" smart black girl who graduated two years before me, had attended. Even though my scholarship funds would have paid for me to go to any college in the world that admitted me, I didn't even think about applying to other schools. Why do you think I didn't consider others?

My background had prepared me to do well academically and socially in college. I interacted easily with white teachers and my white dorm mates, and I participated in many social activities, sometimes with the few other black students on campus. I changed my major three times, from linguistics, to Romance languages, to speech pathology. Notice that I stuck with some type of communication. Also notice that I never pursued a major related to mathematics, even though I had been classified in junior high as math-gifted.

After graduating from college, in a 15-year period during which I worked full-time and attended school, I earned a master's degree and a Ph.D. in organizational communication at Howard University, a historically black college in Washington, D.C. In 1989, I conducted a doctoral dissertation research project on computer-mediated communication (CMC) at the Public Broadcasting System's corporate headquarters. How I got involved in computers is another story, but it's related to my math skills.

.Also in 1989, I was recruited to teach and conduct research on CMC at the University of Colorado at Boulder. Although I was qualified for the position, being a black woman was an important factor in my recruitment and hiring, because the university was actively trying to increase its numbers of minority faculty and women. In 1995, due to a variety of experiences (including the moment with Jason I told you about earlier), I changed my research emphasis to social identity and communication. That same year, I earned tenure (yessss!) and was promoted to Associate Professor. In the Fall of 2001, I accepted a position in the Department of Communication at the University of Colorado–Denver. In the fall of 2003, I became chair of the department. I was promoted to Professor in 2004, and in 2007, I became an Associate Dean in the College of Liberal Arts and Sciences.

Throughout the book, I share more information and stories about myself. I am not trying to brag or to gain pity. I just want you to have a sense of me so that reading the book feels more like interacting with a person than simply viewing printed words. I also provide personal examples to illustrate some of the issues I cover; my examples might model ways for you to explore your experiences. I wish that I could know about you, too. I love getting messages from readers. Feel free to send me e-mail about yourself or your responses to the book. My e-mail address is: brenda.j.allen@ucdenver.edu.

Overview of the Book

In chapter 2, I continue to establish the foundation for the book by defining and describing *power dynamics* and their relationship to difference matters. Chapters 3–8 each concentrate on one of six significant aspects of social identity in U.S. society: gender, race, social class, ability, sexuality, and age. Although each chapter foregrounds one aspect of identity, please remember that social identities are complex and multifaceted. I highlight one category per chapter to illuminate issues and information that are especially relevant to that social identity. However, I urge you *always* to consider that intersections of social identity also matter. To emphasize that idea, I discuss differing consequences and issues for overlapping social identities.

In each social identity chapter I trace the sociohistorical construction of the highlighted category. Although discussing history may seem unusual in a book about communication, I cover history to help you understand social construction and to demonstrate how context matters in communicating constructs of social identities. I want to provide evidence that the social identity categories we assume to be natural and fixed are actually artificial and possible to change.

I also share history to punctuate the point that "past is prologue." People sometimes say about topics like race and gender that we should put the past behind us. However, we need to examine the past to understand its impact on the present and to guide us into the future. By the end of the book, you should recognize commonalities of consequences of social constructions, including privilege for some persons and disadvantage for others, as well as recurring and persistent efforts to change society by members of dominant and nondominant groups.

Insight and information related to history might help you to reflect on your attitudes, beliefs, and assumptions about difference. When you realize that social identity categories can change, you may reconsider some of your attitudes, beliefs, and assumptions, about yourself as well as others. Also, the stories of individuals and groups who imagined and worked to attain social justice might inspire you. I sure hope so.

Each social identity chapter presents examples of relationships between the highlighted identity and communication processes. From the wealth of information that exists, I offer just enough to enlighten you and to stimulate you to learn more. I discuss numerous types of contexts and I refer to a variety of disciplines, including communication, history, sociology, psychology, economics, women's studies, ethnic studies, business, organizational behavior, and anthropology.

I also spotlight research about mass media because they permeate U.S. society. They depict interpretations of social reality, and they socialize us about social identity groups. Media portrayals of social identity groups can influence how we orient to our own as well as other social identity groups. We often receive preliminary information about social identity groups other than our own through mass media rather than through meaningful interpersonal interaction. The media also help to disseminate, shape, and reinforce dominant belief systems, stereotypes, and cultural ideals. On the plus side, media also portray and report resistance to inequalities. They also offer realistic portrayals of nondominant groups.

I tend to concentrate on nondominant groups in each social identity category, primarily to shed light on issues that rarely receive attention. However, I also consider issues and implications for dominant group members. I try neither to bash members of dominant groups nor to idealize nondominant groups. I want members *of all groups* to see themselves as participants in social systems and networks that privilege some people and penalize others. While you did not construct those networks, you inherited them. You can challenge them, and you can even try to change them. I hope that this book helps you to realize that you can choose how you view and do difference. I also hope it provides a blueprint for how to do so.

I share a few "tools" to help you improve how you communicate social identity. These tools can aid intrapersonal, interpersonal, and organizational communication about difference matters. Like all tools, they are optional. You can choose to use them or not, depending on the task at hand. To help you process what you read, I include in each chapter an "ID Check" to allow you to engage in intrapersonal communication. That's right, I want you to talk to yourself! After all, intrapersonal communication matters, too. I also include "Reflection Matters" in each chapter to encourage you to delve into issues that the chapter covers. In the final chapter, I conclude the book and recommend next steps.

Now that I've told you what to expect from the book, I invite you to take a moment to reflect on what you might gain by reading and reflecting on the topics we will cover. I also urge you to open your mind and heart to becoming more aware of how you communicate social identity. Best wishes.

ID Check

1. How do you identify in each of the six social identity categories (gender, race, social class, age, ability, sexuality)? Other categories to list are religion, nationality, and native language.
2. From #1, how many of these place you in dominant categories? How many in nondominant? For religion, nationality, and native language, please consider which tend to dominate in your current context. For instance, English as a native language dominates in the United States.
3. Have you ever been aware of privilege because of any of your dominant social identity categories? Explain.
4. Have you ever felt disadvantaged because of any of your nondominant social identity categories? Explain.
5. Have you ever felt discriminated against because of any of your nondominant or dominant social identity categories?

Reflection Matters

1. What issues raised in this chapter, if any, do you find intriguing? Why?
2. Do you agree that the six categories we're covering are especially important in the United States? Why or why not?

3. Of the six categories that we will cover, which, if any, are most important to you personally? Why?
4. Has "difference" according to the social identity groups with which you identify ever mattered in your life? If yes, in what ways did difference(s) matter?
5. If you had to describe yourself using the labels of only three social identity groups, which would you choose, and why? How do you feel about limiting your description of yourself to three categories?
6. How does the sociohistorical context in which I grew up seem to have affected how my life unfolded? For instance, does the time period of the 1950s and 1960s, or the geographical location of a housing project in Ohio, seem to matter?
7. My brief autobiography demonstrates potential influences of organizations and people in organizational roles on social identity development. For instance, when educators assigned me to an academic track, they reinforced my sense of being a smart black girl. As teachers, peers, and community members affirmed that sense of my self, I became confident and competent in interactions with diverse types of people, particularly black and white peers and white teachers. To explore how organizations or people within organizations have affected your identity development, divide your life into segments, beginning with your birth. For each segment, identify at least one or two organizations (or member[s] of an organization) that affected your social identity development, and explain the effect(s). If you are 35 years old or younger, divide your life into 7-year segments; if you are over 35, divide your life into 10-year segments.
8. In addition to anyone you described in question #7, what other persons in your life have influenced your self-concept? Do you think that your gender, race, age, ability, social class, sexuality, nationality, religion, or intersections of any of these affected how these persons interacted with you, and how you interacted with them? Explain.
9. What do you think of the statement that "-isms," such as sexism, racism, ageism, "are merely behaviors of a 'bad' person"?
10. Have you talked about social identity categories in mixed groups (e.g. talking about race in a multiracial group)? If so, explain the circumstances, and describe your feelings and responses.
11. Have you talked about "others" in homogeneous groups (for instance, in a group of women talking about men, or straight people talking about gay people)? If so, explain the circumstances and describe your feelings and responses.
12. Have you ever experienced any of the obstacles to valuing difference that I cited? Explain.

13. To illustrate how much organizations matter, keep track for one weekday all of the organizations that directly or indirectly influence your life. From the time that you wake up until you go to bed, keep a list of those organizations (or types of organizations). Also keep track of your communication interactions during the day.
    a. Write the list of organizations.
    b. List the communication interactions that you engaged in that took place either within an organization, or with someone representing an organization.
    c. If any of those interactions were cross-cultural, describe them.

• • • • Chapter 2 • • • •

Power Matters

When I was about 25 years old I worked as a secretary in the research division of a national association in Washington, D.C. Two other women in their twenties and I sat at adjacent desks in an open area facing the offices of the male research associates for whom we worked. Betty,[1] the executive secretary, sat at the front of the room. Her desk (which was larger than the other secretaries' and mine) was placed perpendicular to the entrance of the unit director's corner office, which was bigger than those of the three associates.

One time when Betty was going on a weeklong vacation, she asked me to take over her duties. As she listed my responsibilities, she told me to wash her boss's cup each morning and fill it with coffee (with cream) from the vending machine in the break room. I nodded in agreement, but I definitely did not like the idea. Surely this task wasn't listed in the job description. All weekend, the problem percolated in my mind. I just did not want to get coffee for Frank. But if I didn't, what would happen?

That Monday morning, I sat at my desk with butterflies in my stomach. Frank approached me, coffee mug in one hand, and two dimes in the other. He extended both toward me, saying softly, "Betty always gets coffee for me." My heart pounded as I looked up at him and replied softly, "I know." Three seconds later, he headed toward the vending machine area. Things went smoothly for the rest of the week and for the duration of my employment at the association. Frank even intervened on my behalf when Harold, the personnel director, denied my request to revise my work schedule to attend graduate classes. Frank went over Harold's head to ask Henrietta, the executive director of the organization, to grant my request. She agreed. I remain grateful to Frank (and Henrietta) for supporting me.

This chapter continues to set the foundation of the book by exploring matters of power and communicating social identity. Betty, Frank, Harold, Henrietta, and I enacted power relationships in varying ways, for varying reasons. Our behaviors may have been based in part on our social identities. Frank was a middle-aged white male department director. Betty, his secretary, was also middle-aged and white. She had been with the association for many years, and she seemed proud of her position. Both of them probably never had questioned the practice of her serving him coffee.

In contrast, I was a young black woman, working to pay my bills as I figured out what I wanted to be when I grew up. When I did not get coffee for Frank, I may have been acting from my standpoint as a black woman whose mother, grandmother, and great-grandmother had served white people. Maybe I wanted to break that chain. I also could have been playing the role of a budding feminist who objected to any hint of male domination. Or, perhaps I thought someone with a college degree shouldn't get coffee for anybody (what an elitist attitude).

Age also may have mattered. As a woman in my twenties, I probably didn't view my role or my life in the same way as Betty, who was in her forties (which seemed old to me then). The job was a means to an end for me, and I knew I could get another clerical position, whereas Betty seemed settled into her position. Any or all of these aspects of my identity may have affected my response. Believe me, though, I didn't analyze the situation at that time. In fact, my emotions played a much stronger role than my thoughts. It just didn't feel right. What do you think you would have done?

As I noted in chapter 1, when and where events occur can significantly affect those events. My coffee tale took place in the 1970s in Washington, D.C., when you could buy a cup of coffee for twenty cents! More important, many citizens were feeling the effects of the civil rights and women's rights movements. The fact that a first-generation female college graduate from a black working-class family was attending graduate school supports this point. Even my request to adjust my work schedule is time bound, since many organizations now routinely allow employees to work flexible hours. Throughout the book, we will explore examples of interdependent relationships between power dynamics and the sociohistorical contexts where they occur. We will use social construction theory to study ways that humans use communication to construct their realities.

This chapter presents the premise that power matters. First, we will take a close look at the concept of power and its complexities. Next, I explore how concepts known as ***hegemony*** and ***ideology*** operate to establish and maintain control and systems of domination and I describe ***critical theory,*** a useful framework for studying power dynamics. Finally, I show how we enact power relations through communication.

Conceptions of Power

Power is a complex, multidimensional concept. How do you define power? You might think of power as "ability to dominate." This viewpoint usually gives power to persons in powerful positions, which can range from the president of the United States to a boss to parent(s) or guardian(s), and to spouses or partners. Thinking of power in that way implies that certain individuals have "power over" others. The "power over" perspective casts power negatively and neglects to consider positive aspects of power. It also fails to acknowledge that power is a reciprocal process. The "power over" stance simplifies the nature of power by portraying it as overt, conscious behavior, such as using threats, promises, or orders to get what one wants. This focus on the surface overlooks deep structures of power that operate continually, unconsciously, and subtly based on norms and taken-for-granted assumptions.[2] We will study surface and deep levels of power relevant to society in general and in various organizational contexts.

Our primary perspective for studying power relations is ***critical theory.*** In case you're not familiar with this viewpoint, you may think about the everyday meaning of "being critical" as criticizing people and taking a negative approach. That's not what I mean. Critical theory provides a set of frameworks for analyzing power dynamics in society in order to make the world more equitable.[3] Critical theory seeks to liberate and emancipate members of nondominant groups by exploring how and why people comply with dominant belief systems and how they and their allies resist those systems. Critical theorists seek to raise consciousness, to help people realize how power operates. We focus on relationships between communication and structures. We acknowledge the power of communication to create and shape structures and rules and to provide means for resistance. We look at social conditions to uncover hidden power dynamics in surface and deep structures of society. Examples of critical perspectives include feminist theories, which focus on gender inequality; critical race theory, which considers legal aspects and implications of racial inequality; and postcolonial theory, which studies unequal relations between nation-states by examining the dominance of Western knowledge in many countries.

I will refer to these and other critical approaches as I rely mainly on the work of French philosopher-historian Michel Foucault, who depicted power as a behavior or process that permeates all human interaction.[4] In contrast to the "power over" stance, which implies that power occurs occasionally, Foucault asserted that "power resides in every perception, every judgment, every act."[5] Foucault contended that people enact power to produce and reproduce, resist, or transform structures of communication and meaning, in even the most mundane social practices. He used the term "relations of power" to suggest a network of systematic interconnections among people.[6]

Foucault believed that power constitutes all relationships: "We define our relationships and how we should behave in relation to each other in terms of power differences and similarities."[7] In my opening story, when Betty (as my supervisor) assigned me to be her substitute, she assumed I would imitate how she enacted the role of secretary. Frank may have expected Betty and me to get him coffee based on how he viewed the secretary–boss relationship (and maybe even the male–female relationship). Perhaps Betty started getting him coffee because she thought that she had to, or maybe she just enjoyed serving him because she liked him. Regardless of the dynamics of Betty and Fred's relationship, Betty was comfortable with this arrangement, while I was not.

Foucault believed that power can have negative *and* positive consequences. Power is not always oppressive or prohibitive; power also can be productive. Power relationships worked in my favor when Frank asked the executive director to let me change my work schedule, and when she agreed.

Power is not limited to persons in power positions; power "exists in the reciprocal relations of the haves and have-nots."[8] Although some persons are authorized to wield power, everyone engages in power practices, including those who may be lower in an organizational or societal hierarchy. Some secretaries act as gatekeepers, deciding who will or will not have access to their boss. They also may influence their boss. Or, even though teachers have official power over students, students and teachers can police each other. For instance, while teachers may enforce formal dress codes for students, students may verbally and nonverbally express criticisms of teachers' appearance. In response, members of both groups may modify their dress to meet one another's approval. Can you think of other examples where the person who supposedly has less power sometimes controls the relationship?

To explain the complexities of power, Foucault introduced the concept, "discipline." What does the word discipline mean to you? As a verb, discipline means to punish or penalize, as in "the teacher disciplined the unruly child by making her stand in a corner." When used as an adjective, discipline means a strict, self-regulation, as in "I follow a disciplined exercise program." Discipline also can refer to an academic area of study, such as the discipline of communication. Notice that the root of discipline is disciple, or follower. As Foucault conceived it, ***discipline*** refers to "elements of social relations that control, govern, and 'normalize' individual and collective behavior."[9]

The clock is an ever-present example of how discipline operates. In most contexts in the United States, we usually adhere to customs about time, and we rarely question our obedience to them. It just seems "normal" to be mindful of when and how long we engage in certain activities. Just about everyone knows norms about time (they are common knowledge), which we enact in power relations. Students and teachers use norms about time to affect each others' behaviors. In the classroom, teachers expect students to be in their seats at the start of a session. Some teachers will not allow students to enter the class late. One informal rule in universities says that students may leave if the professor hasn't shown up by fifteen minutes after class is scheduled to start. Have you heard that "rule"? When I teach a class, I don't need a watch to know when class should end because students always begin to pack up when the time is almost over. As in schools, in most organizations discipline helps to produce "regular, recurring, functional behavior."[10] Discipline enables organization members to collaborate and to predict outcomes. Discipline can also help prevent chaos. Therefore, discipline can have positive effects.

However, discipline can constrain creativity and spontaneity and help maintain power imbalances. Although we need some degree of discipline for organizations and relationships to persist and thrive, discipline can invite negative consequences. Referring to the example of the clock, patient–doctor relationships show how discipline operates in power dynamics. Although physicians expect patients to arrive on time for appointments, patients often wait well after the appointed time to see the physician. In most organizations, different policies about time apply to employees depending on their status. Some individuals have to punch in and out on a time card and take timed breaks, which illustrates an obvious form of control over the employees. If they don't follow time constraints, their employer may fire them or otherwise punish them. In contrast, other employees can come and go as they wish without paying close attention to time. In some occupations, individuals keep track of their own time. These examples of how the clock regulates human behaviors illustrate Foucault's definition of discipline, which consists of power, knowledge (truth), and rules of right.

Power and Knowledge

Power and knowledge operate recursively: "the exercise of power perpetually creates knowledge and, conversely, knowledge constantly induces effects of power."[11] As a result, what we call "facts" or knowledge often are actually products of political social processes. For example, the act of labeling or defining social identity groups demonstrates power dynamics. Historically, groups in power have named/labeled other groups, whether the other groups agreed with the names/labels or not. "What a group is called and how it is described by other groups, particularly those in power, plays an important role in social relations,"[12] because these labels usually are not neutral. Most often, dominant groups define these names/labels to establish and maintain hierarchy.[13] For instance, definitions of learning ability/disability allow educators (the dominant group) to classify learners (the nondominant group) as either normal or abnormal. Once a person is labeled (e.g., as "gifted and talented" or as "developmentally challenged"), that individual's identity becomes fixed, and the label can forever have positive or negative impacts.

Throughout history, influential disciplines such as medicine, science, law, and religion have developed and instilled many bodies of "knowledge" about social identity groups that became accepted as truth. The Diagnostic and Statistical Manual of Mental Disorders (DSM) of the American Psychiatric Association (APA) is a primary source of information about mental disorders and problems. From their positions of power, medical experts decide which conditions qualify to be included in this storehouse of knowledge, which is presumed to constitute the truth. Anyone who shows symptoms related to disorders cited in the DSM is subject to being categorized and stigmatized because professionals such as psychiatrists and psychologists consult the DSM to make and justify diagnoses and recommend treatment. For over twenty years, the DSM defined homosexuality as a mental condition, and this classification affected the lives of countless people. After concerted effort by groups who challenged that definition, the board of trustees of the APA voted in 1974 to delete it from the DSM.

Rules of Right

The power–knowledge relationship operates through "rules of right," which are "principles and practices we create to govern ourselves, presumably in non-arbitrary, systematic ways."[14] Examples of rules of right include the Constitution of the United States at the national level and employee handbooks at the organizational level. What are examples on your job or at your school? Rules of right "spell out the right way to act in the organization according to the power relationships."[15] They guide and regularize our interactions with others, and they help to maintain power positions. Members of society and organizations routinely and robotically invoke rules of right with statements or sentiments such as "that's the way we do things around here," "these are standard operating procedures," or "it's just common sense." Organization members tend to refer to those meanings that favor certain groups and interests as "common sense." This illustrates the political nature of taken-for-granted knowledge. Relations of power often unfold as struggles over meaning as groups try to "fix" meaning and connect it to their own interests.[16]

> The rules of right provide a formal, structural delineation of power; the exercise of power allows for certain "truths" to emerge and to become the taken-for-granted knowledge base for a social system; the effects of this knowledge base in turn reinforce and reproduce relations of power in the system.[17]

When people create, embed, or express meaning to serve or enhance the interests of some individuals and minimize and/or subordinate those of other individuals, a form of control emerges.

Control in Organizations

Organization members employ a variety of methods to control one another and themselves. Across history, these methods have progressed from simple, direct approaches, to more complex, covert strategies.[18] In early organizations, persons in authority exerted power through ***simple control,*** which includes giving direct orders and engaging in overt observation. As organizations adopted technology, ***technical control*** became an option. For instance, assembly lines partially hid authority relations between workers and supervisors. No longer did the supervisor have to command the worker, because the pace of the line controlled the worker's productivity. Next came ***bureaucratic control,*** enabled through rules, policies, job descriptions, incentives, and so forth. Experts and specialists created standards and operating procedures, which represented a new form of surveillance. Although all three of these types of blatant or obtrusive control still occur, organizations also are exerting more subtle forms of discipline.

Organizational communication scholars Phillip Tompkins and George Cheney refer to unobtrusive forms of control as ***concertive control:*** "In the concertive organization, the explicit written rules and regulations are largely replaced by the common understanding of values, objectives, and means of achievement, along with a deep appreciation for the organization's 'mission.'"[19]

Concertive Control

Because concertive control works best when organization members internalize interests of dominant groups, organizations strive to indoctrinate employees to behave according to the organization's core values and beliefs. A common strategy is to use a rhetoric of ***identification,*** the extent to which an individual, when faced with a decision, will be likely to do what aligns with the organization's objectives rather than with her or his own preferences.[20] Organizations use various methods to gain identification, such as cit-

Tool No. 2

Media Literacy

Media literacy refers to our ability to critique and analyze media and its potential impact. Media literacy education strives to empower us and to transform our usual passive relationship with media to be more active, engaged, and critical. Media literacy education improves how we use critical thinking skills as we "sift through and analyze the messages that inform, entertain and sell to us everyday."[21]

Especially relevant to difference matters, some media literacy curricula critique and analyze power dimensions of how media represent gender, race, class, and sexuality.[22] They focus on recognizing and challenging systematic biases and distortions. They also encourage using media as instruments of social communication and change.[23] They promote producing alternative media that challenge dominant ideologies and portray more accurate and comprehensive views of nondominant groups.

One framework of critical media literacy includes the following concepts and questions to guide critical thinking about media messages:[24]

- **Concept:** All media are constructions. Therefore, they are subject to the biases of their creators.
- **Questions:** Who created this message? What did they hope to accomplish? What are their primary belief systems?
- **Concept:** Different people experience the same media message differently.
- **Questions:** How might different people understand this message differently than me? What do I think and feel about this?
- **Concept:** Media have embedded values and points of view.
- **Questions:** What lifestyles, values, and points of view are represented or omitted in this message? What does this tell me about how other people live and believe? Does this message leave anything or anyone out?
- **Concept:** Media are organized to gain profit and/or power. Furthermore, only a handful of corporations dominate the U.S. media market.
- **Questions:** Why was this message sent? Who sent it? Is this trying to tell me something? . . . to sell me something?

ing metaphors (e.g., "we are family"), telling stories, engaging in rituals, and performing ceremonies.[25] Organizations also try to get members to identify by trying to establish common ground. For instance, they identify a common enemy or glorify a "corporate we," as in "We're number one."[26]

These indoctrinating practices occur formally and informally, through such media as employee manuals, newsletters, meetings, annual reports, social gatherings, Web sites, and electronic mail. As members of organizations internalize organizational premises, control becomes invisible and taken for granted. Concertive control techniques "govern and normalize individual and collective action organizations, particularly to the extent that they are internalized by persons and become, if you will, 'standard operating procedures.'"[27] In essence, members become disciplined.

In a book entitled *The Discipline of Teamwork*, organizational communication scholar James Barker demonstrates the power of concertive control evident in his longitudinal study of a self-managing work team at a mid-size manufacturing company.[28] The company had established participative groups of employees with no assigned leaders by referring to a "team" metaphor. However, through their talk and actions, team members identified, defined, reinforced, and enacted power relationships that looked more like traditional ones. Due to concertive control, four years after converting from a customary bureaucracy, teams had developed formal sets of rules to govern members' workday activities. Team members engaged in self-surveillance behaviors such as developing and enforcing attendance policies that reproduced power dynamics of conventional hierarchy and helped to construct their identities. As one person exclaimed, "Damn, I feel like a supervisor, I just don't get paid for it."[29] Barker's study shows how people impose discipline on themselves and their peers.

As organizations and individuals discipline members, "a well-entrenched power hierarchy is maintained so smoothly that dominant and submissive behavior simply seems natural,"[30] and disciplined members want on their own what the organization wants. The primary means by which these disciplinary processes occur is through hegemony.

Hegemony

Italian philosopher-theorist Antonio Gramsci conceptualized hegemony (if this is a new word for you, it's pronounced hih-jeh′-minny), as "the 'spontaneous' consent given by the great masses of the population to the general direction imposed on social life by the dominant fundamental group."[31] Communication scholars Lee Artz and Bren Ortega Murphy define hegemony as: "the process of moral, philosophical, and political leadership that a social group attains only with the active consent of other important social groups." They elaborate:

> Hegemony addresses how social practices, relationships, and structures are negotiated among diverse social forces. Hegemony offers a template for understanding why women wear makeup, employees participate in

> actions to improve company profits, and homeowners and renters accept segregated housing patterns. In each case, subordinate groups (women, workers, or ethnic minorities) willingly participate in practices that are not necessarily in their best interests because they perceive some tangible benefit. The mass media, educational institutions, the family, government agencies, industry, religious groups, and other social institutions elicit social support for such hegemonic relations through patterns of communication and material reward.[32]

As Artz and Murphy imply, hegemony operates everywhere in a society.

In organizations, hegemony occurs as individuals work to accomplish the organization's goals while being complicit in their own domination. Organization members often support belief systems and enact power relations that may not serve their interests (they may even work against those interests).[33] Thus, a central tenet of hegemony is "domination through consent," as seen in Barker's study.

However, everyone does not always consent to domination. Hegemony also encompasses ***resistance,*** any means by which societal or organizational members attempt to undermine or overthrow the dominant order. Foucault contended that power relations always meet with resistance, as individuals or groups imagine and seek better realities. Moreover, "acts of resistance are as dispersed and innumerable as sites of power."[34] An individual might resist strictly for personal reasons, as I did with Frank. People also resist to seek rights for themselves and/or others, to transform specific organizational contexts, or to cause social change. Recall how Frank intervened on my behalf by going over his supervisor's head. Resistance may be planned and organized, for instance through whistle-blowing, filing a lawsuit, going on strike, or working precisely within guidelines. Resistance also occurs as random acts such as cheating, lying, telling jokes, being late, or stealing. As these examples imply, resistance may be overt or covert.

Resistance also can be "simultaneously resistant and consensual, uniting and dividing, radical and conservative."[35] Although government agencies often control categories of social identity groups, sometimes individuals and groups assert their own names to redefine themselves, to assert power, and/or to reject others' imposing an identity on them.[36] For instance, civil rights groups were instrumental in changing the racial label "Negro" to "black" and "African American." However, name changes can arouse conflict within groups, as all members may not agree with them. I remember some older African Americans responding negatively to the idea of being called "black" because they thought it was a derogatory term. Also, some gay rights activists have embraced the label "queer" as an act of defiance, while others think the label perpetuates oppressive meanings.[37]

To summarize, hegemony is a complex concept about domination/coercion, consent, and resistance/transformation. Hegemony persists within a society and within organizations when most members agree on dominant belief systems, also known as ideologies.

Ideology

Ideology is a contested concept with multiple and sometimes contradictory meanings. For our purposes, think of ***ideology*** as "a set of assumptions and beliefs that comprise a system of thought."[38] Ideology has powerful, intricate influences on all of us. As organizational communication scholars Eric Eisenberg and Lloyd Goodall explain:

> Ideology touches every aspect of life and shows up in our words, actions, and practices. . . . Because ideology structures our thoughts and interpretations of reality, it typically operates often beneath our conscious awareness. . . . it shapes what seems "natural," and it makes what we think and do seem "right."[39]

This perspective on ideology corresponds with how Karl Marx and Frederick Engels focused on ideology as a means for justifying social stratification.[40] For example, the belief that rich people are hard workers and poor people are lazy is ideological.

Dominant ideologies reflect perspectives and experiences of ruling groups, whose members construct and circulate beliefs that will most benefit them. Those who control means to disseminate belief systems usually also control which ideologies become widespread within a society. Over time, ideologies become taken for granted and accepted as universally valid by most members of a society. Ideology thus becomes a "filter to screen out beliefs and proposed actions that do not fit, and to accept opinions and proposed actions that are consistent with the ideology."[41] In essence, ideologies help to validate worldviews that help dictate our attitudes and behaviors. Power and control processes occur as individuals and groups attempt to produce, reproduce, resist, and/or change a society's dominant ideologies.

To further define ideology, here's a preview of some of the dominant ideologies we will examine. Team members in Barker's study were immersed in the ***ideology of organizational hierarchy,*** which arranges job positions in a stratified structure (usually in the form of a pyramid), with power flowing from the top down. Even though a self-managing work team structure empowered the employees not to enact hierarchy, its ideological force was so strong that they reverted to it.

The ideology of hierarchy also is evident in the power-infused interactions between employees, as described in this chapter's opening story. Betty the secretary told me to make coffee for Frank, her boss; Frank's boss, Harold, informed me I couldn't revise my work hours to attend school; Frank went over Harold's head to ask Henrietta, the executive director, to grant my request; Henrietta gave me permission. From my account, you almost can visualize the organizational chart that mapped organization's hierarchy.

Organizational hierarchy exemplifies the ***ideology of domination,*** a fundamental belief system in U.S. society "in a notion of superior and inferior, and its concomitant ideology—that the superior should rule over the inferior."[42] This ideology is so ingrained that most people believe domination is natural.

Systems of domination are common in social structures, which usually are stratified, or "organized [hierarchically] so that one group of people consistently has more opportunity or privilege than another group."[43] Consequences of stratification include unequal, differential distribution of resources, opportunities, status, and services. Structures and systems can be exclusionary and damaging to individuals. This systemic/structural perspective is key to how we will explore difference. I delve deeply into structures of society at large as well as within various contexts to expose power relations that constitute social reality and to discuss how they matter to communicating social identity.

The social identity groups we will study usually are explicitly or implicitly stratified. Social class is layered from upper to lower levels, and not having a disability is usually considered more desirable than having one. Persons in the lower strata of social identity groups tend to occupy lower levels of hierarchies, and to be the lowest paid, while the converse usually is true for persons in higher strata. For instance, women occupy most clerical positions in organizations, and most high-level executives are men.

The ***ideology of patriarchy***—the "structural dominance of men that is built into the institutions of society"[44]—often prompts gender-based assumptions and expectations about organizational roles and behaviors. Returning to my opening story, the roles and expected power relations of (female) secretary and (male) boss exhibit the classic gender hierarchy of U.S. society. This ideology also forms the basis for resistance to those assumptions and expectations, for instance as enacted in women's rights movements or men's profeminist groups.

The ***ideology of white supremacy*** refers to an internalized belief that white people are superior to all other races. This belief stems from power sources in the United States that have steadfastly reinforced and perpetuated a hierarchy of race. Through various actions, including government legislation, groups and individuals systematically have sought to separate white from nonwhite, to glorify whiteness and malign color.

The ***culture of poverty ideology*** contends that poor people collectively embody traits that keep them down. This perspective on social class blames the poor for their plight and ignores the fact that many wealthy people have inherited their wealth and resources or that they were better positioned to attain the "American dream." This ideology does not acknowledge that economic, cultural, and social capital can tilt the playing field in favor of those who have accumulated wealth, knowledge, and/or connections.[45]

Finally, ***heteronormativity*** refers to a belief system that values and normalizes heterosexual identity while marginalizing and stigmatizing individuals who do not identify as heterosexual. This ideology contends that humans are either female or male, and that sexual relations should occur only between a female and a male. This perspective affects related aspects of life, including gender roles, norms of sexual relationships, and marriage.

Whether consciously or not, members of society often allow dominant ideologies like these to dictate their attitudes and behaviors: "the dominant assumptions of a culture establish hierarchical relationships, and as long as the members of a culture *believe* that the hierarchies are *normal* and *natural*, they will tend to act in ways that perpetuate those hierarchies."[46] Although these dynamics matter for everyone, nondominant group members tend to be more negatively affected than dominant group members. Thus, power relations occur in society at large and within organizations as individuals reinforce or resist dominant ideologies. The primary means by which people enact power relations is through communication.

Spotlight on Media

Power and the Media

The media play a powerful role in communicating social identity. Every day, media such as books, newspapers, magazines, radio, recordings, movies, television, and the Internet create and transmit millions of messages to large audiences around the world. Since the 1930s, media scholars in communication have studied a range of topics, including media effects on culture and society, influence and persuasion, and motivations for using media. They've developed a substantial body of work about how media impact our beliefs, attitudes, and actions. For example, social cognitive theory contends that we often learn about life from the media without having direct experience, and we tend to believe that the media accurately represent aspects of life. So, members of dominant groups who don't have much contact with nondominant groups will tend to believe media portrayals of those groups. Cultivation theory says that media shapes our perceptions of social reality through extensive and cumulative exposure to media messages. We develop beliefs, attitudes, and expectations about the real world based on media, and we use those beliefs, attitudes, and expectations to guide how we behave.

Some communication scholars conduct critical cultural studies, which focus on "how the media can be used to define power relations among various subcultures and maintain the status quo. Critical cultural studies researchers examine how the media relate to matters of ideology, race, social class, and gender."[47] They assert that media not only reflect culture, but they also produce culture. They stress how political and social structures influence mediated communication and how that influence helps to maintain or support those with power in society.

These and other perspectives on communication and the media help to inform our study of difference matters. To enhance your understanding of media effects on difference matters, I include a spotlight on media in each of the following chapters.

Communicating Power

We enact power relations through a variety of interrelated communication processes, including: language, everyday talk, and responses to norms and policies about physical appearance.

Language

A primary medium for communicating power is language, which helps to spread ideologies and to reinforce hegemony. Although no language system is superior to another, persons in power tend to value certain systems more than others. Powerful groups usually control language systems and expect all organization members to use vocabulary, jargon, dialects, accents, as well as topics of interactions that the dominant group values and uses.

Communication inequities can arise when members privilege certain language systems and dominant groups tend to place the burden of proof on nondominant group members. For instance, an ***ideology of rationality*** values objective, "cool-headed" behaviors, and devalues emotionally expressive communication styles characteristic of some women and people of color.[48] During ***co-cultural exchanges,*** or communication between nondominant and dominant group members,[49] dominant group members may stigmatize a nondominant speaker as deviant or deficient because the person does not comply with dominant norms. These power relations often occur during routine interactions, or everyday talk.

Everyday Talk

Everyday talk consists of ***discursive practices,*** which are "characteristic ways of speaking and writing that both constitute and reflect our experiences,"[50] that can help to produce, maintain, or resist systems of power. Everyday talk tends to be political. That is, it tends to favor the interests of one group over another. As a result, "all discourse potentially structures relations of dominance and subordination in organizations."[51]

Norms about small talk in everyday situations can inhibit developing harmonious relationships and stifle productivity and creativity. The ease with which a person can engage in small talk—inside or outside the workplace setting—can help or hinder career stability and mobility. For example, some persons might avoid informal networking opportunities, such as company-sponsored social events, because they expect to be uncomfortable about conversing in an informal, nonwork-related context. Some people may also feel inhibited at work. A white male professional described his discomfort in the corporate bank setting where he worked. He let his working-class, Irish-German background restrain him from interacting freely with his middle-class, Ivy League colleagues.[52] Women of color in workshops I conduct often lament that they cannot be "themselves" at their workplaces because they feel obligated to accommodate to "white" ways of communicating.

To "fit into" dominant contexts, members of nondominant groups may engage in ***code switching,*** or adapting their speech to standard English-speaking norms. When nondominant group members do not adapt, power dynamics can become visible. A Chicana told me that her white female supervisor constantly reprimanded her for rolling her r's when she pronounced certain words. Although she told her supervisor the pronunciation was characteristic of her native language, the supervisor repeatedly told her to pronounce words "correctly."

Parents who never attended college or who have limited literacy skills may hesitate to talk with their children's teachers due to a sense of intellectual inferiority. Also, in situations such as doctor–patient encounters, older patients and/or patients who speak English as a second language may not talk openly or ask for clarity when communicating with physicians or other health care providers.

The employment interview represents a common discursive practice in organizations based on dominant ideals: "assumptions about proper interviewing behavior and outcomes exclude experiences of traditionally underrepresented groups and maintain managerial control."[53] Recruiters tend to select new hires based on "fluency of speech, composure, appropriateness of content, and ability to express ideas in an organizational fashion."[54] Furthermore, interviewers tend to rate interviewees more highly when their responses match their expectations. During co-cultural interviews, nondominant group members may feel even more uneasy, self-conscious, cautious, or tense than interviewees who are part of the dominant group. They may struggle to match their language and behavior to meet the expectations of the interviewer.

Most organization members accept dominant ideologies and enact/reproduce them in everyday interactions until they become so embedded that they are invisible, and taken for granted. One consequence is ***discursive closure,*** processes that mute or distort voices of certain persons or groups: "rather than having open discussions, discussions are foreclosed or there appears to be no need for discussion."[55] A prime example of this is the "don't ask, don't tell" policy in the military regarding homosexual identity.

Physical Appearance

A final example of communicating power can be found in how organizations discipline members' bodies. As organizational communication scholar Angela Trethewey explains, "Control, in its most insidious form—discipline—operates simultaneously on employee minds and bodies."[56] Foucault viewed the body as a central object and target of power in organizations. Through disciplinary practices (including self-surveillance), organization members internalize and reproduce dominant ideologies by transforming their own bodies into "carriers" or representatives of prevailing relations of domination and subordination. In essence, they become what Foucault called "docile" bodies.[57]

Members of dominant as well as nondominant groups learn to conform to formalized expectations or unspoken norms about aspects of appearance, such as types of clothing, grooming, and acceptable body weight. Many, if not most, of these policies and norms persist without challenge. Moreover, some policies are based on legitimate business necessity, such as safety issues. For instance, a group of black firefighters claimed that the policy requiring them to be clean shaven was discriminatory. These men suffered from an inflammatory skin condition common to African American men that constrains them from shaving every day. Although the judge indicated that the plaintiffs' concerns were valid, the court ruled in favor of the defendant because respirator masks do not fit properly on firefighters with beards.[58]

However, many policies are based less on necessity than on masculinist, white, middle-class and middle-aged ideals and aesthetics. Furthermore, although the notion of docile bodies affects everyone, it is especially relevant to nondominant group members because rules of right often require them to modify their appearances. Other examples of resistance to traditional norms and policies include lawsuits related to various policies about bodily appearance such as weight requirements for women; men's ponytails or earring(s); young persons' piercings, tattoos, or colored hair; and black people's braided hairstyles.[59]

The preceding discussion only begins to address ways that people enact power relations. In addition to written and oral communication, power relations are expressed through nonverbal phenomena, such as the use of space. Recall, for instance, my description of the office layout where I worked. Research associates worked in offices with windows and doors, while secretarial staff were located out in the open, in the interior of the building. Other examples of nonverbal cues of power include parking privileges, access to bathrooms, and office size and location in the worksite.

Conclusion

Power dynamics are inevitable aspects of communicating in organizations and other contexts. The relationships among power, hegemony, and ideology reveal that organizations are "sites of struggle where different groups compete to shape the social reality of organizations in ways that serve their own interests."[60] Dominant groups rely on various ideologies to maintain and reproduce relations of power, usually through consent of nondominant groups rather than coercion. However, nondominant groups and their allies from dominant groups often strive to develop more equitable realities. Moreover, although power processes can exclude and marginalize people, they also can enable and empower them.[61]

Organizational power dynamics do not occur in a vacuum. Enacting power in organizations resembles and relies on power dynamics in society at large. Major forces such as our families, the government, religion, education, and the media impact how people enact power in organizations, and vice versa.

Throughout history and currently, many individuals and groups in the United States enact(ed) power relations not only to produce and reproduce domination, but also to empower, liberate, and transform. They visualize(d) alternative ways to take us closer to the ideal of liberty and justice for all. Their responses to hegemony and ideology have wide-ranging effects on society at large as well as for organizational communication processes. When Rosa Parks refused to sit in the back of a bus in Montgomery, Alabama, in 1955, a group of citizens formed a grassroots organization whose bus boycott ignited a transformative social movement. This movement formed the backdrop against which power relations unfolded between my coworkers and me in the early 1970s.

Chapters 1 and 2 established the foundation for the remainder of the book by outlining primary concepts and theoretical perspectives. In the following chapters, I describe and analyze the social construction of social identity groups in the United States, and I examine related power dynamics. Throughout, I clarify the power of communication.

Reflection Matters

1. What did you find intriguing or interesting in this chapter? Why?
2. How empowered do you usually feel? Why? Do you tend to feel more empowered in certain situations? Do you tend to feel less empowered in certain situations? Does your sense of empowerment seem related to any of your social identity categories? Explain
3. Recall the example of how the clock disciplines students and faculty in a university setting. Provide another example of discipline (as Foucault conceptualized it) that routinely occurs in educational settings.
4. Offer an example of discipline from your own work experiences, or from the work experiences of someone you know.
5. Discuss examples of simple, technical, and bureaucratic control at workplaces.
6. Does any organization or group that you belong to try to get members to identify with it? What communication strategies did/do they use? Explain.
7. Apply Foucault's conception of power to analyze interaction patterns in significant relationships in your life (e.g., child–parent, supervisor–worker, student–teacher, romantic partner).
8. Narrate a personal example of resistance in an organizational context. In the form of a brief story (similar to my coffee tale), explain what happened, and why. If you do not have a story from your life, obtain a story from someone you know, or from the media (e.g., a movie or television show). Emphasize communication processes that the individuals enacted.

9. Have you experienced any co-cultural communication challenges (i.e., communication between members of dominant and nondominant groups)—as either a dominant or nondominant group member—that I describe in this chapter? Explain.
10. How is language a primary medium for communicating power? Give examples from your experiences.
11. Review the list of dominant ideologies and select any that you have experienced. Explain and give examples.
12. Based on Tool #2 (p. 29), how would you rate your level of media literacy? Explain.

• • • • Chapter 3 • • • •

Gender Matters

Salespersons sometimes refer to me using masculine terms by saying things like, "I'll be right with you, sir," or "I need to help him first." They usually are interacting with a coworker or another customer, or otherwise distracted. Their peripheral vision registers a tall person with short hair, and they assume I am a man. Once they really look at me and realize their mistake, they apologize profusely. One woman moaned, "I feel soooo stupid." I take it in stride because I understand what has happened. One time, though, a cashier looked right at me as she handed me change and said, "Thank you, sir." Now that irritated me. I wanted to correct her, to proclaim that I am a woman. I mean, didn't she notice that I was wearing lipstick and earrings; didn't she see my curves; didn't she hear my feminine vocal tones?

Why do you think I was upset when she didn't recognize that I was a woman? Why do you think people who realized their error were so apologetic? Do you think they would have been more, or less, upset if they had mistaken a man for a woman? Why? A friend of mine who is a lesbian also experiences these types of interactions, although much more frequently because she doesn't wear makeup, and she wears masculine clothing. Another one of my friends is a male-to-female transgendered person who gently corrects service workers when they refer to her using masculine pronouns. One time she did that, a male security guard replied: "OK. Thank you, SIR," putting strong emphasis on the word, "sir." These experiences imply a few matters related to gender that this chapter covers.

Gender is a defining element of everyday interactions, across all social contexts as we routinely rely on verbal and nonverbal cues to "do gender," usually without thinking about it.[1] That is, we enact learned, scripted gender roles. Signs and signals of gender are so ever-present that "we usually fail to note them—unless they are missing or ambiguous. Then we are uncomfortable until we have successfully placed the other person in a gender status."[2] Most of us have a clear, strong sense of our gender that we expect others to acknowledge. Also, individuals sometimes discriminate against others because of their gender.

In this chapter, I explore various matters related to communicating gender to illustrate power relations between and among women and men. I begin by defining gender and distinguishing it from sex, after which I elaborate on why gender matters. Next, I describe how sex and gender have been socially constructed in the United States, and I discuss dominant value systems about gender. Then, I offer a historical overview of gender and labor in the United States. I also explain ways that individuals and groups have challenged perspectives on gender and their consequences. After that, I spotlight educational systems as significant sites of hegemony where we teach and learn about social identities. Finally, I review research on communicating gender, including a discussion about the role of emotion at work. Throughout the chapter, I illustrate that gender and power matter to how women *and* men communicate social identity.

What Is Gender?

What is your sex? What is your gender? Do you think of them as two different ways to say the same thing about yourself? Although many people use the terms interchangeably, gender and sex are distinct though related facets of identity. ***Sex*** is a biological classification. Humans universally tend to label a newborn as either "female" or "male." They designate a baby's sex based on physiological features related to reproduction, including external genitalia, internal sex organs, chromosomes, and hormones.[3] This classification system reflects an essentialist view that stable, innate differences exist between the two sexes. This logic supports the idea that females and males are polar opposites, and that they serve different, complementary roles in society, which leads us to the concept of gender. Gender classifications are based on a "web of socially constructed meanings that differentiate humans on the basis of perceived physical, social, and psychological characteristics."[4] Those classifications depend on societal views of relationships of female to woman and male to man. Thus, ***gender*** refers to cultural norms of femininity and masculinity. In current popular usage, the word *gender* encompasses both biological and sociocultural aspects of identity, while *sex* generally means sexual intercourse.[5]

Most cultures uphold customary conceptions of what women and men are "supposed" to be like. We learn at an early age how to "do gender," based usually on our sex. For instance, we are told that "Boys don't cry," or "Girls should be nice." Did anyone ever tell you either of those things? Gender norms vary across cultures, and they change throughout history. For instance, some languages don't have gender-linked terms for boys and girls or for older people. Some societies classify multiple genders, while others are genderless.[6] And, members of some groups honor individuals who personify multiple genders.

To conclude, sex is based on biology and genetics, while gender is culturally and relationally determined. Thus, "gender is not something we have, but something that we do, over and over again in one setting or another. And these settings are not neutral ground but saturated with gendered assumptions and expectations."[7] These assumptions and expectations can lead to ***sexism,*** discriminatory behavior and attitudes based on a person's gender (including women and men). Although sex classification has remained constant throughout history, conceptions of gender vary across time and within cultures.

Why Gender Matters

Gender is a primary aspect of most individuals' identity that matters throughout our lives. We are not born with a gender. Rather, we learn our gender identity from others. At birth, we enter a world "that is coded and structured in terms of gender."[8] We receive messages from various sources about how to enact a gender role that's usually based on our sex. Most of us develop and solidify our gender identity in early childhood. As we grow up, various sources socialize us about how women and men differ.

In addition to being an important element of identity, gender has considerable consequences for quality of life. Women and men tend to be employed in sex-segregated jobs that are valued differently. Men tend to earn more money and to occupy more positions of authority. Men also tend to have fewer health problems, which may stem from a long history in the field of medicine of concentrating on men's health challenges and men's wellness. However, women live longer than men, and they usually have stronger social support systems. These and other consequences of gender arise from ways that gender has been and is constructed in U.S. society.

Constructing Gender in the United States

A review of how gender has been constructed in the United States reveals that ideas about "natural" differences between women and men are artificial products of "knowledge" created by authorities in disciplines such as science and medicine. Early research and writing about sex and gender tried to rationalize differences between women and men as rooted in natural inferiority or superiority. That essentialist explanation helps to justify women's subordination and men's dominance.[9] In Western culture, a primary approach to explaining differences between the sexes refers to biological constructs such as physical characteristics, reproduction, and sexual activity. These principles certify sex differences as natural, essential, and absolute.

Historical Overview of Ideological Perspectives

Early explanations about sex differences relied on biological reasoning to justify sex-based attitudes and behaviors, including women's purity and men's promiscuity.[10] Scientists conducted numerous tests to discover and demonstrate sex differences. In the late nineteenth and early twentieth centuries, craniometrists (scientists who measured skulls) argued that males were more intelligent than females because females had smaller brains.[11] In 1879, Gustave LeBon, known as the founder of social psychology, said that women "represent the most inferior forms of human evolution . . . they are closer to children and savages than to an adult, civilized man."[12] Also in the nineteenth century, researchers concluded that women should not have access to higher education because university study would deplete the energy they needed for menstrual and reproductive functions, which would prevent them from having babies.[13]

Related to this, Charles Darwin asserted that parental instinct made women naturally more tender and less selfish than men. He based this on the claim that women's hormones make them more caring, while men's hormones make them more aggressive.[14] Therefore, men are more suited to the pressures of the work world. Similarly, religious or quasi-religious beliefs contended that women should not become doctors because menstruation rendered them ritually unclean. "Natural" perspectives on sex and gender like these helped to formulate and perpetuate the belief that men are naturally superior to women and naturally dominant over them.[15]

A historical overview of ideas about femininity and masculinity reflects the persistence of an ideology of patriarchy, or "rule by the fathers." ***Patriarchy*** refers to the "structural dominance of men that is built into the institutions of society."[16] Patriarchal societies enact a hierarchy of gender in which "men as a category have systematic advantages over women whether men desire these advantages or not."[17] In other words, most men enjoy masculine privilege. Moreover, due to persistent power relations, women *and* men reproduce and reinforce this gender hierarchy.

To challenge patriarchy, the women's rights movement in the 1800s sought political rights such as voting, access to employment, and the right to own property and to earn an education. In contrast, an ideal of femininity known as the "cult of true womanhood," or the "cult of domesticity" dictated a middle-class image of correct femininity promoted widely through women's magazines, advice manuals, and novels. "True women" were judged by four prime virtues: purity, piety, submissiveness, and domesticity. They did not seek work outside of their homes; nor did they involve themselves in social or political issues. They were judged primarily by their abilities to serve as wives and mothers, and by their "natural" moral superiority over men.[18] They could not own property, vote, attend college, serve as jurors, or run for political office. Some states even restricted the number of hours that women could work.[19]

Around this time, an ***ideology of separate spheres*** arose to justify the new arrangement of men in the public domain and women in the private sector of society.[20] Basically, women were to confine themselves to the private context of the home. Underlying these attitudes is the idea that women belong in the private domain of society, where they should maintain the household and raise children, while men are responsible for the public sphere of work and politics.[21] However, class differences affected notions of femininity. Being a "lady" was a status symbol of mainly white, middle- and upper-class women, who depended on the cheap labor of working-class women, most of whom were women of color and immigrant women.[22] This latter group of women worked sunup to sundown, often maintaining the residences of wealthier women and their own homes.

Historically, meanings of masculinity usually position men in the public sphere, where they are responsible for production and politics. In the nineteenth century, when certain women were expected to be ladies, and to confine themselves to childrearing and housekeeping, men were expected to be breadwinners. And, men whose wives worked were deemed failures. Thus, a significant sign of masculinity was providing for the family. Indeed, "the very definition of masculinity in American society came to be tied to a man's paycheck."[23] This ideal was difficult for working-class and poor married men to achieve because their wives often needed to work to help sustain the family.[24] For example, many married Latinos who worked on railroad gangs lived apart from their wives, who often worked at low-paying farm or domestic jobs.[25]

Challenging Traditional Messages

Since the late 1960s, research on gender stereotypes has investigated normative beliefs about a "typical" woman or man in the United States. These stereotypes matter because they not only describe characteristics of femininity and masculinity, they also prescribe them.[26] What do you think are characteristics of femininity? Of masculinity? According to some studies, two clusters of traits exist. Femininity traits include expressive-nurturing behaviors such as understanding, compassion, and affection. Masculinity traits encompass instrumental-active attitudes and behaviors, including independence, confidence, and assertiveness.[27] These descriptive stereotypes correspond to prescriptive norms that we traditionally learn from others about our gender roles, as in girls should be caring and relational, and boys should not express feminine emotions.

Feminist communication scholar Julia Wood cites themes of femininity and masculinity that thread through contemporary U.S. society.[28] Femininity themes are: appearance still counts; be sensitive and caring; accept negative treatment by others; and be a superwoman. As women receive contradictory messages about gender, they may struggle with life decisions such as pursuing a career and/or becoming a mother. The wide variety of perspectives on femininity is evident in various forms of feminism, including radical feminism, liberal feminism, social feminism, poststructural feminism, Chicana feminism, ecofeminism, and womanism.[29]

According to Wood, masculinity themes are: don't be female; be successful; be aggressive; be sexual; and be self-reliant. Definitions of masculinity often are the opposite of how we define women or gay men. Boys and men are continually socialized that being a man means first and foremost, *not* being a woman.[30] For instance, men in the military (a highly masculine domain) often refer to defeated enemies, recruits, and passive peers as "girls," "faggots," and other names meant to be derogatory. These constructions show that while views of femininity are changing (although not without tensions), notions of masculinity continue to emphasize male superiority. As many men grapple with changing conceptions of both masculinity and femininity, some have organized themselves to respond to what has been called "a crisis of masculinity."[31] These groups follow a tradition of various women's and men's social and political movements advocating particular versions of femininity and masculinity. They comprise two basic camps: promasculinist, men's rights, which leans toward antifeminism, and profeminists who advocate women's rights.[32] Other examples are "real men," and mythopoetic men (who seek to "rediscover deep mythic roots of masculine thinking and feeling").[33]

Some social scientists critique traditional portrayals of masculinity as always dominant and equally performed by all males. They propose that multiple masculinities exist, which reinforces the need to consider intersections of identity.[34] For instance, the meaning of masculinity in working-class life in the United States differs from its meaning in middle- and upper-class life. Or, some U.S.-born men of Chinese and Japanese descent may associate their masculinity with "caring characteristics such as being polite and obedient"[35] because their cultures revere nurturing as an element of male power. Yet, Western ideas about masculinity would brand these attributes as effeminate and passive and, therefore, unmanly.

A growing area of study known as men's studies or masculinity studies analyzes complexities of masculine identities and acknowledges that some men are not as privileged as others. For instance, ***hegemonic masculinity*** refers to an ideal notion of a man by stressing a plurality of masculinities and noting a hierarchy within masculine identities.[36] This perspective depicts the most powerful version of manhood as someone who enacts traditional characteristics of masculinity and embodies dominant categories of primary social identity groups. That is, someone who is male, white, physically and mentally fit, upper middle class, not too young (and yet not too old), and heterosexual. Consequently, men from all social identity categories may struggle to achieve this ideal as they construct, negotiate, and maintain a masculine identity.[37] Such challenges reinforce the need to consider intersections of identity instead of highlighting only one category.

Recent research in men's studies explores emerging changes in constructions of masculine identity. For instance, "inclusive masculinity" refers to a "softer" version of masculinity among younger men based on reduced homophobia and decreased sexism, as well as acceptance of feminine social behavior among other men.[38] Men who enact inclusive masculinities are more likely to develop emotional relationships with other men.

To summarize, femininity and masculinity are not stable features of individual women and men. Nor are they distinct, clear-cut categories. Rather, members of society create, reinforce, and reconstruct various femininities and masculinities. However, the ideology of patriarchy prevails. Notions of womanhood and manhood are continually constructed within social systems whose members usually rely on hegemonic ideals about gender to teach one another how to perform gendered roles.

Gender and Divisions of Labor

Effects of gender socialization are especially evident in the division of labor. At various points in history, some women and men shared duties such as farming and childrearing, while at other times they enacted distinct roles based on gender norms. The nature and duration of these roles often varied due to other aspects of identity, especially race and social class. Roles also changed due to historical events such as the beginning and end of slavery, the world wars, the Industrial Revolution, the Civil Rights Movement, the Information Revolution, and legislative reforms.

For instance, prior to the Civil War, 90 percent of white men were independent farmers, businessmen, or artisans. After the war, many men could not make a living, so they moved to the cities to find work in factories. By the early twentieth century, fewer than one-third worked for themselves. Simultaneously, newly freed black slaves migrated north, and large numbers of southern Europeans immigrated to the United States. As these newcomers looked for work, they competed for white men's traditional power positions.[39]

In the first half of the twentieth century, many women were demanding equality in education, voting, work, and sexual matters, including birth control and reproduction.[40] During World War II, unprecedented numbers of women entered the workforce. When men returned from the war, they thought women should return to their "natural" place in the home. During this era, expectations of women shifted:

> In the 1940s, [white, middle-class] women were told that they shouldn't work outside the home if they were married, then that it was patriotic to work outside the home, then that their real job was to cook and take care of their kids and husband. In the 1950s and 1960s, movies glorified male war heroes and the sweethearts they left behind. Hollywood and the country selectively forgot women in the factories and the armed forces. It was as if their jobs as riveters, welders, nurses and pilots—along with the emergent feminism—never happened.[41]

One of the most significant developments related to gender and labor has been the increasing number of women entering the paid workforce. Note, however, that most women always have engaged in various forms of unpaid labor within their homes and in agricultural settings. At the beginning of the twentieth century, fewer than one of every five workers was a woman; at the beginning of the twenty-first century, almost one of every two was a woman. Statistical projections predict that 61 percent of women 16 years of age and over will be in the workforce by 2014.[42] These increases apply to all women, although more women of color and white working-class women always have worked for pay than white and/or middle-class women. Currently, about half of the workforce in the United States are women, due in part to a recession that has decreased numbers of male-dominated jobs such as construction and manufacturing, and increased numbers of jobs in health care, education, and government (traditionally dominated by women). Although more women are entering the labor force, most women and men work in occupations where the same sex predominates. An occupation that is at least 75 percent female or male usually is considered female or male dominated.

Throughout the twentieth century, occupational rates of ***sex segregation,*** "the extent to which women and men are concentrated in different industries, establishments, occupations, and jobs, and in the extent to which any particular job is dominated by workers of one sex,"[43] remained consistent and high. This phenomenon demonstrates the prevalence of gender hierarchy in the workforce.

Assigning women and men to certain occupational roles based on societal notions of "natural" capabilities and responsibilities is known as ***sex role spillover.*** Jobs deemed as "typically female" tend to be extensions of women's domestic roles, while masculine jobs are extensions of men's provider roles. In the health professions, males dominate the higher-paying specialties such as brain surgery, heart disease, and plastic surgery.[44]

The origin and persistence of sex segregation stems in part from internalized gender ideologies, which we learn from teachers, peers, parents, and counselors. These and other socialization sources direct girls and boys toward traditional gender-role jobs. Sex segregation of occupations also occurs due to conscious or unconscious grooming or weeding out practices in educational and training settings. Recruitment and hiring practices, as well as on-the-job dynamics, also can influence occupational choices on the part of both the employee and the employer.

Close inspection of sex segregation patterns reveals the influence of patriarchy. When the sex segregation of an occupation changes, it usually shifts from male to female domination rather than vice versa. For instance, men used to dominate clerking positions[45] and elementary school teaching.[46] Usually a job is resegregated from male to female domination due to a shortage of male workers. Men tend to leave jobs that have become less attractive due to decreased prestige, pay, or other job rewards. As women assume those jobs, the occupation often becomes less valued, thereby reinforcing the gender hierarchy.

Patriarchy is also evident in the fact that jobs at the top of the hierarchy of all job categories (white-collar, pink-collar, and blue-collar) tend to be male dominated.[47] Moreover, workers in male-dominated jobs earn more in general than women in female dominated jobs.[48] Also, men persistently have earned more than women: after World War I, the federal government paid men $5 and women $3 per week for public works programs; in the 1970s women earned 59 percent of what men were paid.

In 1999, a woman earned 72 cents when a man earned a dollar.[49] Ten years later, that amount had barely changed to 77 cents per dollar.[50] And, racial differences affect these statistics. In 2009, Asian women and men earned more than other racial groups, and Hispanics earned less than all groups.[51] White workers in general earned more than their black or Hispanic counterparts, although women's differences in earnings within racial-ethnic groups were smaller than those among men. For instance, black men earned

74.5 percent of white men's salaries, and black women earned 95.3 percent of black men's salaries. On average, Hispanic women with a high school diploma earned 33 percent less than white men with the same level of education.[52]

In the early twenty-first century, more white middle-class women are in managerial and professional jobs than ever before. However, these women are clustered at lower levels of management, and they comprise less than 4 percent of workers in the highest levels of Fortune 500 companies. These statistics imply the invisible barrier to women attaining higher-level management and executive positions known as the "glass ceiling."[53]

As more women enter the workforce, gender roles reveal their impressive staying power. With a majority of adult women in the workforce, very few men are sole providers; most are coproviders. However, middle-class white men, on average, perform only about a third of the total family work. Therefore, most married working women face a "second shift" when they get home from their jobs. The old cliché that "a women's work is never done" rings true. Some changes are occurring, however. A small body of research reveals that some men who are fathers are struggling to manage work and family due to rising expectations that they become more involved in caring for their families. This research responds to questions about fatherhood and fathers' roles within and outside of the home. As men negotiate competing discourses about their identities, they may "construct varied masculinities and fatherhoods depending on class, race, occupation, economic (in)stabilities, national origins, and other factors so that they can, for example sustain breadwinner status even when they are not engaging in wage work."[54] Men also may have to negotiate their masculinities "when they are stay-at-home fathers or employed in female-intensive or stereotypically feminine work."[55]

This brief overview of gender and labor demonstrates that because of expectations about who should perform which types of jobs, we're all "prisoners of gender."[56] However, women seem to be doing harder time than men, and nondominant men are worse off economically, in general, than dominant ones. Meanwhile, poor women and/or women of color tend to suffer more economic hardships than middle- to upper-class women and/or white women.

Attempts to correct sex and gender discrimination have resulted in several solutions. Equal opportunity laws include Title VII of the Civil Rights Act of 1964, which focuses on employment discrimination, and the 1972 Title IX, which prohibits discrimination in government-funded educational programs. Other legal initiatives include Title IV of the Civil Rights Act, and the Women's Educational Equity Act of 1974 and 1978. These laws focus on discrimination against individuals rather than groups of persons. They also consider only current circumstances. Consequently, as communication scholar Julia Wood observes, these laws do not redress the impact of sociohistorical patterns of discrimination against groups of people.[57] To address these patterns, President Lyndon Johnson initiated affirmative action policies in 1965 to advocate preferential treatment of historically disenfranchised groups.

The goal is to increase numbers of qualified women and minorities (as well as other traditionally marginalized groups) in education and in the workplace.

Other initiatives include the 1963 Equal Pay amendments to the Fair Labor Standards Act, which requires employers to pay the same wages for the same jobs. A more recent development for gaining equal pay for women is ***comparable worth,*** which requires employers to pay the same wage for dissimilar work of equivalent value. For instance, if their job within an agency requires a similar amount of complexity, a female food service worker should be paid the same as a male truck driver.

The Role of Education

To further explore gender socialization, let's look at educational systems. As you read this, please remember that no one source of socialization is necessarily more influential than another. I highlight educational systems because of their obvious potential impacts. Through numerous disciplinary practices, schooling is a deeply gendered process in which people tend to enact dominant ideologies of society. Fortunately, education also can help to transform gender roles and relationships. Schools are primary arenas where we produce, reinforce, and perpetuate gender ideologies through interactions between and among teachers, administrators, students, parents, and staff members. Schools help to create and affirm normalized institutional definitions of femininity and masculinity. Students in school experience gendered interactions with teachers, other persons in authority, and their peers.

Most young women and men are exposed to differing discourses concerning sexuality, domesticity, vocation and career options. What students "learn" about gender roles in schools is likely to stick with them for the rest of their lives, as well as have a deep impact on their emotional and psychological selves. Note that issues related to gender are tempered by race and social class distinctions among students and teachers, as shown in a growing body of research.[58] From preschool through college, females' and males' experiences in educational settings tend to differ significantly. Structures of educational systems tend to reproduce the gendered hierarchy of the larger society as teachers play central roles as socialization sources. They frequently reinforce and reproduce gender inequalities without realizing it. They may not be conscious of perpetuating gender differences or of presenting curricula that reinforce traditional gender norms. However, teachers' behaviors frequently inscribe and model traditional gender stereotypes.

Teachers are more likely to give boys attention, to call on them more, and to give them more criticism, praise, help, and correction. These actions imply that boys are more valuable—more worthy of attention than girls. Teachers also are more likely to encourage girls to focus on feelings, fairness, and connections to others, and to comment more on girls' clothing and appearance. This latter may correspond with research findings that girls become concerned about body weight as early as elementary school; over 50 percent of girls in high school say that they have been on diets.[59] Appearance concerns vary according to race and ethnicity, with white girls tending to be more concerned about weight than others.

Teachers usually are more accepting of "bad-boy" behavior than "bad-girl" behavior. Related to that, teachers are likely to question boys' masculinity when they are quiet and attentive, thereby marking such behaviors as inappropriate for boys but proper for girls. Boys who are good students may be subject to ridicule from other students. Teachers may use gender as a means of control. They may shame a boy by telling him he is "acting like a girl." Such behavior corresponds to the themes of masculinity described above, where boys are taught not to be female, and to be aggressive. Punishment, too, is liable to be gendered. When corporal punishment was legal, administrators and teachers beat boys much more often than they did girls.[60]

Gender infuses the institutional functions of schools, including divisions of labor, control of resources, and authority patterns. A prevailing pattern is associating masculinity with authority. Men dominate authority positions in school systems.[61] Although 75 percent of the educational workforce is female, approximately 22 percent of school superintendents are female.[62] Notice the hierarchy in school assignments for women principals: 37 percent of them headed elementary schools, 23 percent ran middle schools, and 8 percent were in charge of high schools. A similar pattern is evident at the college and university level; in 2007, women comprised 26 percent of full professors, 40 percent of associate professors, and 48 percent of assistant professors.[63] The good news is that percentages of women have increased at all levels since 2003.

Gender differentiation in educational contexts includes spatial arrangements and segregated, separate work and play areas. Gender bias is evident in textbooks and other curricular materials across all levels. Male characters and depictions of traditional gender roles and behaviors dominate these materials. For instance, social studies curricula rarely include information about the voting rights movement for women or other gender issues.[64]

Although schools import many symbols of gender from the wider culture, they also develop and maintain their own symbol systems, as seen in uniforms and dress codes and in formal and informal language codes. A particularly important symbolic structure in education is the gendering of knowledge, the defining of certain areas of the curriculum as masculine and others as feminine. Industrial arts (shop) teaching, for instance, is historically connected with manual trades where there has been a strong culture of workplace masculinity that excluded women.

Sex segregation and gendered division of labor recur in educational settings. Work specializations among teachers concentrate women in domestic science, language, and literature teaching, and men in science, mathematics, and industrial arts. Men typically are not encouraged to teach elementary school because society feminizes the role of elementary school teacher with substitute mother. A study of male elementary school teachers revealed that people often treated them negatively, for example by questioning their sexuality and suspecting them of being pedophiles.[65] No wonder only 9 percent of elementary school teachers are men.[66]

Although educational contexts produce and reproduce gender hierarchy, they also are potential sites of transformation: Educational reform initiatives include programs to help teachers understand the effects of gender, race, and class on curriculum and classroom interaction. The No Child Left Behind Act of 2001 authorized public schools to apply funding for single-sex schools and classrooms, and the U.S. Department of Education amended Title IX regulations in October 2006 to allow school districts additional flexibility for implementing single-sex programs.[67] Some schools have established separate-gender academies or offer sex-segregated classes in subjects like computer science, which boys traditionally dominate. Although initial findings are mixed, research indicates multiple benefits for single-sex schooling for girls and boys, including decreased distractions to learning and improved student achievement. In addition, girls may benefit more than boys due to better interactions with their peers and more order and control in the classroom.[68]

Power Dynamics and Gender

Two recurring areas of study about gender and communication that reveal power dynamics are language and gender differences in communicating.[69]

Language

As communication scholars Diana Ivy and Phil Backlund observe, "English is a patriarchal language."[70] However, as they also note, we did not invent this male-dominated language; we inherited it. Therefore, referring to English as patriarchal and sexist doesn't blame those of us who use it: "It's nobody's fault (nobody alive anyway) that we have a language that favors one sex over the other, but it's also not something that we 'just have to live with.'"[71] As I share examples of the sexist nature of English, I invite you to reflect on how you might avoid them.

Language reflects patriarchy and sexism in numerous ways. Some of these are subtle; others are blatant. A widespread example is the use of generic masculine pronouns to refer to individuals who might be female or male (e.g., referring to a doctor as "he" in television ads). Although some people contend that terms like "he," "him," or "his" are neutral and inclusive of women and men, research indicates that exclusively using masculine pronouns helps to maintain sex-biased perceptions and shape attitudes about appropriateness of careers for women or men. Such usage also helps to perpetuate gender hierarchy. What do you think? Why?

Another example of sexism and patriarchy in language is the higher number of derogatory words in English for girls and women than for boys and men. I won't list any here, but I invite you to make a mental list to see for yourself. Among negative synonyms for females and males, many have sex-

Spotlight on Media

Gender and the Internet

The Internet has become a powerful medium for creating, producing, sharing, storing, and processing information about almost any topic. Thus, the Internet is both a prime site for disseminating dominant belief systems and an empowering tool for challenging and changing them. For instance, members of hate groups around the world can use the Internet to spread their doctrine, while the lack of nonverbal cues like sex or race might help anonymous online communicators avoid stereotyping one another.

Researchers interested in gender and sex stereotypes have studied differences in computer use and attitudes between women/females and men/males. They recognized the potential of the Internet as a gender-neutral space that could help to reduce gender discrimination. Early studies showed that males had more access to the Internet and tended to use it more frequently than females. According to recent statistics, females and males now have equal access. However, users tend to reproduce gender roles and attitudes that we are socialized to enact, and social stereotypes persist in computer-mediated communication.

In a large-scale project of forty U.S. higher education institutions, males reported spending more time online than females.[72] Males also spent time online differently: they used the Internet for a wider variety of applications than females did—including entertainment (e.g., checking sports scores, listening to music or watching music videos, downloading music), trying online dating, and visiting adult Web sites. Females in this sample used the Internet more for communicative and academic purposes, such as using the library online. The latter uses may be related to differences in study time in general: females reported studying more hours than males. Females also used the Internet more than males for communicating socially. A study on how students use creative aspects of the Internet found that women in general are less likely than men to share their content (e.g., stories or poems) on the Web than men.[73] Men also were much more likely to post music and share videos.

Why do you think these differences occur? Females and males tend to have different formal and informal educational experiences with computer technology. They tend to be socialized differently about how to use computers and about their ability to use them. Also, the Internet historically has been a male domain, which may influence behaviors and attitudes. So, it seems that gender and sex matter for how we use the Internet. Not surprisingly, age also seems to matter: female and male college students reported similar uses of e-mail and blogging. Both groups seem to use the Internet for social interaction, as communicating socially was the most frequent use of time online for females and the second most frequent use for males.

ual denotations or connotations. As I noted earlier, belittling terms for males include negative labels for females, and most males learn that one of the worst insults is simply to call them a girl or a woman, or accuse them of feminine behavior.

Gender hierarchy and differences in connotations also are implied in gendered pairs of words such as "old maid" and "bachelor." Notice that although each of these refers to an unmarried person, the one for a woman is more negative than the one for a man. Additional examples include gendered titles such as Mrs., Ms., Miss, and Mr., which differentiate women according to marital status, but not men. Man-linked terminology such as "mankind," "chairman," "foreman," "man-hours" and feminine suffixes (-ette, -ess, -enne) are other examples. These uses of language help to instill the idea that men are more valuable than women.

Linguistic practices also reveal patriarchy. For instance, in everyday talk and writing, communicators usually place masculine words before feminine words. Consider the following phrases: "boys and girls," "he or she," "his and hers," "husband and wife," and "masculine and feminine." While writing this chapter, I found myself routinely enacting that norm. To resist this tendency, I conscientiously placed the feminine in the first position. Exceptions to this rule include "ladies and gentlemen," "bride and groom," and "mom and dad." Why do you think these are exceptions? Although these and similar uses of language may seem trivial, their recurrent use helps to subtly reinforce notions of female inferiority and male superiority. They reflect deep structures of power that most people do not even realize exist.

Communication Differences

One stream of research investigates differences in women's and men's communication styles. Such studies rarely assess similarities between women and men's communication. They focus on sex or gender differences in: (1) communication styles and (2) perceptions about the function of communication.

A recurring depiction of women's speech as tentative encompasses several patterns. Women sometimes use tag questions such as "isn't that right?" or "don't you think?" Or, they employ question intonation in declarative contexts; that is, they say a statement as if it were a question and as if seeking approval. Other examples include hesitation forms such as "um" or "like," overuse of polite forms, and frequent use of intensifiers like "very," "definitely," or "really." Have you ever observed or used these styles of speaking? Some communicators overuse these ways of speaking to the extent that listeners may not take them seriously.

Rather than view these differences in speech styles as gender-based, some scholars refer to them as "powerless" speech styles that anyone can employ.[74] Although women tend to use powerless language more frequently than men, other users include poorly educated or lower status individuals. Thus, some linguists argue that this speech style is related more to women's relatively powerless position in society rather than to essentialist characteristics of females.[75] Experimental courtroom research found that jurors and judges were less likely to view powerless speakers, regardless of gender, as credible.[76]

Results of research on functions of communication tend to correspond with the femininity/masculinity clusters (nurturing-expressive/instrumental-active). For example, Ivy and Backlund offer a "relational/content" differentiation: "We believe that men approach conversation more with the intent of imparting information (the content aspect) than to convey cues about the relationship (the relational aspect)."[77]

Sociolinguist Deborah Tannen offers similar perspectives on gender differences in her influential book entitled *You Just Don't Understand*.[78] Tannen labels female communication style "rapport," meaning that women establish connections and negotiate relationships. In contrast, she terms the male style of communication "report" to indicate men's need to preserve independence and to impart information.[79]

Communication differences between women and men may be due to socialization processes, including the abundance of literature asserting such differences (consider, for instance, the popular series of books about women being from Venus, and men from Mars).[80] Men tend to be socialized to use language that is valued, while the opposite usually occurs for women. Several research conclusions support this claim: men tend to talk about their accomplishments using comparative and competitive terms, while women may understate their contributions and acknowledge others' assistance.[81] Women often are more relational and dialogic; men tend to be more competitive and monologic.[82] Women tend to provide support; they often provide verbal and nonverbal encouragement, ask questions returning to points made by earlier speakers, and attempt to bring others into the conversation.[83]

Communication scholars Daniel Canary and Kimberley Hause criticize research on sex differences in communication for: relying on and perpetuating sex stereotypes, using invalid measures of gender, a dearth of theory, and a tendency to polarize the sexes.[84] In a meta-analysis of communication studies, they conclude, "given this research, we should *not* expect to find substantial sex differences in communication"[85] [emphasis added]. Indeed, they did not.

Communication scholars Daena Goldsmith and Patricia Fulfs draw a similar conclusion in a critique of Tannen's claims about gender differences. From their analysis of Tannen's evidence, they report that communication differences between women and men are typically minimal and contextual. They conclude that differences tend to be nonverbal rather than verbal. Basically, they assert that women's and men's communication behaviors are more similar than different.[86]

Some scholars challenge researchers' tendency to denote females and males as a dualism, with each embodying clear-cut, uniform characteristics. Rather than assuming a "two worlds" approach to gender interaction, they advocate research that explores different forms of femininity and masculinity.[87] In a book entitled *The Myth of Mars and Venus: Do Men and Women Really*

Speak Different Languages? Deborah Cameron problematizes the tendency to homogenize women's and men's communication behaviors.[88] She contends that we have overrelied on white, middle-class conversational patterns to identify gender differences. She asserts a need in gender studies of language to consider contextual factors such as cultural norms, setting, purpose of communication, and relationship between communicators, as well as complex facets of communicators themselves.

Instead of focusing on differences *between* women and men, some studies examine differences *among* women or among men. For example, men in all-male groups such as sports teams or in combat situations may exhibit caring characteristics that usually are attributed to women. Women in positions of authority often are more assertive than those who are in powerless jobs. Finally, gender differences in communication styles also can be related to other aspects of social identity, including race, nationality, age, sexuality, religion, social class, ability status, and occupation.

Communicating Gender in Organizations

A growing body of work on gender and organizations and organizational communication rests on the premise that organizations are fundamentally gendered: "doing gender is an ongoing and communicative accomplishment of everyday organizational life and, as such, it embodies issues of control, resistance, and transformation."[89] Feminist organizational communication scholar Patrice Buzzanell asserts that "gender organizes every aspect of our social and work lives including how we formally and informally communicate in organizational settings.[90]

The language and discourse practices I described earlier help to reproduce stereotypic feminine and masculine belief systems, as we are likely to confront practices in organizations that confirm our perceptions of gender distinctions. Moreover, through gender relations, women and men "construct and perpetuate confining roles, practices, and meanings that preserve asymmetrical power relations between them."[91] For instance, pink-collar roles (which women tend to occupy disproportionately) are defined by relationships to other organizational roles (e.g., secretary–boss). In organizational contexts, roles and relationships require us to react in appropriately gendered ways. We reproduce gender as we perform gender, through language, small talk, joking, dress, body language, marketing materials, advertising campaigns, use of space, and so on. In essence, organizations are gendered.[92] The gendered nature of organizations is evident in many communication practices, policies, and preferences. Women and men learn to conform to formal expectations or unspoken norms about aspects of appearance, such as types of clothing, grooming, and acceptable body weight. Many, if not most, of these policies and norms persist without challenge and are based on masculinist, white, middle-class and middle-age ideals and aesthetics.

Organizations tend to value masculine ways of communicating more than feminine ways. Feminine styles such as being inclusive, collaborating, and cooperating often are linked to subordinate roles. We also can see a preference for masculine styles in military and sports themes within organizations.[93] Organizational structures tend to emulate military models by operating under rigid hierarchies and chains of command. Traditional masculine sports often serve as the impetus for work (i.e., to win) and as a root metaphor in language that organization actors routinely use. Examples include: "ballpark figures," "score a touchdown," and "come up with a game plan." Military terms such as "battle plan," "big guns," and "plan of attack" also prevail.[94] Metaphors with masculine sexual implications include "he has balls" and "screw the competition."

A masculine ethic of reason and rationality underpins images of professionalism in organizations. This perspective reinforces the public–private dichotomy of femininity and masculinity. It also excludes and devalues femininities and women. These perspectives are evident in this common profile of how someone behaves "professionally":

> acts with restrained civility and decorum; wears a convincing shell of calmness, objectivity, and impersonality; thinks in abstract, linear, strategic—in a word, "rational"—terms; covers the body in conservative, mainstream attire; keeps bodied processes (e.g., emotionality, spontaneity, sexuality) in check; has promising, upwardly mobile career track; derives primary identity and fulfillment from occupation and work accomplishments; speaks standard English; and so on.[95]

As this profile implies, ideas of professionalism usually encompass masculine ways of being, including assertion, independence, competitiveness, confidence, competition, domination, and winning.[96]

Not only do workplaces discipline women and men to enact these ways of being, but women and men also discipline themselves. A study of white professional women revealed three themes of how these women view and modify their bodies in order to appear "professional."[97] First, they believe a professional body must be "fit," which means that women must engage in disciplinary regimes such as exercise and diet or using laxatives or diuretics. Second, they view the professional body as a "text" that others will read. To display and control their bodies, women develop and enact certain disciplinary practices such as monitoring their posture, offering a firm handshake, crossing their legs properly, and so forth. Finally, according to these women, a woman's body is excessive (or undisciplined) because it may leak, be overweight, or appear to be unruly. Their bodies may leak menstrual blood, protrude due to pregnancy, or display emotion through tears. Concerned that an undisciplined body might draw attention to their femaleness, these women constantly self-discipline.

Participants in a study of Latina public relations practitioners reported challenges with professionalism.[98] Some of these women try to counteract stereotypes of being highly sexualized by wearing dark clothing to avoid standing out. One woman said that a male colleague advised her: "to become much more bland. Less makeup. Less vocal. Less use of my hands. . . . This is the corporate game and you have to learn how to fit in."[99] They also experience pressure to be "feminine." Many of them reported dress codes that required them to show their legs. One woman explained that she would be fired if she didn't wear a dress or skirt, while another said that a client told her, "Oh, next time why don't you wear a skirt instead of pants."[100]

Sometimes, women resist attempts to discipline them. Latinas in the study described above gave examples of standing their ground, demanding respect, and confronting attempts to control them. Some women flight attendants share information with one another regarding high-risk areas where supervisors are likely to be watching them; when they are going to be in those locations, they wear appropriate shoes, makeup, and so forth. A group of flight attendants successfully contested their airline's weight requirements to gain a change in policy.[101]

Policies and practices also perpetuate gender hierarchy and role specializations. Employers tend to prefer women applicants for stereotypical feminine jobs, and men for masculine work. During job interviews, female applicants may face a double bind. They may hesitate to assert their accomplishments and abilities because they have been socialized to downplay them. Interviewers may rate them unfavorably because they do not exhibit these classic ways of describing themselves. Yet, if women interviewees are assertive, interviewers may perceive them as too aggressive and unfeminine.[102]

Men also face conflicts related to expectations about their gender. They may feel obligated to endure sexist language to maintain their masculinity. A white male colleague told me that he attended all-male meetings with higher-level university administrators who routinely made sexist, sex-oriented comments. Similarly, men may assume that other men share similar masculine interests, such as sports, and that they are interested in and available to participate in extracurricular activities such as happy hour or golf. Organizations that allow leave for childbirth usually offer time off for women but not for men. The prevalence of maternity leave rather than paternity leave reinforces the notion that child care is primary for women and secondary for men.

However, the number of fathers who take time off for their children's births is rising, in part due to the passage of the Family and Medical Leave Act (FMLA) in 1993. To comply with this law, many medium- and large-sized firms had to offer paternity leave for the first time, especially since men tend to be more eligible for the leave than women.[103] In addition, some corporations, including Timberland, IBM, Microsoft, and Merrill Lynch, have begun to offer one to two weeks' paid paternity leave.[104] Ernst & Young offers up to six weeks of paid paternity leave and flexible work arrangements.

A study of 4,638 fathers found that 89 percent took some time off work after the birth of their child. Among those, 64 percent took leave for one week or less.[105] Some men are taking off when their children are born, but they aren't using policy.[106] Instead, they're negotiating time off with their boss. They seem to be responding to cultural and economic pressures that discourage them from taking extended time off, for fear of repercussions. In 2008, the Army instituted a new paternity leave policy that gives fathers up to ten consecutive days of leave with their families when a child is born. Some men have filed workplace discrimination complaints with the EEOC for not granting leave for child care that they have granted women employees.

Emotion(al) Labor

A relatively new area of study reveals relationships between discipline and how people perform gender at work. Sociologist Arlie Hochschild coined the term ***emotional labor*** to refer to "the effort to seem to feel and to try to really feel the 'right' feeling for the job, and to try to induce the 'right' feeling in certain others."[107] Similarly, organizational communication scholar Sarah Tracy uses the term ***emotion labor*** to characterize "a type of work wherein employees are paid to create a 'package' of emotions."[108] Although most jobs require some degree of controlling one's emotions, the concept refers to jobs where emotional displays during face-to-face or voice-to-voice interactions are almost essential. Examples include flight attendant, waiter or waitress, wedding coordinator, police officer, bartender, bill collector, administrative assistant, sales clerk, teacher, physician, Disney employee, detective, cruise ship employee, health care worker, financial planner, and trial lawyer. As the workforce increasingly emphasizes customer service, employers increasingly are requiring employees to perform emotion labor—for instance, "a flight attendant who is required to smile politely even when passengers are surly, and a bill collector who must be stern and unpleasant even though he or she might feel great pity or sympathy for the debtor."[109]

Although this area of research is rife with issues related to communicating gender, organization scholars have only recently turned attention to emotion in the workplace. Emotions were typically viewed as private, feminine, and irrational, and therefore not relevant to the public, masculine, and rational domain of work.[110] However, some researchers have begun to investigate how employers monitor and try to control workers' expressions of emotions.[111]

Certain emotions are viewed as both experienced and expressed more often by women. Often referred to as "feminine" emotions, they include happiness, shame, fear, and sadness. Other emotions, such as pride, contempt, and anger, tend to be viewed as "masculine." "Neutral" (not necessarily related to gender) emotions include displays of detachment and objectivity.[112]

Many scholars contend that emotion labor is gendered because of traditional gender expectations and stereotypes, for both employees and their clientele.[113] Even when women and men hold the same position, customers or clients may expect them to display different emotions. For instance, victims may expect female police officers to be more caring and empathic than male officers. Women attorneys reported that male judges sometimes ordered them to smile.[114]

Jobs that require negative or neutral emotions tend to be more consistent with normative views of masculinity and professionalism, and men usually fill such positions. Women usually occupy jobs that require positive emotion. One quarter of men's jobs can be classified as requiring emotional labor, as contrasted with more than half of women's jobs. This makes sense, since most emotion labor jobs call for positive emotion.[115]

Not only are women and men segregated by emotional labor jobs, but gender affects assignments of job tasks. Although most service work usually requires displays of positive emotions, women generally are expected to be nicer than men. In fact, people expect women employees in general to be nicer and friendlier and to smile more than their male counterparts.[116] Female professors tend to spend more time teaching, advising, and being involved in service activities, while male professors often spend more time in research activities. Students also seem to rate female professors higher on friendliness than their male counterparts. Notice how these expectations align with gender role stereotypes that women are nurturing, while men are objective and rational. They also correspond with the hierarchical system in many research universities that values research more than teaching, while supposedly attributing equal weight to both.

Emotion labor jobs can be demanding and stressful, especially if compensation depends on customer approval. For example, a server's tip may be at risk, or a job evaluation may include customer ratings. Many people assume that emotion labor involves natural abilities and little effort rather than skills and considerable effort. Yet, emotion labor can be hard work. A worker who does not genuinely feel the emotion required by the job must conjure up the emotions while suppressing actual feelings. Consequently, organizational burnout often is associated with emotion labor.[117]

Transgender Issues

A final topic related to communicating gender at work is an identity category known as "transgender" that arose in the mid-1990s to describe various experiences and conditions of persons whose identity or behavior does not meet stereotypical gender norms. Transgender—a contested term with complex political and social implications—includes pre-operative, postoperative, and nonoperative transsexual individuals, as well as cross-dressers and intersexed individuals.[118] I focus in this section on transsexuals and workplace issues related to transitioning from one sex identity to another. These persons must choose to undergo transition while remaining in their job, or they have to find new employment. Transgender persons in mid-transition face tremendous challenges.

Employers sometimes terminate employees who intend to undergo gender corrective surgery, who have completed sex-change surgery, and/or exhibit behaviors that do not correspond with their perceived gender identity (e.g., wearing gender-"inappropriate" clothing).[119] Jennifer Blair, a male-to-female transsexual, works as a support group facilitator at a gender identity center. Her experiences and those of other transgender individuals indicate that employers often find pretexts for terminating gender-variant workers. One male-to-female transgender person told me that her boss fired her the day after he encountered her outside of work dressed as a woman. She was following a procedure that requires individuals who intend to undergo surgical sex change to "present" (i.e., dress and behave) for one year as a member of the "other" sex. Coworkers or managers sometimes harass or taunt individuals who are in process of transforming their identity. Blair observes, "To transition gender is almost certain professional suicide. This harsh reality no doubt keeps many if not most of us in the closet, living inauthentic lives."[120] Employers justify their reactions by citing concerns with potential disruption of work routines, such as negative responses or confusion for clients, students, or other stakeholders.

Numerous transgender persons have filed lawsuits against their employers or potential employers. The first statute prohibiting discrimination against transgender individuals was passed in Minneapolis, Minnesota, in 1975. Although only three additional cities had instituted similar ordinances by 1990, at least 108 cities and counties have passed laws prohibiting gender identity discrimination including Atlanta, Buffalo, Cincinnati, Dallas, El Paso, Indianapolis, Kansas City, Louisville, Nashville, New Orleans, and Pittsburgh.[121] Many states have introduced bills to update antidiscrimination laws to add gender identity and expression as protected categories in employment and in public accommodations.[122] Also, numerous states have passed specific laws to prohibit discrimination against transgender persons, although their protections vary. While Hawaii's law bans discrimination only in housing, Minnesota's law covers housing, employment, education, and public accommodations.

More companies are addressing gender identity and discrimination in their nondiscrimination policies. Some organizations have developed policies and procedures to facilitate transition for transsexual employees and their coworkers, including awareness training and designating some restrooms (a touchy issue for many coworkers of transgender persons) as "gender-neutral."

Conclusion

Gender is a primary aspect of identity. We create, negotiate, and maintain gender through communication. Notions of gender have varied across time, and they continue to change. Conceptions of gender also differ depending on other aspects of social identity. However, discourse about femininity and masculinity persistently has reflected an ideology of patriarchy. We often engage in gender construction in organizational contexts, where we produce, reproduce, and sometimes challenge and change expectations and stereotypes about femininities and masculinities.

1. What is your gender?
2. How important is your gender to you? Explain.
3. What primary sources have taught you about your gender?
4. How, if at all, do you express your gender (e.g., through language, communication style, dress, accessories, music, and so forth)?
5. Does your awareness of your gender ever help you communicate with others? Explain.
6. Does your awareness of your gender ever hinder how you communicate with others? Explain.
7. What situations, if any, do you avoid because of concerns related to your gender?
8. What situations, if any, do you seek because of your gender?
9. What advantages, if any, do you enjoy based on your gender?
10. Do you know of any stereotypes about your gender? If so, list them.
11. Are you ever aware of stereotypes about your gender as you interact with others? Explain.
12. How do the media tend to depict your gender? Do media depictions correspond with your sense of your gender? Explain.
13. Do you think your attitudes toward gender intersect with any other facets of your social identity, for instance: your age? your race? your sexual orientation? your nationality?

Reflection Matters

1. What did you find intriguing or interesting in this chapter? Why?
2. Do any current news stories where you live involve issues that this chapter covers? If yes, what points do they exemplify?
3. According to the sociohistorical overview, what are examples of how people used communication to construct gender throughout the history of the United States?
4. What are examples of power relations in the construction of gender in the United States?
5. For an entire day, imagine that you are a woman if you self-identify as a man, or that you are a man if you self-identify as a woman. If you identify as another gender category (e.g., bigender or genderqueer), please imagine that you are either a woman or a man. As you go through your day, think seriously about what you or others who interact with you might do differently. Pay attention to details about

your thoughts, your feelings, and your behaviors. Also, focus on interactions between yourself and others. Write a narrative essay (a story) about how your day might have gone differently, from the time you wake up until you go to bed. However, understand that *you never really can know what it's like to be someone else.* The point of this exercise is to help you analyze how you view gender.

6. During the course of a day, try to identify examples of sexist language.
7. As you reflect on your educational experiences, can you recall examples of any of the gender dynamics that I described?
8. Do you think that women and men communicate differently? If so, why do you think they communicate differently? Also, what are examples? Do these vary according to other aspects of social identity or based on context? Explain.
9. Do you agree with the notion that emotion(al) labor is gendered? Explain. What have your experiences been as related to the concept of emotional labor? You may refer to jobs you or someone you know has held, and/or you may refer to your experiences as a customer or client.
10. If you use the Internet, have you observed any differences in how women and men communicate online, or use various applications? If so, explain.
11. Conduct an Internet search on transgender issues and write a brief reflection on what you find.

Chapter 4

Race Matters

While teaching a course on critical thinking and race, I picked up a copy of a local newspaper. The front page displayed a large color photo of three men who appeared to be Latino. As I looked at the picture, I wondered what they had done. Reading the caption, I was saddened to learn that these men were relatives of a group of young people who had died in a car crash. Deeply ashamed for assuming they had committed a crime, I whispered an apology to them. This distressed me because even though I know better, my social conditioning had kicked in. However, I was glad I caught myself TUI (remember, that's "Thinking Under the Influence" of dominant beliefs).

Why do you think I assumed the men had committed a crime? Do you think I would have thought that if they had been black? (I'm pretty sure I would have.) What if they seemed to be Arab? (Probably.) Or, if they appeared to be white, or Asian? (I'm not sure.) What if they were women (of any race)? (Probably not.)

This story denotes some of the race matters I discuss in this chapter. Race, like sex or gender, is one of the first things we notice about a person, whether consciously or not. We often depend on race to provide clues about a person.[1] This tendency becomes obvious when we can't classify someone: we wonder and sometimes even ask, "What *are* you?" In this case, I figured the men were Latino because of their skin color, hair texture, and body types. But, I could have been wrong.

My story also illustrates how we may rely on stereotypes to interpret media representations of racial groups. I probably figured the men had committed a crime because the mass media often offer negative portrayals of minority racial groups, especially of black and Latino men as criminals.[2] My story also shows how intersections of identity matter, since I relied on cues of race *and* gender to infer that the men had done something wrong. Come to think of it, signs of social class also could have affected my response, because the men wore what seemed to be working-class clothing. Their clothing might also have helped me conclude that they were Latino.

In this chapter, we will explore the significance of race, racial stereotypes, media depictions, intersections of identity, and other race matters. After I define race, I describe how race has been socially constructed in the United States. Next I outline the history of race and labor in the United

States, and I discuss a variety of issues related to race and communication, including how the media socialize us. In addition, I connect historical developments to contemporary communication processes. As you will see, power and ideology affect (and have always affected) how we communicate race in the United States.

What Is Race?

What is your race? How do you know? When and how did you learn your race? Do you remember? Most people, especially people of color, become conscious at an early age of their racial identity. And, most people in the United States perceive race to be an important facet of identity. As ethnic studies scholar Michael Omi and sociologist Howard Winant observe, "Everyone 'knows' what race is, though everyone has a different opinion as to how many racial groups there are, what they are called, and who belongs in what specific racial categories."[3]

Definitions and classifications of race vary across time and contexts. When I was born in 1950, hospital personnel classified me as "N" (for Negro). During my younger years, I considered myself "colored" because that's what people like me in my community called ourselves. When I was a teenager in the 1960s, my friends and I gleefully obeyed the godfather of soul, R&B singer James Brown, who declared, "Say it loud, I'm black and I'm proud." The concept of black pride was an empowering force against ways I had been taught to dislike being black. In college, I designed a poster with "B-L-A-C-K" as an acronym for "Beauty, Love, Ability, Creativity, Knowledge." Because of these experiences, although the newer label of "African American" is an option, I still prefer "black."

Changes in my personal history of race labels show how the concept of race can vary. You also can see why some people are confused about what to call members of racial groups. For instance, if "colored" is taboo or outdated, why is "people of color" acceptable for some people? The difference rests partially in the historical-political contexts where people use the terms. For some people, the word "colored" brings up negative notions of blackness during postslavery times, while "people of color" can signify solidarity among groups of nonwhite persons.[4] While writing the opening story, I debated about how to refer to the men pictured in the newspaper. I could have said they were Latino, Hispanic, Mexican, Mexican American, Chicano, Dominican, or Puerto Rican, among many choices. I often feel awkward when speaking about racial groups because I'm not sure of the proper term. Has that ever happened to you?

But I still have not defined race, have I? We typically view race as an aspect of identity based on physiological features known as ***phenotypes,*** including skin color, hair texture, body type, and facial features. We use these physical attributes to assign an individual to a racial category. However, scholars from many disciplines conceptualize race as an artificial construct that varies according to social, cultural, political, legal, economic, and historical factors within a society. This social constructionist stance frames how I view race.

As I developed this chapter, I wrestled with how to refer to various racial groups because so many choices exist. And, I do not want to offend anyone. I selected the scheme that communication scholars Mark Orbe and Tina Harris use in their textbook on interracial communication.[5] They refer to the primary racial groups in the United States as "African-American," "Asian-American," "European American," "Latino/a," and "Native American." Where applicable, I specify groups within these categories, for example, I may refer to an Asian American as "Korean," to a Latina or Latino as "Mexican American," or to a European American as "Italian American." Sometimes I refer to African Americans as "black," or European Americans as (non-Hispanic) "white." When I cite research that employs other labels, such as "Hispanic," or "Anglo," I use the author's terminology.

I also struggled with how to distinguish European Americans from African Americans, Asian Americans, Latinas and Latinos, Native Americans, and other groups, because historical and current labels pivot from power dynamics between these two groups of groups. Each of my choices ("white/nonwhite," "majority/minority," "dominant/nondominant," "white/people of color") is potentially problematic. For instance, "white/nonwhite" implies that white is the preferred status because it designates other groups as *not* white. Or, "majority/minority" is currently accurate as a statistical descriptor, since European Americans currently outnumber other races in the United States. However, in terms of the world's population, that term is incorrect. It's also not accurate in some parts of the U.S. Finally, "dominant/nondominant" does not allow for contextual constraints and intersections of identity. A white woman may be the dominant person in one setting, but not in another. These distinctions typify language matters related to race that often confront policy makers, legal experts, and scholars, among others. I decided to selectively use most of these terms, depending on what I am discussing.

A final point related to defining race: although sometimes people use "ethnicity" as a synonym for race, I differentiate the two terms. Ethnicity refers to "categories of people who are distinctive on the basis of national origin or heritage, language, or cultural practices."[6] To elaborate, ***ethnicity*** refers to a common origin or culture based on shared activities and identity related to some mixture of race, religion, language, and/or ancestry. Therefore, ethnicity may encompass race, while race is a distinct socially constructed category. For example, Middle Eastern Americans (whom the census classifies as white) comprise a wide variety of cultural, linguistic, and religious groups descended from many countries in Europe and Asia.

Why Race Matters

Race has always mattered in the United States, at both societal and individual levels. Many societal developments have arisen, and they persist, due to the relentless significance of race, "a *fundamental* axis of social organization in the U.S."[7] Omi and Winant explain: "In American history, racial dynamics have been a traditional source, both of conflict and division, and of renewal and cultural awareness. Race has been a key determinant of mass movements, state policy, and even foreign policy in the U.S."[8] Historian Thomas Holt offers a similar conclusion: "Issues of group difference—and especially *racialized* differences—have informed most of the major conflicts of the century."[9] Race also is a primary facet of individual identity for many people, especially members of racial minority groups. Racial categories have "facilitated a sense of identity and common experiences for racial groups."[10] I once gave a talk entitled "Twice blessed, doubly oppressed" to celebrate being both black and woman, even as I acknowledged the potential for discrimination based on my race and/or gender.

Although racial pride can encourage a sense of empowerment and solidarity, it also can elicit ***balkanization***, or breaking up into smaller, hostile groups. Racial groups may compete among each other for resources and recognition. In addition, promoting one racial group may be seen as rejecting others. While some individuals and racial groups like the Ku Klux Klan (KKK) and Black Nationalists operate from that premise, that is not always the case. My sense of pride in black womanhood does not mean I disrespect whiteness, white womanhood, black manhood, or any other race-gender identities. Rather, my pride helps me to resist negative ideas about black women.

As Omi and Winant explain, most of us are socialized "to use race as a central cue for perceptions about others: temperament, sexuality, intelligence, athletic ability, aesthetic preferences and so on are presumed to be fixed and discernible from the palpable mark of race."[11] Numerous sources socialize us about our own race as well as how to classify others: "from census interviews to job applications to school reports to affirmative action reporting, Americans are bombarded with presumptions about their racial identifications. The media and schools teach racial categorization through visual and written language."[12] Therefore, race matters because it is an ongoing organizing principle of our lives.

Numerous political events illustrate the continuing significance of race in contemporary U.S. society. In 2003, the Supreme Court ruled on a controversial affirmative action suit that was brought against the University of Michigan Law School; the Court's 5–4 decision supported the school's affirmative action policy.[13] During the U.S. presidential election of 2008, race became a controversial issue as the first black candidate from a major party ran for the office, and won. Moreover, many people seem to think that having a black president means that the United States has overcome racial inequality: the popular, contested term, "post-racial America" alludes to a color-blind society where race is insignificant.[14] This perspective corresponds to a persistent difference in attitudes toward race, as whites are less likely than people of color to think that race and racism still matter. However, evidence demonstrates that persons of color continue to experience various forms of prejudice and discrimination, even as the U.S. can celebrate electing a black president and many other examples of racial progress.

In recent years, racial-ethnic minority groups filed class action lawsuits for employment or consumer discrimination against large corporations such as Walgreen Company, Coca-Cola, Eastman Kodak, Texaco, FedEx, and Sara Lee Foods, resulting in payouts of billions of dollars.[15] The problem is so serious that the Equal Employment Opportunity Commission (EEOC) launched an outreach, education, and enforcement campaign known as "E-RACE" (Eradicating Racism And Colorism from Employment) "to advance the statutory right to a workplace free of race and color discrimination." E-RACE focuses on new and emerging race and color issues in the twenty-first-century workplace.[16] In 2009, over 36 percent of cases filed with the EEOC alleged race-based discrimination.[17] These race-based claims reveal new forms of discrimination that allege intersecting areas of identity such as age, disability, gender, national origin, and religion. In addition, overt forms of race and color discrimination are resurfacing. Claimants report nooses, swastikas, KKK propaganda, and other racist symbols or insignia in their workplaces.[18]

Race also matters because the United States is undergoing an unprecedented racial transformation. Between 2000 and 2050, most of the population growth will arise from racial minorities, based on increasing numbers of immigrants (especially Hispanics and Asians). Currently, one in five children under the age of 5 is Hispanic. By 2050, whites will comprise less than 50 percent of the population, and Latino and Asian populations will have tripled.[19] The percentage of mixed-race individuals is climbing and is predicted to continue to grow: mixed-race marriage rates are rising, and a 2005 Gallup Poll found that almost 60 percent of teens had dated someone of another race or ethnic group.[20] As more people identify as being of mixed race, Americans' traditional ideas of racial identity will be challenged.

These transitions will impact all areas of our lives, including employment, education, politics, voting, immigration, and so forth. For instance, as I discuss later, considerable growth of immigrant populations impacts interactions at work and in school, as many persons will have varying degrees of skill in speaking English. Related to this, many groups are advocating policies and laws to ensure that English remains the dominant language in the public sphere. These initiatives "seem to embody a pattern of concern among largely white, middle-class individuals about their position relative to other ethnic groups—particularly Latinos."[21]

Race also matters because significant gaps persist between whites and persons of color in terms of socioeconomic status and related aspects of life. In 2008, the poverty rate for non-Hispanic whites was 8.6 percent; for Asians, 11.8 percent; for Hispanics, 23.2 percent; and for blacks, 24.7 percent.[22] Whites are more likely than blacks and Hispanics to have college degrees and to own homes. In 2005, 75 percent of white households owned their homes, compared to 48 percent of Hispanic households and 46 percent of black households. Thirty percent of the white population had at least a bachelor's degree as compared to 17 percent of blacks and 12 percent of Hispanics. Median incomes were $50,622 for white households, $36,278 for Hispanic households, and $30,939 for black households. Although Asian Americans had higher median incomes ($60,367) and college education levels (49 percent) than whites, they also had lower home ownership and higher poverty rates overall.[23] In essence, "racial inequality remains a robust feature of American life by nearly any commonly accepted measure of well-being."[24]

Constructing Race in the United States

Race always has been an important issue in the United States. How long do you think the concept of race has existed? Many scholars contend that race is a modern phenomenon that did not exist in the ancient world.[25] Race as a concept originally referred to breeding stock. A "race" of horses categorized common ancestry and distinctive physical features.[26] What we think of as races of humans seems to have emerged in the sixteenth century when Spanish explorers first encountered natives in the Americas. English travelers adopted the term for similar purposes to refer to people who looked different from them. Biological anthropologist Anthony Goodman notes that although Europeans previously had demonstrated an "us" vs. "other" mentality about non-Europeans, no formal classification schemes of humans based on phenotypes (physical characteristics) had existed.[27]

Scientific concern with human differences seems to have arisen only after Europeans encountered people during their travels who looked and acted differently from them. Based on explorers' accounts, European scientists and philosophers began to develop prejudiced theories of European superiority over non-Europeans.[28] The concept of race helped to establish Europe as the center of the world and to justify European capitalist expansion. In early colonial days, contrived categories of race helped to rationalize oppressive treatment of native peoples as well as the institution of slavery. Later, the concept justified similar mistreatment of other groups who immigrated to the United States.

Relying on the animal husbandry perspective that physical characteristics predict behavior, temperament, and capability, European scientists sought to identify and rank perceived variations among human beings. They claimed that racial groups evolved separately in various parts of the world, with no common lineage. They also asserted European superiority. The first classificatory system often is credited to French naturalist Georges-Louis Leclerc in 1749. Botanist Carolus Linnaeus based his work on Leclerc's system and specified four racial groups partially based on skin color: red, white, yellow, and black. In 1795, Johann Friedrich Blumenbach, a German anatomist and naturalist student of Linnaeus, developed a social hierarchy of race that identified Caucasian as the ideal: "I have allotted the first place to the Caucasian . . . which makes me esteem it the primeval one."[29]

Hierarchical arrangements of human groups created an ideology of race that placed whites in the supreme position. The process of naming groups illustrates how power and knowledge connect, as scientists used their positions of authority to fabricate information about groups of people. Moreover, this "knowledge" about race became a powerful source for explaining, predicting, and controlling social behavior. For example, these arbitrary claims of distinctions within species justified treating slaves and native people as animals.

Scientists conducted countless studies to present concrete proof of differences between races. The animal husbandry perspective infuses one scientist's claim that "superior races produced superior cultures and that racial intermixtures resulted in the gradation of the superior racial stock."[30] To substantiate these claims, scientists measured body parts, including brains, lips, jaw muscles, and noses, to link "inferior" races with apes.[31] Their efforts were inconclusive.

The preceding examples demonstrate that race is an artificial artifact that persons in dominant positions created to explain observed differences among human beings, to establish their superiority over other groups, and to justify mistreating other humans.

A telling example of race as a social construction is evident in the chronology of how the U.S. Census Bureau classified racial categories. Census forms always included questions of race, whether referring to them implicitly or explicitly. Although the first census in 1790 had no category for race, it distinguished black slaves from white people. In the nineteenth century, the census identified blacks based on percentage of African "blood." A person with one black and one white parent was typed as *mulatto*; *quadroon* and *octoroon* were used for one-quarter and one-eighth black lineage. Race became a more explicit category in the 1900 census, when census takers—known as enumerators—were required to put a check mark next to white, black, Chinese, Japanese, or Indian (American Indian). These options were listed under a category labeled "color" or "race."[32] "Color" was used from 1830 until 1940, and dropped in 1950, when the category asked for race only. "Color" was reinstituted with "race" in 1960 and 1970, and dropped thereafter. Enumerators provided information for these categories strictly based on visual cues; they did not ask individuals to state their race. In 1960, responses were based on direct interviews, self-classification, and enumerators' observations.[33] Since 1970, respondents have indicated their own classification by checking a category on census forms. These categories mainly delineated various labels for whites and blacks until 1870, when Chinese and Indian were added, although Indian also was a category in 1800 and 1820. Across the twentieth century, census forms listed twenty-six different schemes to categorize race or color.

Developers of census categories relied on varying principles and criteria to classify the population according to color or race. At one point, they defined Jews as nonwhite. In 1980, Asian Indians successfully lobbied to change their census classification from white to Asian American. In 2000, for the first time in its 210-year history, the census allowed individuals to identify mixed lineage by introducing an option to choose more than one racial category.

Due to increased numbers of interracial marriages and relationships, a community of self-identified multiracial citizens exists. Many of these individuals have formed support groups and advocacy organizations.[34] Nearly seven million people (2.4 percent of the population) identified as multiracial in 2000, and that number will probably escalate in the 2010 census. The 2010 census also includes the option to choose more than one race, with 15 racial categories and places to write in specific races not listed on the form.[35]

Challenges of constructing racial categories persist for the Census Bureau, which is trying to resolve whether to develop a separate category for people from North Africa and the Middle East. Although Arab Americans and other Middle Eastern Americans (e.g., Iranians, Lebanese, Egyptians, and Syrians) may classify themselves as white, some do not. Moreover, many of them do not "look white." In November 2009, the U.S. Senate blocked an amendment that would have required the Census Bureau to add a question on citizenship and immigration status to the 2010 census form.[36]

This brief overview of racial categorization according to the United States census exemplifies how race is a social construction. However, this artificial construction has real ramifications. Power sources in the United States have steadfastly reinforced and perpetuated a hierarchy of race that reflects an ***ideology of white supremacy,*** an internalized belief that white people are superior to all other races. Through individual actions and government legislation, individuals systematically have sought to separate white from nonwhite, to glorify whiteness and malign color.[37]

For example, in the 1920s, the infamous "one-drop" rule (initiated during slavery) was formalized, stating that if you had one ancestor of African origin, you were black. Along with the classifications of octoroon, quadroon, and mulatto, categories based on percentage of blood implicitly distinguish whiteness as a standard of genetic purity. This perspective seems to still affect African Americans, who are least likely among people of color to identify as being multiracial, even though many of them know that they have Native and white ancestors. Furthermore, non-Hispanic whites are least likely among all groups to identify as being multiracial.[38] Until 1966, over half of the states prohibited black–white marriages in order to preserve racial purity and to prevent "racial mongrelism." These examples reveal race to be an ideology based mainly on a hierarchy of skin color, usually the most defining characteristic of race in the United States.[39]

These examples also illustrate that government legislation often was based on preference of white to nonwhite people, helping to enforce discrimination and segregation. Consider, for instance, the time line for citizenship privileges:

- 1789: Native-born white persons automatically became citizens after the Constitution took effect. The Constitution classified blacks as three-fifths human.
- 1790: The Naturalization Law of 1790 reserved citizenship for free white immigrants only.[40]

- 1868: Blacks were allowed to become citizens.
- 1882: The Chinese Exclusion Act was the first immigration law to specify race, and to prohibit immigrants from entering the country on the basis of nationality.[41]
- 1924: Native Americans were granted citizenship. In that same year, the National Origins Act allowed citizenship rights only to emigrants from the Western Hemisphere.
- 1952: Asians were granted permission to become citizens.[42]

The ideology of white supremacy also is evident in immigration history. The "melting pot" assimilationist model of the late nineteenth century was premised on whiteness. During the height of this model, immigrants who looked white were pressured to assimilate into the mainstream of Western European-based white culture of the United States. However, many groups classified as white today were initially considered to be nonwhite. For instance, in the South, dark-skinned Italians were forced to go to black schools.[43] To be accepted as white, some members of these immigrant groups changed their names, religious practices, and ethnic traditions.

In the late nineteenth century, an anti-immigrant nativist movement arose to preserve fundamental "American" values. Native-born European Americans of Anglo-Saxon, Teutonic, and Scandinavian descent comprised these groups. These secret societies of men believed that the economic downturn of the nineteenth century was due to the influx of Caucasian immigrants from Ireland and southern and eastern Europe (Italy, Russia, Poland, Bulgaria, Yugoslavia, and Hungary). Because these newcomers were willing to work for lower wages, nativists decried them as "cheap labor." They also described them as "riffraff," "scum," "immoral," "drunken hoodlums," and "niggers turned inside out."[44] Due to a strong Protestant ethic, they were particularly derogatory toward the Irish, since most Irish were Catholic.[45] Magazine and newspaper editorials printed pejorative portrayals of the Irish as blacks and equated them with apes and savages.[46]

During those times, government and legal practices also focused on American values that reinforced racial hierarchies. For instance, the federal government decided that education was the best way to assimilate Native Americans into "American" ways. From 1870 to 1933, many Native American children were forced to attend boarding schools. These institutions were based on the philosophy of "kill the Indian, save the child."[47] Many children were taken against their parents' will and prevented from returning home until their education was complete. School administrators gave the children Christian names and cut the children's hair, which many tribes considered sacred. They also prohibited children from speaking their native language. Around 1933, the schools were abolished after public outcry.

While the government was enforcing policies for educating Native Americans, blacks began to make progress during postslavery Reconstruction. However, they suffered a significant setback due to the Supreme Court's landmark *Plessy v. Ferguson* decision. Based on the appeal of Homer Plessy, an octoroon from Louisiana who challenged separate train facilities for blacks and whites, this ruling established the "separate but equal" doctrine. This doctrine legalized segregation of blacks from whites in the South.

During a half-century time frame known as the "Jim Crow" period, blacks were subjected to second-class citizenship. Black children attended schools with inferior textbooks, lower paid teachers, crumbling buildings, and so forth. However, due to black educators' committed, concerted, and caring efforts, many blacks believe they had better educational experiences in these segregated settings than when they eventually went to integrated schools. Most other public facilities, including swimming pools, libraries, drinking fountains, passenger trains, buses, state universities, and many private institutions, such as hotels, restaurants, and movie theaters, were also segregated, and the black sections usually were considerably inferior to the white ones. Thus, although "separate but equal" was the law, the practice was "separate but unequal."

In February of 1942, following the Japanese bombing of Pearl Harbor, President Franklin Roosevelt signed Executive Order 9066, which authorized evacuating Japanese Americans to concentration camps.[48] Over 110,000 Japanese Americans were transported to various locations in the United States, where they were retained until 1944–1945.

Throughout history, as individuals and groups tried to enforce white supremacy through laws and other means, other individuals and groups successfully challenged this ideology. After the Civil War, President Ulysses S. Grant sent federal troops to the South to protect newly freed blacks. In 1865, Congress passed the Thirteenth Amendment to abolish slavery. The Fourteenth Amendment granted citizenship rights to former slaves in 1868, and in 1870, the Fifteenth Amendment granted voting rights to black men. (This ratification, however, had little impact for almost a century, with virtually no effect in the South where whites used various methods—from physical force to the poll tax and grandfather clauses—to keep blacks from voting.)

In 1943, Congress repealed the Chinese Exclusion Act. The Japanese American Evacuation Claims Act in 1948 authorized the government to pay Japanese Americans who suffered economic loss during internment. In 1952, the McCarran-Walter Immigration and Naturalization Act granted naturalization rights for all races.

Movements also arose to remove other legal barriers to full participation in U. S. life for racial minority groups. In another landmark decision, on May 17, 1954, the U.S. Supreme Court ruled unanimously that racial segregation in public schools violated the Fourteenth Amendment to the Constitution, which says that no state may deny equal protection of the laws to any person within its jurisdiction. The *Brown v. Board of Education of Topeka* decision declared that separate educational facilities were inherently unequal, thereby reversing the *Plessy v. Ferguson* ruling.

Tool No. 3

Cultural Competence

"Cultural competence" refers to how well you can interact effectively with people from cultures other than your own.[49] Cultural competence includes "an experiential understanding and acceptance of the beliefs, values, and ethics of others as well as the demonstrated skills necessary to work with and serve diverse individuals and groups."[50] The concept of cultural competence originated in health care professions, where providers became aware of communication challenges based on cultural differences while working with diverse patient and client populations. Members of these professions and others have created a wealth of information about how to deal effectively and humanely with challenges in cross-cultural communication through cultural competence training. Training often includes four components of cultural competence:[51]

1. **Awareness:** Become more aware of how culture operates in your life. Reflect on and examine your own cultural background and values, as well as biases and prejudices. Also become more aware of how you perceive and respond to other cultures. Recognize impacts of your cultural background on your perceptions and communication style.
2. **Attitude:** Increase your level of respect for different heritages. Become comfortable with differences between your culture and other cultures' values and beliefs; be sensitive to cultural differences. Be open-minded about cultural differences.
3. **Knowledge:** Understand power structures in society and their impact on nondominant groups. Learn more about other cultural groups *and your own*. Recognize and acknowledge societal and institutional barriers that prevent members of disadvantaged groups from using organizational and societal resources.
4. **Skills:** Develop, use, and improve skills for cross-cultural communication that include a wide variety of verbal and nonverbal responses. Select and use various media to communicate accurately and appropriately. Intervene and advocate on behalf of individuals from different cultures (i.e., serve as an ally).

I encourage you to seek and create opportunities to develop these components of cultural competence. By becoming culturally competent, you learn more about yourself as well as others, thereby expanding your horizons and gaining a better understanding of multiple views and experiences that form the foundation from which others see the world. A culturally competent individual can think critically about power and oppression and work to foster fairness and appropriate actions that apply in all contexts.

Embedded in all of these events is ***racism,*** a complex concept with multiple meanings. Different types of racism exist around the world. However, the most prevalent and pernicious form of racism has historically been European racism against non-European peoples. Early versions of this brand of ***racism*** referred to "any theory or belief that a person's inherited physical characteristics, such as skin color, hair texture or facial features, determine human intellectual capacity and personality traits."[52] Blatant racist attitudes flourished in the early days of the United States due to a pseudoscience that declared whites to be superior to all other races. Racist attitudes and behaviors intensified and deepened from the late nineteenth to the early twentieth centuries, as seen in a variety of legislative measures against various racial groups, the inception of the Ku Klux Klan, forcing Native American children to attend boarding schools, innumerable lynchings of blacks, internment of Japanese Americans, and so forth.

Currently, the concept of racism is both political and personal. To be called racist is one of the most disturbing accusations for most people in the United States, sometimes leading to irreparable damages to reputations and careers.[53]

Basing their connotations of racism on our horrific history, as well as notable progress since the civil rights movement, many whites and some persons of other races contend that racism no longer exists, except for isolated, individual, brutal crimes. Moreover, some whites may believe that their contempt for such crimes and the beliefs that provoke them disqualifies them from being racist. Many people do not understand that racial biases permeate practices and norms in organizations and institutions as well as individual attitudes and behaviors, whether intended or not. They do not understand the concept of systemic racial issues that became known as ***structural or institutional racism.*** In the late 1960s, Black Nationalist Stokely Carmichael coined this term to refer to collective patterns and practices that help to entrench racial inequality. Institutional racism is a product of "the systematic allocation of resources, privileges, and rights differentially by race: it is distributed across the whole range of social institutions both historically and in the present, and it does not require intention or agency to be perpetuated."[54] Institutional racism results from "the social caste system that sustained, and was sustained by, slavery and racial segregation. Although the laws that enforced this caste system are no longer in place, its basic structure still stands to this day."[55] In other words, the history of white supremacist ideology and racial hierarchy influences and maintains institutional patterns and practices that reproduce inequalities.

Institutions enact this type of racism through blatant behaviors, such as specifically excluding people of color from services, or covertly, such as adopting policies that can unintentionally exclude people of color. A policy of "seniority rules," or "last in, first out," which tends to apply to jobs that white persons historically have held, makes it difficult for more recently appointed persons of color to advance or to retain their jobs. Another example of institutional racism is the prevalence of standardized academic tests or criteria unrelated to job requirements or success, which measure cultural and educational norms of middle-class white males.

Racism can arise from individuals' behaviors, as well as from institutional or corporate policies. Both can be conscious or unconscious. For instance, individuals who realize that they may face sanctions may consciously veil discriminatory behaviors, or they may unconsciously enact biases based on how they have been socialized about race. On the other hand, perpetrators may genuinely be oblivious to the racist nature of their behaviors, and they will protest that they are not racist. Yet, "even people who are strongly motivated not to be racist are subject to automatic cognitive activation of stereotypes that can unconsciously influence behavior."[56] Psychological research, particularly studies using the Implicit Association Test (IAT),[57] provides convincing proof of the unconscious impact of living in the U.S., "where we are surrounded every day by cultural messages linking white with good."[58]

Meanings of racism are further compromised by people of color who indiscriminately label any negative behavior as racist. Sometimes called "playing the race card," these promiscuous charges of racism have "devalued the currency of the term."[59] Also, when some whites experience anything that smacks of favoritism for people of color, they will claim "reverse racism." These connotations and developments indicate that "U.S. society is presently engaged in a highly politicized struggle to define and redefine the meaning of racism."[60]

Concurrent with struggles over the meaning of racism are debates about definitions of race. The prevailing position corresponds with the premise of this chapter that race is an artificial construction. Most social scientists reject biological notions of race. Anthropologists in particular have challenged "essentialist" explanations of racial difference that have pervaded Western thought. In 1998, the American Anthropological Association (the official professional organization of anthropologists in the U.S.) released an official statement about race as a social and historical construction and that race should not be considered a valid biological classification:

> The "racial" worldview was invented to assign some groups to perpetual low status, while others were permitted access to privilege, power, and wealth. . . . Given what we know about the capacity of normal humans to achieve and function within any culture, we conclude that present-day inequalities between so-called "racial" groups are not consequences of their biological inheritance but products of historical and contemporary social, economic, educational, and political circumstances.[61]

In 2001, the Human Genome Project concluded that the human genome sequence is almost exactly the same in all people; that is human beings share 99.9 percent of their DNA.[62]

This discussion about the construction of race in the United States demonstrates that race is a social concept: "Racial categories and the meaning of race are given concrete expression by the specific social relations and historical context in which they are embedded."[63] We cannot consider race to be a scientific construct because society constantly changes its categories. This process is known as ***racial formation,*** "the sociohistorical process by which racial categories are created, inhabited, transformed, and destroyed."[64] In this process, social, economic, and political forces determine the content and importance of racial categories. Consequently, meanings and categories of race depend more on the social relations and historical context in which they operate than actual physical differences between human beings. Moreover, meanings and categories tend to reflect and reinforce dominant ideologies about "superior" and "subordinate" groups. Members of society enact these belief systems in all aspects of their lives. Next, we'll explore how race-based ideologies have operated in the labor market.

Race and Labor

The history of race and labor in the United States shows relationships between white supremacist ideology and how various racial groups are treated in the labor market. Common themes have been domination, discrimination, and segregation, which affected indigenous people who occupied the land prior to the Europeans, as well as members of different racial groups who came or were forced to come to the United States under varying circumstances. Combined with ideologies about race and their effects, those circumstances affected these groups' experiences in the labor market.

In the Virginia colony, most workers were white indentured servants who were outcasts (e.g., convicts) from England, Germany, and Ireland. Many of them were brought to this country involuntarily. By 1808, over 330,000 Africans populated the United States as unfree, unpaid laborers. Slave traders crammed them into ships and transported them against their will to the United States. African slaves received much harsher treatment than white indentured servants. They were doomed to be slaves for life, while indentured whites served for a contracted period of time. However, indentured whites also suffered discrimination, and many died before their contract expired. In 1850, Congress passed the Fugitive Slave Law, which obligated citizens to help capture runaway slaves and established harsh penalties for anyone who helped runaways.

White colonists employed various means to use persons of color to help build the "New World." Some Europeans forced indigenous peoples to work for them in addition to making payments of corn and animal skins. During the 1880s, Mexican cowboys *(vaqueros)* taught their ranching and cattle-herding skills to the colonists. Mexicans also worked as laborers in railroad construction and mining. These worksites always were racially stratified: on the ranches, managers and foremen were white, while cowhands were Mexican. In the mines, whites operated machines, while Mexicans did the dangerous work. On rare occasions when whites and nonwhites did the same work, their pay was unequal.[65]

During that time, many Chinese voluntarily came to the U.S. for sanctuary from conflicts in their native land. Concentrated in low-paying jobs, Chinese laborers built the agricultural industry in California, and they worked in gold mines. They also played a pivotal part in constructing the Central Pacific Railroad line.

Once railroads were completed, jobs on the West Coast became scarce. As numbers of jobs decreased, white workers often used physical force to shut Chinese immigrants out of farm, factory, or construction work. Many Chinese started laundry businesses because they were easy to establish and maintain and because whites were not interested in that type of work. In 1900, one of four employed Chinese men worked in a laundry.[66]

Around this same time, the federal government decided to train native people to become agricultural workers. Governmental interventions designed to "help" indigenous people often relied on "scientific" knowledge, and coerced them to abandon their ancient ways, which often were more effective. Whenever the government's forced initiatives failed, many Native Americans were forced to take temporary government employment to earn minimum wages. One last example: in 1912, President Woodrow Wilson issued an executive federal order to segregate (by race) eating and toilet facilities of civil service employees.

These are but a few ways that persons in power or members of dominant groups, often with the help of the federal government, oppressed nondominant racial groups. They illustrate the potency and persistence of the ideology of white supremacy.[67] However, across history, members of all racial groups challenged this perspective. The abolitionist movement, which was the first large-scale movement in the United States, consisted of women and men of all races who condemned the practice of slavery of any group. Abolitionists advocated abolishing all forms of involuntary servitude.[68] In 1903, Mexican farm workers formed a coalition with Japanese laborers known as the Japanese-Mexican Labor Association. In addition, members of *Sociedades Mutualistas*, an association established to instill a sense of pride among the members of various Mexican American communities, resisted labor exploitation and racism. Chinese workers not only went on strikes, but they also took their struggles to court, and sometimes they won their cases.[69] Individually and in groups, many other people of color and their allies exercised their legal rights by attempting to settle their grievances related to labor and employment through the court system. Sometimes, they succeeded.

In the 1930s, all-black unions enacted a movement against racial segregation and discrimination in the workplace. A. Philip Randolph, the president of the Brotherhood of Sleeping Car Porters, collaborated with other black leaders to organize a march on Washington, D.C., in 1941 for labor solidarity. Their actions culminated in Executive Order 8802, which President Franklin Roosevelt signed to end discrimination in defense industries and government employment. In 1944, the Supreme Court ruled that labor unions had to represent *all* employees. Randolph also helped persuade President Harry Truman to issue an executive order to integrate the armed services.

As reported earlier, the Supreme Court overturned the separate-but-equal doctrine in 1954. This momentous decision was the impetus to the civil rights movement, which spawned a series of laws to end racial discrimination related to voting rights, housing accessibility, employment, education, and public accommodations. These formed the foundation for most other social movements in the twentieth century and also encouraged initiatives such as the development of women's studies and ethnic studies in college curricula.

Equal opportunity laws include Title VII of the Civil Rights Act of 1964, which forbids discrimination in employment based on race, color, religion, national origin, and sex, and Title IX (1972), which prohibits discrimination in government-funded educational programs. In 1965, to remedy the impact of persistent patterns of discrimination and to advocate preferential treatment of historically disenfranchised groups, President Lyndon Johnson encouraged the government to take "affirmative action."

Consequently, the Equal Employment Opportunity Commission (EEOC) developed affirmative action policies to end discrimination in hiring, college admissions, and awarding contracts. Affirmative action is based on the premise that current conditions arise from centuries of systemic inequalities in education, training, and preparation for work, as well as racist stereotypes and white supremacist ideologies. When affirmative action was first created, most people endorsed it because they thought it was a fair way to remediate past injustices. However, by the mid-1970s, many people, particularly whites, had become disgruntled because they felt that minorities were receiving unfair opportunities and advantages. In 1978, in the midst of backlash, Allan Bakke sued the University of California Medical School at Davis because admissions personnel denied him admission in favor of black candidates whom he claimed were less qualified academically than he was.[70] Bakke called this action reverse discrimination, contending that preferential treatment of blacks meant discriminating against whites. The Supreme Court ruled in Bakke's favor, and this became the basis for an ideological campaign against affirmative action policies. Other lawsuits followed, with similar conclusions by the Supreme Court. However, as discussed earlier, the Supreme Court ruled in 2003 to uphold affirmative action policies.

In the 1960s and 1970s, Native Americans and their allies also sought justice and equal rights. For instance, they challenged treaty violations. In 1967, they won the first of many challenges to land and water rights. The first Native American Senate member, Ben Nighthorse Campbell, was elected in Colorado in 1992. The American Indian Movement, founded in 1968, remains an active force against discrimination.

This overview of race and labor in the United States shows how power dynamics operate to construct race, to reinforce racial hierarchies, and to make changes in favor of equality. Due to countless acts of resistance by groups and individuals, and based on related legislation, the plight of persons of color in the labor force has improved. While we have made notable progress, current statistics expose an enduring, race-related division of labor, opportunity, and power in the United States. People of color persistently and disproportionately occupy menial service-sector jobs, and women of color (especially Latinas) remain the lowest paid labor group.

Although members of all racial groups helped to build the United States, persons of color in general have not reaped the benefits of their contributions. Minorities often are placed in powerless positions or departments or in dead-end jobs. People of color in management positions tend to be concentrated in public relations; community relations; personnel/human resources, which deals with affirmative action issues and equal employment opportunity mandates.[71] I do not mean to demean these jobs, which are important in their own right. Instead I wish to punctuate the persistent paucity of persons of color in powerful, decision-making positions across many types of organizations. These conditions arise and are either reinforced or resisted, as individuals communicate race in various social contexts.

Spotlight on Media

Communicating Race on Television

Television is an omnipresent form of contemporary media. One television show can reach 20 million or more households.[72] Moreover, television is "a crucial location in which relationships between social groups, stereotyping, group identity, and the like, are played out."[73] Television programs tend to condense and oversimplify characters, which helps to perpetuate caricatures and stereotypes. TV shows regularly "assign and reassign racial characteristics to particular groups, both minority and majority."[74] These characteristics often convey stereotypical ideas about racial groups.

Such stereotypes are especially powerful for persons who have limited interactions with other racial group members, because they may unconsciously believe what the media broadcast. Research shows that viewers from all racial groups are likely to believe televised portrayals of minorities to be realistic and representative.[75] Thus, television may help to validate false ideas about racial minority groups, and negatively affect self-esteem of minority groups.[76]

Television programs always have overrepresented whites in contrast to their proportion in the population, while they tend to underrepresent other racial groups. (However, class distinctions permeate portrayals of poor or working-class white characters, who often embody negative stereotypes.) They also depict whites in a greater variety of roles. These distinctions matter because, for example, if we see only a few Native American characters, the few images that we do see may seem more significant and have more of an impact; also, if the media present a limited range of characters, we are less likely to understand that a wide range exists.

(continued)

The imbalance in numbers and types of roles persists. Recent studies show that persons of color in general tend to play more negative roles than whites. Also, although Hispanics are currently the largest ethnic minority in the U.S., they comprise only about 3 to 4 percent of characters on prime-time television. Furthermore, they tend to be restricted to a few roles such as comics, criminals, law enforcers, or sex objects. Plus, these characters frequently exhibit negative characteristics, such as limited intelligence, inarticulate speech, laziness, and verbal aggression. And, most Latinos are cast in service status roles (more than any other racial-ethnic group on television).[77] Thus, mainstream television depictions don't begin to capture the complex cultural, linguistic, gender, and social class heterogeneity of Hispanics in the U.S.

The rare portrayals of Native Americans tend to be negative, representing them as vicious, cruel, and/or lazy. They also fail to convey the heterogeneity of Native American groups. Instead, depictions promote homogeneous notions of poverty, alcoholism, and folklore. Although some recent images are more realistic, they substitute past stereotypes for newer ones, including the gentle, peaceful, noble, or passive Native American who has a "natural" connection to the environment.[78]

Similar racial distinctions operate in television news, which historically depicts whites more often and in more positive light.[79] Whites dominate coverage on national news programs, which overrepresents whites as victims of crimes, and persons of color as perpetrators of crimes. An in-depth analysis of nightly newscasts from three national networks ABC, CBS, and NBC in 2005 found that whites comprised 77.3 percent of on-camera sources.[80] Sources who were racial minorities included blacks, Middle Easterners (most of whom were of foreign descent, part of international stories), Hispanics, and Asians. American Indians were virtually nonexistent. Elite news sources such as experts, company spokespersons, government officials, and attorneys were predominantly white. Most of the persons of color who were news sources were private individuals providing personal accounts of news topics, such as disaster/accident stories and crime stories. Among racial minorities, Asians appeared most often as experts, (e.g., doctors and scientists in highly specialized fields), usually in stories about health and medicine. Minorities appeared more often in stories about crime and sports/entertainment than in any other topics.

On a more positive note, prime-time news magazine programs such as *20/20* and *Dateline NBC* have offered compelling hidden camera programs about racial dynamics that expose ways that people both enact and resist prejudice against minority racial groups, including Middle Easterners and African Americans in everyday settings. Also, numerous cable channels focus exclusively on various racial, ethnic, and linguistic groups. Although these alternatives strive to offer cultural sanctuary to members of minority groups, they also may perpetuate negative representations, as media studies scholar Beretta E. Smith-Shomade discusses in an in-depth analysis of positive and problematic aspects of Black Entertainment Television.[81]

Communicating Race

Communication research offers insight into relationships between the history of race in the United States and communication processes. Intercultural communication and mass media communication studies delve into topics such as racial/ethnic identity, co-cultural interaction (communication between members of dominant and nondominant groups), and media depictions of race. Combined with research from organizational behavior and organizational communication, this body of work implies intriguing relationships between racial dynamics and organizational communication processes. To get a better idea of how we communicate race, let's look at everyday interactions and personnel procedures in organizations.

Everyday Interactions

Within various settings, individuals tend to expect everyone to enact dominant norms and communication styles during everyday interactions. As a result, they may negatively judge persons who do not meet (or do not seem to meet) expectations related to white, middle-class values and attitudes. Standard-English-speaking listeners usually evaluate nonstandard speakers unfavorably based on status-related traits. They may respond to variations in verbal and nonverbal communication by equating them with speakers' levels of intelligence and personal characteristics. One group of listeners evaluated Spanish-accented, Appalachian-accented, and vernacular black English speakers as being of low status, while they evaluated British-accented speakers as being of high status.[82] According to one study, inner-city blacks speak less standard English than they did three generations ago.[83] Negative views of their speech styles can negatively affect black children's education in inner-city schools.

A major controversy about language in the U.S. centers on Spanish. Some groups want to abolish or restrict Spanish in the workplace and education, while others advocate extensive bilingual or multilingual training and curricula. For instance, a hotel owner in New Mexico forbade Hispanic workers from speaking Spanish in his presence because he thought they were talking about him. He also ordered some of them to Anglicize their names: Martin (Mahr-teen) would become Mar-tin, and Marcos changed to Mark. He fired those who did not go along with his demands. The New Mexico chapter of the League of United Latin American Citizens has protested the owner's behaviors.[84]

A large-scale study of diverse U.S. Latinos found that the more English that Latinos and Latinas speak, the more likely they are to interpret co-cultural interactions as discriminatory.[85] Speaking English was associated with twice the rate of reporting everyday discrimination, such as being treated with less courtesy or respect, receiving poorer service, and people acting like they were afraid of them or thought they were dishonest. Respondents also reported being called names, insulted, threatened, or harassed. As Latinas and Latinos achieve higher social status and become more assimilated, they seem to be more sensitive to discrimination than their less-acculturated counterparts. Basically, "as immigrants assimilate, they may lose their idealized view of America as the land of equal opportunity and therefore have higher expectations of fair treatment."[86]

Sometimes dominant group members enact skeptical attitudes toward people of color by challenging them, questioning their authority, or not inviting their input. Consequently, many people of color are guarded, cautious, and/or suspicious during interracial interactions. They sometimes find themselves second-guessing others' behaviors. For example, they may wonder whether another person's comments or behaviors are based on prejudiced attitudes or if they stem from a harmless misunderstanding. Communication scholar Mark Orbe developed ***co-cultural theory*** to describe a variety of verbal and nonverbal communication practices that nondominant people use while communicating with dominant groups.[87] They may use "conscious communication" strategies such as "mirroring" the language practices and appearances of dominant group members. They may also prepare extensively. For instance, persons of color may engage in cognitive rehearsal prior to interacting with members of dominant groups. They also may censor themselves. Although they may feel offended by dominant group members, they may choose to remain silent because they fear their response might magnify differences or alienate them from dominant others.

In addition to mirroring and extensive preparation, members of racial minority groups may respond to potential and actual stereotyping and discrimination by consciously avoiding interaction with dominant group members. They also might try to avert controversy by deflecting potentially controversial or charged topics, such as affirmative action or any current event that implicates race. Furthermore, persons of color may emphasize commonalities among all human beings and downplay differences based on race. Or, they may contend with others' preconceptions by simply being themselves: "Instead of worrying about the stereotypes that others place on all members of a co-cultural group, these persons do not allow such considerations to affect their behaviors."[88]

Stereotypes can influence everyday co-cultural interactions. Dominant group members may expect a Latina to be an expert on race relations and to speak Spanish fluently. Moreover, they may believe she is not qualified to perform any roles other than stereotypical ones, such as working with members of "her" community. Thus, executives may relegate persons of color to community liaison/relations positions rather than to more powerful executive roles.

Expectations based on stereotypes and their consequences can vary according to racial group. Organization members may expect Asian Americans to enact the "model minority" role by being docile, passive, and compliant. Asian Americans are characterized as "model" because they tend to assimilate into U.S. society without challenging mainstream ethos. This stereotype mistakenly assumes that Asian Americans do not identify as a racial minority group with specific grievances. Yet, in 2005, 31 percent of Asians reported incidents of discrimination—the largest percentage of any ethnic group.[89] Stereotypes of passivity also undergird managerial discourse that Asian Americans are not interested in climbing the corporate ladder. This reasoning may explain low numbers of Asian Americans in higher-level executive positions and their slow entrance into high-level positions in society, known as the "bamboo ceiling effect."[90]

In addition to impeding career advancement of people of color, race-based stereotypes can influence co-cultural interactions between service providers and clients or patients. For example, anthropologist Geri-Ann Galanti's book, *Caring for Patients from Different Cultures*, chronicles more than 200 case studies, illustrating how lack of cultural competency can cause cross-cultural conflicts and misunderstandings that affect the quality of health care that a person receives.[91]

Racial dynamics also can affect interactions within educational contexts. Communication scholar Patricia Covarrubias' in-depth study of Native American college students' everyday experiences revealed the prevalence of ***discriminatory silence,*** "the public or private withholding of speech, specifically the withholding of voiced objections to statements that dismiss, disconfirm, or alienate a person because of racial, ethnic, or cultural origin when the ethical action would be to speak up."[92] Students described numerous classroom moments when their white classmates, professors, or presenters made discriminatory or dismissive comments about Native Americans that everyone else ignored. One student reported crying through a whole class as a guest speaker interspersed his speech about injustices against Native Americans with frequent references to "drunk Indians," and no one questioned the speaker's assumptions and stereotyping. Another student said that while she "poured her soul out" in a class where everyone else was white during a speech about a need for increased federal funding for health care on Indian reservations, white students made negative remarks and exhibited negative nonverbal cues. When she concluded, a white student said, "I don't think Indians deserve to have free health care. My grandfather had to pay for his own." The professor and other students said nothing, although the professor supported her outside of the class. As Covarrubias concludes: "it is up to all of us to collaborate to invent more just selves by deciding when it is ethical to exercise silence or to speak up."[93]

As some persons of color negotiate co-cultural interactions, some white people also struggle with racial dynamics. White males sometimes feel targeted and stereotyped as the source of racial strife. They believe that others equate "white male" with being racist, sexist, homophobic, and insensitive.[94] During everyday interactions, white persons' anxiety about being perceived as racist can inhibit communication. In a multiracial consulting firm, white employees actively avoided conflict or confrontation with persons of color because they feared they would be seen as racist.[95] These apprehensions constrained interracial relationships to the extent that white managers hesitated to offer constructive criticism to people of color. In contrast, people of color resented the conflict-avoidant behaviors of their white colleagues.

Some white people are not conscious of race because of their historical power position. Whites as the privileged group have tended to take their identity as the hidden standard for measuring other groups. In early communication studies, being white was the unspoken norm. As a result, when scholars and researchers referred to an individual or a group as "different," they usually meant as compared to a white person or white people. When an identity is the norm, it is thereby invisible, "to the extent that many whites do not consciously think about the profound effect being white has on their everyday lives."[96] This lack of consciousness about white racial identity is changing due to racial demographics, responses to affirmative action, perceptions of "reverse discrimination," diversity training/teaching initiatives in corporations and on college campuses, and scholarship on whiteness.[97] Similar to work in gender studies that considers men's experiences, research about race now includes whiteness. This body of work seeks to challenge the reality that "whiteness often has gone unnamed and unexamined because it has been uncritically and unthinkingly adopted throughout society."[98]

A pioneer in whiteness scholarship named Peggy McIntosh introduced the concept of ***white privilege*** to refer to the unearned, unacknowledged entitlement one receives in everyday life simply because of white skin. In a groundbreaking article, McIntosh offers a list of forty-six invisible advantages she enjoys as a white person, including the ability to choose to be oblivious to the effects of race. Her list includes ordinary conditions of daily experience that she "once took for granted, as neutral, normal, and universally available to everybody."[99] The list illuminates issues and circumstances that people of color tend to routinely confront, but that most white people are unaware of. Most of the items she includes in her "knapsack of privilege" have obvious implications for communication. As you read the following examples, consider if and how they apply to your life.

1. I am never asked to speak for all the people of my racial group.
2. I can do well in challenging situations without being called a credit to my race.
3. I can turn on the television or open the front page of the paper and see people of my race widely and positively represented.
4. I can go shopping alone most of the time, pretty well assured that I will not be followed or harassed by store detectives (because of my race).
5. I can worry about racism without being seen as self-interested or self-seeking.[100]

These sample items illustrate how race can matter during everyday interactions and events in various contexts. As items 1 and 2 imply, persons of color often encounter situations where others view them as representatives of their race. In college classrooms on predominantly white campuses, black,

Latina, and Latino students sometimes feel a sense of hypervisibility when it comes to discussions about race, as others in the classroom turn to them for "expertise" when the topic of race arises. On the other hand, they may feel hyperinvisible during discussions about any other topics, as others seem to believe that they are not intelligent enough to participate in discussions about other subjects.

Item 3 refers to the influence of the media's documented tendency to depict people of color and white persons in ways that reinforce dominant ideologies. Item 4 refers to discriminatory practices that some persons of color experience while shopping. It's happened to me more than a few times, and I always feel frustrated, humiliated, or angry. Finally, item 5 alludes to race-related differences in how people respond when an individual makes comments about race and racism.

The concept of white privilege illustrates how U.S. society institutionalizes racial hegemony. The purpose of raising consciousness about white privilege is not to make white people feel guilty or ashamed. Rather, the goal is to increase their understanding of how others experience race, and their commitment to using their privilege to combat racism. Understanding white privilege also may help people of color understand why some white people seem oblivious to the issues that frequently occur for people who are not white. Furthermore, the concept does not assume that ALL white people enjoy maximum benefits of white privilege because it recognizes that privilege operates in degrees, according to other aspects of identity such as gender, sexuality, social class, and so forth. Thus, exploring whiteness and white privilege has positive potential for achieving racial equality.

Personnel Procedures

Racial dynamics often unfold during personnel procedures such as recruiting, hiring, evaluating, and promoting employees. To recruit employees, organizations often rely on informal hiring practices, and applicants often learn about jobs through friends or relatives. As a result, organizations that use employee referrals to fill job vacancies tend to hire workers of the same race as current employees, which helps to maintain racial segregation patterns of employment across all levels of organizations. Recruitment through informal methods such as word-of-mouth reinforces racial homogeneity because employees usually tell people like themselves about job opportunities, and companies often hire applicants who are referred by current employees.[101] Furthermore, research shows that race-based social networks can affect racial inequality in attaining jobs, as well as pay levels and retention rates.[102] Regardless of how people apply for a job, employers may base hiring decisions on race-based stereotypes and attributions. A large-scale research project on employment screening behaviors found that school principals were more likely to invite Asian American applicants to interview for an assistant principal position than they were to invite Hispanic or older Native American applicants, although their credentials were identical.[103] The principals may have relied on stereotypes that Asian American candidates are more intelligent and capable than other racial minorities.

In a similar project, resumes of applicants with "white-sounding" first names (e.g., Neil, Brett, Greg, Emily, Anne, and Jill) elicited 50 percent more responses than ones with "black-sounding" names (e.g., Ebony, Tamika, Aisha, Rasheed, Kareem, and Tyrone). Researchers mailed five thousand resumes in response to want ads in the *Chicago Tribune* and the *Boston Globe.* "White" applicants received one response—a phone call, e-mail, or letter—for every ten resumes mailed, while "black" applicants with equal credentials received one response for every fifteen resumes sent.[104]

Once hired, persons of color may face differential treatment. Contrasted with whites, they tend to receive fewer rewards, resources, or opportunities to advance. In general, employee evaluations are significantly higher for persons of the same race or gender as the evaluator, even when they are based on "objective" performance standards, although black raters may evaluate blacks lower than whites.[105] Although supervisors may not realize their perceptions or how their attitudes toward people of color influence their evaluations, tendencies toward differential performance evaluation can limit career mobility for persons of color and increase opportunities to advance for white employees. However, white males also can experience limited career mobility if they do not personify the image of a promotable employee, which often is based on the ideal of white masculinity that I discussed in the chapter on gender.

Research repeatedly reveals that discriminatory practices in organizations can block minorities' advancement to top management positions. Persons of color may have limited access to critical information and they may experience lower levels of acceptance into work groups or teams. The Federal Commission on the Glass Ceiling reported that areas in which minorities and women experience obstacles to advancement include managerial preparedness, mentoring, management training, and career development.[106]

A key to successful career development is networking. Establishing relationships with persons who can help you advance is essential for moving up the organizational ladder. Employees may join formal groups at work or engage in informal networking. Informal networking often occurs outside of the organization during sporting events, cocktail hours or happy hours, and parties. Persons of color may not participate in these extracurricular social activities because they think they will be uncomfortable due to anticipated "culture clash." In addition, they may simultaneously contend with in-group pressure not to align with the "good old boys." White colleagues may not invite persons of color to participate because of outright discrimination, or due to apprehension about interacting with an "other" outside of work.

In addition to formal and informal networks, another key to advancement is mentoring relationships, which also may suffer from racial dynamics and politics. Employees of all races might hesitate to initiate cross-race mentoring relationships: persons of color may worry that others in their racial group will consider them to be an Uncle Tom or Aunt Jane (someone who kisses up to white people), while whites may feel similar apprehensions about other white people's opinions. Cross-race/cross-gender mentoring relationships—for example, between a white man and a Latina—may be fraught with concerns about sexuality issues, given increased attention to sexual harassment in organizations, as well as cultural differences in attitudes toward sexuality (I discuss organizational romances and sexual harassment in chapter 6).

The good news is that many organizations have instituted formal practices and policies that seem to address many of these challenges to career advancement for employees of color (and members of other nondominant groups, including women, GLBTQ employees, and persons with disabilities). For instance, many businesses support employee resource groups (also called advocacy groups, affinity groups, or employee networks), which focus on issues germane to underrepresented groups. Most groups do not limit membership to those who self-identify with the focus of the group; they welcome anyone who wishes to join. About 90 percent of Fortune 500 companies have employee resource groups, and 100 percent of the organizations honored as the *2010 DiversityInc Top 50 Companies for Diversity* finance employee resource groups (contrasted with 62 percent in 2005).[107] These 50 organizations consider resource groups to be crucial assets to accomplishing business goals, and all of them allow groups to meet during the workday (contrasted with 73 percent in 2005). Earlier versions of resource groups tended to provide in-group networking, and to focus on social or cultural networking and activities, such as cultural potluck lunches or Black History Month events. However, current groups serve much more productive functions, including employee recruitment, retention, and advancement, as well as marketing to diverse communities and achieving supplier diversity. Moreover, 74 percent of CEOs from the Top 50 meet regularly with these groups, and 92 percent of the groups have a senior executive who is a formal member (this person usually reports to the CEO). A few companies support affinity groups for white males; most of these address diversity issues and strive to include white males in diversity initiatives. A group at IBM formerly known as the white male network changed to a men's network that supports diversity efforts and fatherhood.[108]

Because companies such as the Top 50 realize the value of diversity to their bottom line, they are investing monetary and human resources into a variety of initiatives. In addition to employee resource groups, these initiatives include formal mentoring programs and mandatory diversity training (which often focus on communication and cultural competence). Many companies also are making diversity more central to their missions and strategic goals, and they are factoring accountability into their efforts. For instance, Sodexo (number 1 on the list), implements a Spirit of Mentoring program: "a focused, practical and extremely comprehensive mentoring effort that includes advance training and benchmarks at regular intervals to examine how mentoring pairs are relating to each other and accomplishing goals."[109] Sodexo also measures progress in diversity through a scorecard that tracks hiring, retention, and promotion of underrepresented groups.

Our exploration of communicating race highlights numerous issues that confront members of nondominant and dominant races. Organizations that embrace/support racial diversity can reap numerous rewards, including enhanced co-cultural interactions, decreased complaints and lawsuits, less turnover, increased innovation, greater market performance, and improved productivity. Valuing racial difference requires concerted effort at all levels of an organization. Members must assess and be willing to reconstruct everyday practices and policies. The process can be challenging and time consuming. However, the potential positive outcomes seem well worth the efforts.

Conclusion

Race is an artificial construction of social identity based on an ideology of white supremacy, a belief in a racial hierarchy with white people at the top. Various power sources have used communication to construct categories of race to reinforce and reproduce this ideology. However, persons of all races have also used communication to envision and enact more positive perspectives on race. Across the history of the United States, labels for race have often changed, due to political, social, cultural, and economic developments. Currently, actual and anticipated changes in racial demographics (i.e., numbers of persons of color are increasing) have heightened awareness of racial dynamics in all sectors of U.S. society. In the labor market, race has been, and continues to be, a significant factor, as minority racial groups and their advocates vie for equal employment opportunities. Consequently, race remains an important aspect of social identity in the United States. Furthermore, communication plays both oppressive and liberatory roles in the quest for racial equality and harmony.

ID Check

1. What is your race?
2. How important is your race to you? Explain.
3. What primary sources have taught you about your race?
4. How, if at all, do you express your race (e.g., through language, communication style, dress, accessories, music, and so forth)?
5. Does your awareness of your race ever help you communicate with others? Explain.
6. Does your awareness of your race ever hinder how you communicate with others? Explain.
7. What situations, if any, do you avoid because of concerns related to your race?
8. What situations, if any, do you seek because of your race?
9. What advantages, if any, do you enjoy based on your race?
10. Do you know of any stereotypes about your race? If so, list them.

11. Are you ever aware of stereotypes about your race as you interact with others? Explain.
12. How do the media tend to depict your race? Do media depictions correspond with your sense of your race? Explain.
13. Do you think your attitudes toward race intersect with any other facets of your social identity, for instance: your gender? your age? your social class? your sexual orientation?

Reflection Matters

1. What did you find intriguing or interesting in this chapter? Explain.
2. Do any current news stories involve issues that this chapter covers? If yes, what points do they exemplify?
3. According to the sociohistorical overview, what are examples of how people used communication to construct race throughout the history of the United States?
4. What are examples of power relations in the construction of race in the United States?
5. How much does your race matter to you? How much does your race seem to matter to others? Explain and give examples. How strongly do you identify with your ethnic heritage? Explain.
6. How is the "melting pot" metaphor based on whiteness?
7. What do you think of the concept of white privilege? How did you respond to the sample questions from Peggy McIntosh's list? Explain.
8. How much do you know about races or ethnic groups other than your own? How did you attain this knowledge?
9. Are you aware of any stereotypes about your combined race-gender identity (e.g. white woman, or Asian man)? If yes, what are they? Has anyone ever seemed to respond to you based on your combined race-gender identity? Explain.
10. If you watch prime-time television, how do the programs that you like portray race and race relations? How accurately do you think they tend to portray racial groups?
11. Do you ever watch cable channels that target a specific racial or ethnic group? If so, how well does their programming represent those groups? What criticisms, if any, would you offer about these channels?
12. How do you think you would have responded if you were a student in the class that I described where a Native American student was visibly distressed by a speaker's presentation?

Chapter 5

Social Class Matters

I would get excited when my grandma brought home hand-me-down clothing from the white families she worked for as a maid. I would eagerly sift through the pile to find something I liked. Although I proudly wore secondhand outfits, my friends and I would mock members of a family in my neighborhood who often rummaged through dumpsters for castoffs. Even though I knew the government housing project where we lived was restricted to low-income families, I do not remember feeling stigmatized. Every year my elementary school would send "care" packages to needy families overseas. Happy to help poor children, I would eagerly donate small items like a bar of soap, a handkerchief, or a box of crayons.

I used to wish my family could get surplus government food like some of my friends' families. Even though Ma was raising my brother, sister, and me on her own, her income was slightly higher than the maximum allowed. Fortunately, her income was low enough to qualify me for the Comprehensive Employment Training Act (CETA) program. In junior high, CETA employed me as an assistant to the home economics teacher; in high school, I worked in the guidance counselors' office. I used my income to start a bank account and help Ma pay for my school clothes.

Kids in the projects enjoyed lots of recreational activities, thanks to government social programs that provided facilities, staff, and other resources. We flocked year round to the settlement house (a recreation and social services center) to do arts and crafts, play sports, perform in variety shows, and watch movies. I was a member of the girls' basketball team and an award-winning drill team. During the summer, we played in fully equipped and staffed playgrounds. Thanks to the Associated Neighborhood Centers (a city-sponsored program), I worked one summer as a day-camp counselor, where the kids nicknamed me "Big Bird."

My experiences encompass some of the issues that I cover in this chapter. They show how class-power dynamics unfold in macro-level structures as individuals engage in everyday micropractices. The fact that my friends and I made fun of the family who could barely afford clothes demonstrates the enduring nature of class consciousness. Combined with my home training, the annual charitable drive at my school socialized me to care about less-fortunate people. Yet, attitudes toward class vary according to sociohistorical context. When I was younger, the media did not bombard me with ads tailored for my age group, although they had begun to target teenagers. I distinctly remember the jingle for Wrangler stretch jeans. I begged Ma to get me a pair, and she did. However, my friends and I were not as concerned about style and brand names as many young people nowadays seem to be. I suspect that few children who now live where I was raised would welcome hand-me-downs. Due to peer pressure, the hype of brand names, and fashion trends, most of them are probably way more picky than I was about clothing.

My story illustrates how use of space can indicate class. Geographic location can denote class position. "Housing projects" are class symbols of being poor, and trailer parks often signify poverty.[1] Race also matters, since the projects symbolize people of color (especially blacks), and trailer parks symbolize white people. The familiar saying that the most important aspect of real estate is "location, location, location" implies a class bias. Prices of comparable homes can vary sharply based on neighborhoods. Most major U.S. cities have identifiable communities of wealthy people, as well as "the other side of the tracks" (or the "wrong side") where poor people reside. Was that true where you grew up?

Throughout history, the federal government and state and local agencies, to varying degrees and with varying criteria for qualifying for assistance, have intervened to assist lower-class groups. When I was growing up in the 1960s, the United States was in the midst of social reform. Due in large part to social activists, the government initiated programs for socioeconomically disadvantaged families. As a result, many lower-income families had jobs, affordable housing, and food. The programs that employed me as a teenager helped to reinforce the strong work ethic my mother instilled in me and to empower me. Yes, my peers and I were poor, but we enjoyed a rich childhood and a strong sense of community. We were among countless beneficiaries across the country of the settlement house movement that offered services to poor citizens and poor immigrants. Many of us are proud to be from the neighborhood we affectionately call "Brick City." We were fortunate to grow up during a time when public attitudes toward the less fortunate were benevolent.

My memories imply relationships between hegemony and social class. For example, income often dictates where people live.[2] The United States comprises a class-segregated society with poor and rich people residing in different types of "gated" communities, with different ramifications. To live in the projects, we had to follow rigid rules and policies or risk eviction. Members of homeowner associations in other types of neighborhoods also have to comply with rules and regulations.

I delve into these and related issues in this chapter to show how power relationships and ideology affect constructions of social class in the United States. First, I discuss conceptions of class, after which I explain why class matters. Next, I trace the social construction of class in the United States. Then, I explore relationships between class and communication.

What Is Social Class?

What is your social class? If you are like most people in the United States, you consider yourself to be middle class. Whatever class you identify with, what do you base your category on? Many people equate class with money or economic status.[3] However, class consists of more than economics. The word "class" comes from the Roman *classis*, a system used to divide the population into groups for taxation purposes.[4] Since Roman days, class consistently has been based on social stratification—the ranking of groups according to various criteria, with higher positions afforded more value, respect, status, and privilege than lower positions. Placement in a class system can occur through ***ascription,*** based on conditions at birth such as family background, race, sex, or place of birth, or ***achievement,*** as a result of individual effort or merit such as running a profitable business or earning a college degree.[5]

Most social science ideas about class stem from Karl Marx and Max Weber, who based their work on economics. Marx conceived of two classes related to the means of production: the bourgeoisie, which includes those who own the means of production, and the proletariat or working class (everyone else).[6] Class labels initially were based on objective factors, such as amount of ***capital*** (accumulated goods and their value).

Believing that class is more than just economics, Weber claimed that stratification is based on property, power, and prestige (the three Ps).[7] Property refers not only to ownership, but also to the *control* of property. Weber conceived of power from a "power over" standpoint. He viewed power as the ability to control resources and behaviors of others, contending that this form of control and its results affect social stratification:[8] "Class is about the power some people have over the lives of others, and the powerlessness most people experience as a result."[9] Prestige means esteem or social status. One type of prestige in contemporary society is occupation. Because amount of income and advanced education and training can influence the prestige level of occupations, white-collar occupations generally imply higher prestige than blue-collar, pink-collar, or brown-collar occupations, which include service and clerical jobs.

Weber's ideas about class correspond with contemporary views that it consists of both economic factors and more subtle variables. French sociologist Pierre Bourdieu elaborated the concept of capital to emphasize ideological conditions plus how people use capital to compete for position and resources. He specified three types of capital: ***economic capital,*** which includes financial assets; ***cultural capital,*** which encompasses specialized skills and knowledge such as linguistic and cultural competencies, passed down through one's family or from experiences in social institutions, such as an Ivy League education;[10] and ***social capital,*** which consists of networks, or connections among people who can help one another.[11] Here's a brief example of Bourdieu's conception of capital. When I won an all-expenses-paid scholarship for college, I could have gone to any college in the world that admitted me because I had earned access to economic capital to pay tuition, room, board, and travel costs. Because I was clueless about how to select a school, I picked the one that another black female student (who had won the same scholarship two years earlier) had chosen. I was not savvy about the college selection process, and the guidance counselors at my school did not offer any assistance, even though I worked in their office. (Research persistently reveals a pattern of differential counseling according to a student's social class.)[12]

In essence, because I was a member of a poor family whose members had never gone to college, I had not gained the appropriate cultural or social capital to navigate the college admission process. Fortunately, I did acquire an important bit of cultural capital because I was tracked according to intelligence and placed in classes with middle- to upper-class white students who knew the ropes of getting into college. I took my cues from them as they discussed the SAT and the ACT (college entrance exams I did not know about), and I persuaded Ma to pay for me to take those tests. Also, I dared to dream about going to college because of my friendships with white peers; if they could do it, so could I. Unfortunately, my black friends from the projects did not have similar exposure and experiences, and none of them planned to attend college immediately following high school.

My experiences and Bourdieu's perspective on class reveal "linguistic, social and communication processes that foster class membership and consciousness."[13] For example, an increasing emphasis on educational credentials reflects the strength of cultural capital in U.S. society. Members of the middle and upper class increasingly seek access to elite universities that signal a more superior educational experience than other types of institutions of higher education that increasingly are available to the masses.[14] People in higher socioeconomic brackets often rely on "connections" to gain admission to preferred institutions, illustrating an underlying premise of social capital: "It's not what you know, it's who you know." Another example of social capital permeates the standard practice within elite institutions of higher education of "legacy admissions," or giving preferential treatment to children of alumni. Yet, few people challenge this longtime form of "affirmative action."

When I asked you about your social class, what categories did you consider? Although dozens of classification schemes exist, most charts refer to variations of "upper," "middle," and "lower" classes. Some subdivide these, for instance: "upper-upper," "lower-upper," "upper-middle," "lower-middle," "working class," and "poor." Synonyms for the upper class include "owning," "capitalist," or "overclass." And, the lowest of the lower class has been labeled the "underclass."[15]

These classifications explicitly indicate power relationships. Members of the working class tend to have relatively little control over their jobs, and they usually do not supervise anyone. At the top level, the capitalist class includes those who control the means of production. Furthermore, "as of 2007, the top 1 percent of households (the upper class) owned 34.6 percent of all privately held wealth, and the next 19 percent (the managerial, professional, and

Tool No. 4

Networking

The old saying, "It's not what you know, but who you know" is true, to a certain extent. According to many sources, nearly 80 percent of job openings available at any one time are never advertised. These jobs exist in the "hidden job market." You can access this invisible market through networking. Networking seems to come naturally to many members of dominant groups because they have been socialized to make and use connections. However, many people may not feel empowered to network or they may not know how to network. Yet, anyone can build and maintain an effective career network. Here are some tips:

- Build a local career network of anyone who has helped you or who might help you with your career in any way—regardless of where you are on your career path. For instance, list current and former teachers, employers, classmates, and coworkers. (I got my first job when I finished college from my 8th grade English teacher, who was directing a citywide library program.)
- Be inclusive in building your career network. Don't limit yourself to people who are like you. Consciously include people from varying social identity groups and with diverse professional interests.
- Consider adding variety to your routine so that you're exposed to new people, places, and ideas.[16] Attend workshops, conferences, seminars, job fairs, and other career-oriented events. Also, network during social functions. When you meet someone new, exchange business cards (if you're not employed, create a basic card with your name and contact information), and follow up with an e-mail saying that you were pleased to meet her or him.
- Stay in touch with members of your network. Drop an occasional line to check in, or schedule a beverage break. Also, send them information related to their professional interests. Don't wait until you need something to contact individuals in your network.
- Be generous within your career network. Tell your connections about job openings or opportunities for career development.
- Use the Internet. Sign up for online social networking tools (I won't name any because they change so rapidly; ask people in your network to recommend online social networks relevant to your interests). Also, find out which sites and organizations are active among people in your career area and browse these for information and insight.[17]
- Consult resources on career networking. If you're in college, your campus probably has a career services office. Don't wait until you're about to graduate to use this resource. If you've graduated from college, check to see if your university's office offers services to alums. If you're not affiliated with a university (and even if you are), a great reference for networking is *What Color Is Your Parachute,* by Richard Bolles.[18]

small business stratum) had 50.5 percent. . . . leaving only 15 percent of the wealth for the bottom 80 percent (wage and salary workers)."[19]

The preceding ideas correspond with our working definition of ***social class:*** "an open (to some degree) stratification system that is associated with a systematically unequal allocation of resources and constraints."[20] "Resources and constraints" can refer to various types of capital, including financial net worth, savoir-faire or "know-how," social skills, authority, experience, and networks. Social class is dynamic; we can change our location in the hierarchy, though not always easily.

Why Social Class Matters

Class difference and class struggle represent significant themes in U.S. history. Social class embodies a powerful, persistent predictor of accessibility to resources, potential for longevity and success, and self-esteem. Most people remain in or close to the class position of their family, which may affect their personal identity: "estimation of self-worth, degrees of confidence and feelings of entitlement or lack of entitlement permeate the experience of belonging to one class or another."[21] Social class also can be "a major determinant of individual decisions and social actions."[22]

From womb to tomb, social class can make a major difference in one's life. Most working-class mothers see a doctor for the first time in the last month of pregnancy, whereas most wealthy women get top quality prenatal care throughout their entire pregnancy.[23] As a result, rates of infant mortality, birth defects, and illness are higher among poor families. Poor children lack basic resources and suffer distressing material conditions, such as constant moving, poor nutrition, lack of warm clothing, and inferior living conditions, which can constrain their potential to develop physically and mentally. Lower-class communities more often are built in old industrial areas, and residents are exposed to environmental hazards such as air pollution, lead paint, and asbestos.[24]

Class is the strongest predictor of achievement in schools.[25] The higher the social class, the more likely the student is to succeed academically. Social class also is the strongest predictor of whether or not an individual will go to college, as well as the type of college a student will attend. Suburban schools in wealthy neighborhoods work with budgets two to three times higher per student than poor urban and rural schools. Poor students are disproportionately labeled as low-status and segregated from mainstream students and education. In one poor, Hispanic district, more than one-quarter of the students were classified as "special education," and teachers believed that students' poverty caused their failure rates.[26]

Compared to patients in higher-level social classes, those from lower classes tend to receive more inferior medical care and have limited access to care.[27] Incidents of injury at work and work-related fatalities are higher for lower-class workers.[28] Older poor people suffer more from chronic illness, and wealthy people in general live longer than poor and working-class individuals. These distinctions across classes are not limited to stark differences between the poor and the rich. Throughout the life span, health declines with each successive class group.[29] Of course, class intersects in stark ways with other aspects of identity. Although all working-class people might tend to have some similar experiences, they can vary according to race, ethnicity, sex, and sexuality because we experience class through multiple lenses.[30] Although social discourse implies that the United States is classless, class-based stratification persists.[31] As the preceding paragraph suggests, quality of life varies according to ***socioeconomic status*** (SES), which is determined by the combination of income, education, and occupation. Even though the United States is an affluent society in general, measured by the median income for a family of four, wealth (defined as total value of money and other assets, minus outstanding debts) is distributed much more unequally than income.[32]

In fact, the United States has the most unequally distributed wealth and income in the world. About 34.2 percent of all people in the U.S. are classified as living in poverty at least two months out of the year.[33] In 2003, the average poor family had an income of $8,858, or $738 per month.[34] Economic statistics indicate that the rich are getting richer, and the gap is widening between the haves and the have-nots. In 1982, CEOs of large corporations earned 42 times the salary of the average factory worker; in 2005, their salary was 431 times greater.[35]

Social class matters because it affects the political system. Political candidacy and being elected are tied to class issues. Running for office requires a big bankroll and extensive social networks. Most candidates for national office gain funding from elite corporations, and most congressional representatives are lawyers or established business persons. In addition, political candidates recognize that class matters. Most of them either tout the fact that they grew up poor, or in working-class families, implying that they understand the plight of the poor, or they admit that they are rich, invoking proof of the American dream.[36]

Finally, a number of startling statistics confirm why we should concern ourselves with social class. Approximately one out of four children is born into poverty in the United States. This rate is 1.5 times greater than that of comparable democracies in the world. The United States provides fewer tax-supported services for infants and youths than other developed countries.[37] Furthermore, 40 percent of people living in poverty are under 18 years of age. Approximately 17 percent of children or 12.1 million under 18 are poor by federal standards. Nine million U.S. children suffer from malnutrition.[38]

Nondominant members of society, such as women, children, and people of color, are more likely to be poor than are dominant members. These numbers illustrate once again that intersections of identity matter. Similar to other aspects of social identity we are studying, current conceptions and conditions of social class arise from a variety of developments across history.

Constructing Social Class in the United States

Power dynamics related to the social construction of social class are evident in the history of how the United States was established and built. In early stages of the country, many white male newcomers arrived with high social and economic status. Others experienced "shipboard mobility," simply by leaving poor circumstances in England to take advantage of opportunities across the ocean. In the seventeenth century, over half of English immigrants were indentured servants who worked five to ten years to pay for their passage to the New World. Almost one-third of them died before paying off their contracts. Those who survived were able to improve their status, though not to a substantial extent.[39]

Meanwhile, Native Americans, white women, and blacks had few economic opportunities. Chances for upward mobility were available primarily to certain white men who capitalized on slavery, immigrant labor, tenant farming, sharecropping, farm mortgages, and land grabs from Native Americans, French immigrants, and Mexicans. Consequently, only a few persons accumulated wealth.

The so called "New World" was unlike Europe, which operated under feudalism and a formal class hierarchy. In contrast, the land that would become the United States seemed egalitarian, and numerous authors wrote about abundant opportunities for mobility. Yet, the main persons who climbed the economic ladder were offspring of wealthy colonialists. During the financial panics in the 1800s, descendants of the colonial elite survived because they could afford to capitalize on economic prospects, such as buying up land offered for sale below market value. In the mid-1800s, 95 percent of New York City's wealthiest one hundred persons were born into their wealth.[40] Thus, class was primarily ascriptive.

The government and politicians have played major roles in creating, reinforcing, and changing conceptions of and attitudes toward social class. During World War I, President Woodrow Wilson appealed to values of thrift and savings to persuade citizens to make personal sacrifices. When times became more prosperous after the war, political figures invoked and inculcated ideals such as individualism, materialism, and hedonism. A consumer ethic arose, encouraging people to acquire material possessions. Mass advertising campaigns aimed to convince middle- and working-class people to use credit or installment plans to buy products.

After World War I, the government mainly served the interests of the wealthy. For example, the tax on earnings of one million dollars decreased from $600,000 to $200,000.[41] Consequently, inequalities in the incomes of the rich and the poor became even more pronounced. During the Great Depression (1929–1933), the gross national product dropped by 29 percent and consumer spending fell 18 percent. Unemployment rose from 3.2 percent in 1929 to 24.9 percent in 1933. In essence, "the American dream had turned into the American nightmare."[42] The economic cycle turned again after the bombing of Pearl Harbor, with the beginning of World War II. Spending and investment increased in the defense industry. Once again, politicians implored citizens to make sacrifices for patriotism.

During the twentieth century, the government established numerous programs to improve economic and material conditions, including the Social Security Act implemented in 1935 to provide retirement income for workers, and the GI Bill of 1944 to benefit veterans of World War II by opening up educational opportunities for young men of all races from poor backgrounds. By the 1950s, the country was poised to return to prosperity and materialism. Although boundaries of race and gender blocked mobility, class lines became more permeable in the 1950s and 1960s. Many working-class families were able to purchase a modest home and a car and to plan for extended summer vacations. Many also could afford to send their children to college. In addition, the government created opportunities such as CETA (which employed me during high school) to remove obstacles to class mobility.

Numerous developments have affected class location since the 1960s. In the 1980s, under Ronald Reagan's administration, the tax structure shifted to benefit the wealthy and to decrease domestic programs for low-income families and children. In 1996, Congress passed the Personal Responsibility and Work Opportunity Reconciliation Act (PRWORA) and the Temporary Assistance for Needy Families (TANF) program to initiate welfare reform that requires recipients to work in exchange for time-limited assistance. A health care reform bill, the Patient Protection and Affordable Care Act, was signed into law by President Barack Obama on March 23, 2010. One of its goals is to provide affordable, quality health care to all Americans.

Across history, whenever the federal government created and administered social policies and programs, they often were responding to concerns and demands of citizen groups and individuals, whose attitudes toward poor people and poverty fluctuated. Early perceptions of social inequality reflected a Christian attitude of benevolence and compassion toward the less fortunate. This mind-set changed drastically in the late nineteenth century, when most people viewed poverty as a blight on society. Social programs during those times distinguished "deserving" poor, such as the elderly, orphans, and widows with young children, from the "undeserving" poor, such as vagrants. Crimes of vagrancy were punishable by flogging and even death.[43]

During the late nineteenth century, a discourse arose about survival of the fittest and eradicating the unfit. This social Darwinist approach to poverty endorsed the idea of helping nature run its course by weeding out "undesirables," for instance, through sterilization. Included in the list of undesirables were persons with disabilities, people of color, and poor white people. Stereotypes portrayed poor whites as incestuous, alcoholic, stupid, and "genetic defectives." White Anglo-Saxon Protestant families who moved West from the Oklahoma dust bowl during the 1930s were held with contempt and antagonism. Known as "Okies," they were called "dirty, shiftless, ignorant, breeders." This "white trash" stereotype blames the poor for being poor, and it helps to solidify for middle- and upper-class whites a sense of cultural and intellectual superiority.

Across the twentieth century, societal discourse fluctuated between portraying poor people as genetically defective and depicting them as helpless victims of macrosocietal economic conditions.[44] By the beginning of the twenty-first century, attitudes had shifted yet again, as some analysts contend that "poverty" has lost its meaning and that most citizens are apathetic toward poor people.[45]

However, grassroots groups are springing up to narrow the widening gap between the rich and the poor. The living wage movement, established in the 1990s, seeks to raise wage standards at local levels. Advocates of this movement encourage cities and counties to develop ordinances for organizations that contract city and county services. These ordinances require employers to pay workers enough to "survive on what they earn and support their families without relying on welfare for emergency health care and food stamps and other public assistance."[46] Over 117 local living wage ordinances have been adopted across the United States.

Another example of efforts to improve class positions of citizens is the "I Have a Dream" Foundation.[47] Philanthropist Eugene Lang created this remarkable intervention program in 1981 after returning to the elementary school he had attended 50 years earlier in New York's Harlem. When the school's principal told Lang that three-quarters of the students would probably never complete high school, Lang was so moved that he vowed to pay the college tuition of every sixth grader who would graduate from high school. Lang's program has blossomed. Across the country, local groups adopt an entire grade from an elementary school or an entire age group from a housing development and offer a variety of services and support systems to children and their families from elementary school through college. Most "Dreamers" who go to college are the first in their families to do so. More than 15,000 Dreamers have gone to college in 27 states, Washington, D.C., and New Zealand.

The U.S. Department of Education has developed a replication of Lang's model called GEAR UP (Gaining Early Awareness and Readiness for Undergraduate Programs), which employs partnerships committed to serving and accelerating the academic achievement of cohorts of students. In 2009, the program funded 747,260 students in 209 programs across the U.S.[48]

The Myth of a Classless Society

Social discourse often portrays the United States as a classless society.[49] Compared to ascriptive class system in England and the caste system in India, the "classless" United States certainly would seem preferable to most people. However, an irony infuses this myth of classlessness. As feminist scholar bell hooks observes, many people in the U.S. have wanted to "hold on to the belief that the United States is a class-free society—that anyone who works hard enough can make it to the top. Few people stop to think that in a class-free society there would be no top."[50] Furthermore, the language we use to denote class differences implies hierarchy as well as power differentials, as seen in the terms "upper class" and "lower class."

From its colonialist beginnings, the United States was praised as the land of opportunity. This image, etched into the psyche of many people, helped to generate the fundamental class-based ideology of the American dream: "an American social ideal that stresses egalitarianism and especially material prosperity."[51] This premise arises from a culture of individualism and autonomy, which affirms that *anyone* can get rich because our society is open and competitive. This ideology rests on an achievement orientation to success rather than ascription. The concept of equal opportunity implies that individuals are responsible for success or failure: "wealth is seen as the result of superior individual effort and talent and poverty as the product of deficiencies in these areas."[52]

The rags-to-riches myth valorizes the few people who manage to beat the odds. Popular since the seventeenth century, this recurring narrative promotes a picture of the United States as a utopia. It focuses on individuals and their potential, claiming that everyone can participate and advance equally, *if only they work hard enough*. This narrative associates success with virtue and merit. Thus, this perspective ignores the fact that a person's starting point can affect success and overlooks the fact that success often depends on access to education, health care, safe living conditions, legal protection, books, contacts, professional jobs, travel beyond one's neighborhood, and other forms of economic, social, and cultural capital. The rags-to-riches perspective fails to acknowledge structural barriers and systemic obstacles to employment, housing, education, and health care.

Related to this, the ***culture of poverty*** ideology contends that poor people collectively exhibit traits that keep them down. This perspective on class blames the poor for their circumstances and ignores the fact that many wealthy people have inherited their wealth and resources or that they were better positioned to attain the American dream. This ideology does not acknowledge that economic, cultural, and social capital can tilt the playing field in favor of those who have accumulated wealth, knowledge, and/or connections. Instead, victim-blaming narratives attribute persistent intergenerational poverty to immorality and family dysfunctions.[53]

Belief in the dream seems to be alive and well: 94 percent of Americans think that "people who work full-time should be able to earn enough to keep their families out of poverty."[54] Many people in the United States also hesitate to even entertain the topic of social class: "if we identify and recognize a class system in the United States, we are challenging and questioning the very fiber of democracy. To some of us it may even seem unpatriotic to consider an American class system."[55]

Social Class and Labor

The overview of the social construction of social class implies several issues related to labor. By the late nineteenth century, due to large corporations and railroads, the United States had become a capitalist society. Capitalist expansion impacted class formations as the Industrial Revolution provided opportunities for thousands of workers to produce a multitude of goods. As the U.S. became more industrialized and urban, more people depended on wage-paying jobs for food, clothing, and shelter. Rapid industrialization fostered the rise of a large class of white-collar workers. By the end of the 1920s, corporations controlled almost half of industry, and publicly financed corporations owned two-thirds of industrial wealth.[56]

During the depression, job discrimination escalated for women and blacks, 50 percent of whom became unemployed. Desperate for any type of work, whites took over so called "Negro" occupations such as bellhop, street cleaner, and elevator operator. This type of response recurred across the history of labor in the United States: "the roots of ethnic and racial antagonism usually lie in economic inequality and conflict . . . because subordinate racial and ethnic minorities represent an economic threat to many members of the dominant majority."[57]

As the number of factories rose, workers' safety and health were often threatened. Also, factory owners did not have to pay workers the wages they deserved because a large labor pool provided a steady supply of employees. Consequently, workers began to organize for safe working conditions as well as reasonable compensation. They formed labor unions and took actions such as strikes and organized protests to secure their demands. To retaliate, some capitalist owners took coercive measures. They enlisted local or federal law enforcement groups who used physical force against the workers. Many persons were killed or injured during these interventions. For instance, in 1937, National Guardsmen killed eighteen strikers and arrested two hundred in my hometown (Youngstown, Ohio).[58]

Resistance through organized protests and strikes marks an important era in the labor history of the United States. These activities, usually initiated by unions, resulted in changes in opportunities for economic mobility. Labor union movements helped to gain significant aspects of employment that we take for granted, including an eight-hour workday, a forty-hour workweek, occupational safety laws, wage minimums, unemployment benefits, and so forth. However, many union groups barred racial minorities and women from their membership.[59] In addition, corporate bosses sometimes used class and race antagonisms to secure consent to domination. Henry Ford mounted a conscious campaign of racial division between black and white workers. To dissuade blacks from joining unions, he reminded them that the United Auto Workers' opposed black membership.[60]

On the other hand, groups also formed interracial coalitions because they realized that economic opportunity and political and civil rights were interrelated. Predominantly white members of the unions representing automobile workers, electrical workers, and garment workers joined with the predominantly black Brotherhood of Sleeping Car Porters to donate money and organize members to travel to Washington, D.C., in 1963 to march for jobs and freedom.

A pivotal figure in the labor movement was former migrant worker Cesar E. Chavez. In the 1960s, he and Dolores Huerta founded the United Farm Workers union and worked tirelessly for almost three decades to gain better pay and working conditions for laborers. Basing his efforts on Gandhi's non-violence approach, Chavez went on extended hunger strikes and coordinated numerous boycotts. In 2000, California made his birthday, March 31, a paid holiday for state employees. Nine other states (Arizona, Colorado, Illinois, Michigan, New Mexico, Texas, Utah, Wisconsin and Rhode Island) have established optional and commemorative Cesar Chavez Days, and a campaign is under way to create a paid federal holiday to honor Chavez.[61]

Communicating Social Class

We use communication to disseminate and internalize ideologies and myths about social class. Power dynamics operate, as "those in control of linguistic and communicative resources use these to manage the impressions of others."[62] In essence, communication is a fundamental aspect of class formations, and the experience of class occurs primarily through communication. Individuals consciously or subconsciously "read" one another's appearance and behaviors to discern class position. We look for cues such as clothing, accessories, speech style, mode of transportation, and so forth to make decisions about other people's class location. And, we perform class by our (conscious and unconscious) choices of clothing, accessories, speech style, manners, food preferences, home décor, mode of transportation, and so forth. Persons in similar class positions usually share similar symbols and language systems. Most organizations reflect the class system of society where class dynamics are evident in organizational structures, practices, policies, and norms.

Educational Settings

Educational systems are primary sites of social class dynamics:

> The educational system replicates the class structure and corporate system of capitalist societies. That is, schools prepare a labor force to assume the tasks demanded by the corporations. Some schools, dominated by low-income and minority youth, teach the skills of punctuality needed to maintain the assembly line. Other schools, populated by majority and high-income youth, teach the skills of independent thought and personnel management necessary for higher levels of the corporation.[63]

Basically, educational experiences "from preschool to high school differentially prepare students for their ultimate positions in the workforce, and a student's placement in various school programs is based primarily on her or his race and class origin."[64] For instance, school personnel counseled students to enroll in either college preparatory or trade-technical courses based on students' social class and assumptions of their parents' ability to pay for their education.[65]

Because members of the middle and upper classes have always controlled educational systems and content, their values dominate curriculum structures and materials and placement procedures. Consequently, education processes differ for children according to their social class, and these differences help to reproduce inequalities.

Most children attend schools segregated by race, ethnicity, and class. Was that true for you? Even when schools are integrated, students often are resegregated by tracking or ability grouping, like I was. Lower-track classes

Spotlight on Media

Communicating Social Class in the News

The news media rarely report on working-class or poor persons and their concerns, mainly because a class divide exists between most journalists and members of the lower levels of social classes in the United States.[66] Fewer than 30 percent of citizens have a college degree, as contrasted to over 80 percent of journalists. These journalists decide what and whom to portray regarding social class, and they increasingly report stories of wealth rather than poverty. Their articles align with publishers' and advertisers' perspectives on social class that values middle- to upper-class readers. As a result, "the poor have become increasingly invisible."[67]

When reporters cover poor people, they often portray them as "a problem, victims and perpetrators, the face of failed social policies."[68] Consequently, "millions of people in this country see little of themselves and their lives in the media, unless they are connected somehow to a problem."[69]

Journalists occasionally offer thoughtful insights into complexities of social class issues. In 2005, *The New York Times* published a series entitled "Class Matters." For this project, "A team of reporters spent more than a year exploring ways that class—defined as a combination of income, education, wealth and occupation—influences destiny in a society that likes to think of itself as a land of unbounded opportunity."[70] Also, *Chicago Tribune* columnist Mary Schmich has written over two dozen columns about everyday experiences in a poor/working-class neighborhood in Chicago. She explains how the press tends to deal with poor people: "We bite off a huge project every few years, and that has the effect of reducing the poor to a problem. Then they disappear largely until the next big project."[71]

These sporadic, one-dimensional approaches to covering poor and working-class people can affect their self-esteem and further disempower them. Moreover, because public opinion can affect public policy, "if attitudes on poverty-related issues are driven by inaccurate and stereotypical portrayals of the poor, then the policies favored by the public (and political elites) may not adequately address the true problems of poverty."[72] Thus, a need persists for more balanced reporting of lower social class groups in the United States.

tend to consist mainly of working-class and minority students. Separating and segregating students by social class can perpetuate class distinctions and socialize students about "their place" in society. For instance, teachers who work with lower-class students often apply an approach known as a "pedagogy of poverty," which stresses teacher control and student compliance.[73] Many teachers expect all students to comply and respond in similar ways. They may not employ alternative methods such as cooperative learning, student-devised learning contracts, individualized instruction, or peer tutoring. Rather than assign students problem-solving, group/team-oriented, or creative classroom activities, they give repetitive, nonintellectual tasks.[74]

In contrast, children from upper-class families often experience enrichment outside of the classroom. They usually come to school better prepared, and better socialized to be educated. Their access to cultural and social capital places them in positions of privilege. Working-class or poor students do not always perform well on standardized tests written and geared toward higher SES members. Therefore, how well someone speaks and understands white, middle-class English becomes a common measurement of intelligence, and students not proficient in standard English may have limited opportunity for advancement.

Class differences may also affect parent involvement, a pivotal factor for student success. A review of literature concludes that "low-income parents and working-class parents, as compared with middle-class parents, receive less warm welcomes in their children's schools; their interventions and suggestions are less respected and attended to and they are less able to influence the education of their children."[75] The study cites repeated reports of teachers and administrators who discount and devalue any information that working-class parents might try to share.

However, many teachers in low-income schools strive to develop relationships with low-income parents. Educator Bernice Lott recommends ways to improve parent–teacher relationships that have obvious communication implications and also imply effects of power and ideology. Lott believes that schools should initiate building relationships because they have the resources and power. She advises teachers to encourage informal communication rather than focus only on scheduled meetings that frequently do not correspond to lifestyles of working parents who may not be able to take time off work, or who may work during nontraditional hours. She also recommends that teacher training programs help prospective teachers to communicate effectively with parents from varying class backgrounds.[76]

These issues also matter in higher education, where some students enter with a great deal of class privilege, and others have virtually none. Will Barratt refers to this as ***academic capital,*** which some students attain at home and apply unconsciously to succeed at college. Elements of academic capital include "can afford supplemental school material; has expansive life experiences; has good social skills to develop and maintain relationships with faculty, staff, and students; has good study, critical thinking, reading, and writing skills."[77] Basically, "whether young people go on to college and the type of postsecondary education they pursue is a class-based process."[78]

Students from working-class backgrounds will more likely have had inferior resources and fewer mentors or role models. They also may have a more difficult time transitioning to higher education than students from middle- or upper-class families. Moreover, college tends to be a middle-class experience. Some universities offer resources for first-generation college students to help them acclimate. They try to ease culture shock and isolation that some students experience.[79] They orient students to the unwritten norms and expectations in college. Basically, these programs try to increase students' cultural capital related to being a college student.

Some students won't hesitate to contact a professor to discuss the course or their grades, while others may equate visiting a professor with the negative connotations of visiting the principal's office. Students also learn different attitudes toward questioning authority figures, or thinking for themselves. Some students exhibit a greater sense of entitlement and self-confidence than others. Some working-class students hesitate to ask for assistance or use resources like a writing center or student tutors because they fear that others will think they are inferior.

Texas passed a Top 10 percent Law in 1996 to increase diversity at their public colleges by guaranteeing admission to the top 10 percent of graduating seniors from each high school, thus opening the gates to students at low-income-serving high schools. However, students from low-resource high schools are significantly less likely to apply than their more well-to-do peers. How would you explain this?

Communicating Class at Work

The workplace is a crucial site of class production and reproduction: Within organizations, classism occurs in numerous ways. Organizations tend to exercise varying degrees and types of control of employees depending on their place on the organizational chart. Lower-level workers usually have to account for when and how they expend their time. In contrast, higher-level employees may be less accountable. Because I am a professor, I can come and go freely on campus. I do not have to fill out a time sheet or punch a time card, and I do not have to take timed breaks. If I do not feel well, I can cancel class without consulting anyone, and my pay for that period will not be affected. Yet, most nonfaculty staff members at the university have to call their supervisor by a specific time in order to be paid for sick leave; they also might be required to provide proof of illness. When we have "snow days" in Colorado, I can stay at home without worrying about losing a day's pay, as many workers might.

Organizational hierarchies are necessarily class based, and some are more explicit about distinctions between levels than others. The federal government designates occupations according to a grade system that divides civil servant employees into eighteen ascending categories. Usually, the higher one's position in a hierarchy, the greater that person's status and access to resources, including compensation, benefits, leave policies, parking privileges, bathrooms, dining facilities, and even office furniture.

Physical aspects of the workplace also signify class distinctions and forms of control. The higher one is in the hierarchy, the more space one gets, and vice versa. Within office buildings, space is usually assigned according to class location. Executives tend to occupy larger, private offices furnished with more expensive or status-loaded artifacts. Consider, for instance, the symbolism of the corner office or the key to the executive washroom.

Lower-level personnel not only tend to have less privacy but also less control over their work space. Higher-level employees are more likely to have window(s) and door(s), individual light switches, and even a thermostat—whereas lower-level employees tend to have limited (if any) control of climate conditions. Yet, employees sometimes challenge or subvert control mechanisms by altering their spaces or creating new ones.

Class biases appear in many routine practices in organizations. Employee recruitment processes often occur through social networks based on class similarities. In some organizations, hiring criteria favor recruiting Ivy League or private college graduates, an example of more obvious class discrimination. As I mentioned in the race chapter, interview expectations for certain jobs value dominant language codes, which usually correspond with speech styles used by dominant group members, who tend to belong to middle or upper classes. Requiring employees to pay for items needed for doing the job, such as uniforms, may prohibit some individuals from taking a job. Other examples of practices that reflect class bias include requiring employees to pay their business travel expenses in advance and be reimbursed later or issuing company credit cards, possibly excluding persons with bad credit histories.

When organizations schedule mandatory events such as training or retreats during off-hours, employees responsible for children or other family members may incur family care expenses (e.g., for their children or elderly parents). Organizations may assume that members have cultural capital, for instance by expecting employees to attend and participate in social events such as black-tie affairs in country club settings. Even though these events may not be mandatory, they can be important sites for networking. Employees who do not attend because they may feel out of place, or because they can't afford to buy proper clothing and/or to pay child care costs, or those who do attend but are unsure about etiquette, may not gain networking advantages.

Some staff members, such as janitors, perform their work backstage and/or after-hours, which renders them invisible. Even when they are visible, others in the workplace may tend not to acknowledge them. However, some of these employees don't mind being backstage because they have autonomy and independence, and are less likely to experience degrading interactions with other employees.[80]

Formal and informal dress codes also signify class. Common distinctions like "blue collar" (less formal: clothes might become soiled on the job) and "white collar" (more formal: clothes are likely to retain a clean, pressed appearance) illustrate a class distinction connected to appearance. Newer labels combine status and other aspects of social identity. For instance, "pink collar" refers to clerical workers and implies a female focus. "Brown collar" refers to low-level, physically demanding occupations, such as domestic workers, farm workers, and low-level machine operators, who are most likely to be Latino/a.[81] Thus, "brown" refers to the ethnicity of the disproportionate number of Latino/as who are employed in those types of jobs.

Dress style often signals a person's organizational status. Most executives are expected to wear business suits or business attire. Many organizations require employees to wear uniforms, which can reveal and conceal statuses, certify legitimacy, establish conformity, or suppress individuality.[82] Uniforms "vary in legitimacy and prestige, conferring different degrees of honor on members."[83] Military uniforms may evoke different responses than working-class uniforms. In addition, "the very existence of a uniform implies a group structure."[84] For example, uniforms clearly signify the hierarchy of armed services personnel. When I was in high school, I kind of envied the girls who went to Catholic school because their uniforms looked "cool." My envy probably was related to the positive image of those schools, which were private.

Think for a moment about different types of uniforms, and what they signify. Among working-class employees such as hotel maids or bellmen, a uniform signals a person's role to customers, clients, and patrons. For members of the working class, a uniform forces conformity and constrains individuality of dress among an occupational group. It also highlights the wearer's status and differentiates the wearer from other people in an organizational setting. Author Katherine Boo contends that working-class uniforms are not made for the workers, but rather for "the rest of us." Boo reports that a backlash about dress is building among the working class, following members of occupations who have substituted uniforms for street clothes. Nurses report an increase in respect from both patients and doctors when they wear clothing other than a white uniform, and anthropologists repeatedly find that persons wearing business suits evoke more respect and better responses than those who wear other clothing.[85] However, working-class individuals may resent people whom they call "suits" because "the business suit represents the ability of members of the middle class to command respect for their kind of work. The business suit in our society loudly proclaims that the wearer is involved in dignified work."[86]

In contrast, a working-class uniform may invoke a different response. Parking attendant Jimmy Killens asserts that he would not accept an invitation to go after work to dinner at a fancy restaurant in Washington, D.C., because he feared that patrons would disdain him: "I wear a uniform," he declared, "so it does not matter that I make an honest wage. I'm looked down on in this town. A uniform—it says you're nothing."[87]

Conclusion

Social class encompasses a socially constructed category of identity that involves more than just economic factors; social class includes an entire socialization process. Across history, attitudes toward social class have varied, as have the communication processes that create, reinforce, and challenge class distinctions. Although the United States claims to be a classless society, social class distinctions have become solidified, due in part to dominant ideologies such as the culture of poverty and the American dream. To achieve the American dream, many groups have organized and fought to improve important aspects of employment, including equitable pay and safe working conditions. Their efforts have had significant, positive impacts on the quality of work life for many people. However, organizations of all types—from schools, to factories, to health care facilities, to corporations—continue to be sites where members reproduce dominant perspectives on social class. Consequently, a strong need exists to identify and develop strategies for reducing blatant and subtle forms of classism and its effects.

•••• ID Check ••••

1. What is your social class?
2. How important is your social class to you? Explain.
3. What primary sources have taught you about your social class?
4. How, if at all, do you express your social class (e.g., through language, communication style, dress, accessories, music, and so forth)?
5. Does your awareness of your social class ever help you communicate with others? Explain.
6. Does your awareness of your social class ever hinder how you communicate with others? Explain.
7. What situations, if any, do you avoid because of concerns related to your social class?
8. What situations, if any, do you seek because of your social class?
9. What advantages, if any, do you enjoy based on your social class?
10. Do you know of any stereotypes about your social class? If so, list them.
11. Are you ever aware of stereotypes about your social class as you interact with others? Explain.
12. How do the media tend to depict your social class? Do media depictions correspond with your sense of your social class? Explain.
13. Do you think your attitudes toward social class intersect with any other facets of your social identity, for instance: your gender? your race? your age?

Reflection Matters

1. What, if anything, did you find intriguing in this chapter?
2. According to the sociohistorical overview, what are examples of how people used communication to construct social class throughout the history of the United States?
3. What are examples of power relations in the construction of social class in the United States?
4. Do any current news stories involve issues that this chapter covers? If yes, what points do they exemplify?
5. What type of neighborhood did you grow up in? Did your neighborhood affect your sense of self? Did your neighborhood seem to matter to anyone else (your peers, your teachers, other family members)? Explain.
6. Has class ever mattered (in a positive or a negative way) in your life? Explain. Refer to Bourdieu's notion of capital to reflect on how class matters or has mattered to you. Please think carefully about this question. People who are middle class often say that class does not matter. They take for granted the privileges they enjoy because of their class position.
7. Interview someone who is at least 10 years older than you. Which social class did the person grow up in? How does the person describe that level of social class (i.e., what are distinguishing variables)? Has the person's class changed since s/he was a child? If so, how? How does the person define "The American dream"? Does the person believe that s/he can achieve the American dream? Why or why not? Does the person believe that *anyone* in the United States can achieve the American dream? Why or why not? Write an essay about the interview, including your response to it.
8. What is your family's social class history? How, if at all, does it reflect any concepts from this chapter?
9. What is the difference between economic, social, and cultural capital? How do they interact to produce socioeconomic class?
10. Do you believe, "It's not what you know, but who you know?" Explain.
11. Have you ever used cultural capital? Explain. How about social capital?
12. The "white trash" stereotype blames the poor for being poor, and it helps to solidify for middle- and upper-class whites a sense of cultural and intellectual superiority. Can you think of examples of how this stereotype operates?
13. What are some examples of media portrayals of class? Do they shape and define class relationships and values? Explain.

14. Have you ever "passed" as a member of a social class different than your own? Explain.
15. Have you or anyone in your family worn a uniform? What did or does the uniform signify?
16. Have you had any experiences that illustrate how organizations reflect the class system of society? Explain.
17. Have you developed a career network? If yes, does your network consist of diverse members (e.g., persons from varying professional backgrounds, ages, races, and so forth)?

Chapter 6

Sexuality Matters

Several years ago, an administrative assistant telephoned me on behalf of the dean of the college where I was teaching. The dean wanted me to meet with a black woman student who was struggling to adjust to university life. I gladly agreed, because one reason I had accepted the job at the predominantly white university was to be a role model for students of color. Later that day, a black woman professor called me. The student was enrolled in her department, and the dean had told her he thought I could relate to the student's struggles as a lesbian, since I was a lesbian. The woman professor and I were friends, and she was pretty sure that I was heterosexual. She wanted to tell me about the dean's misperception.

I didn't know how to respond. A part of me wanted immediately to correct the misunderstanding. I didn't want to be identified as gay. Yet I also didn't want to care what the dean or anyone else thought about my sexual orientation. That was nobody's business. Should I tell the dean he was mistaken? Would denying that I was gay seem homophobic? Why did he even think I was gay? Was it my short hair, or maybe it was because I was single with no children and had never brought a date to campus social events? Could it be how I dressed for work (I usually wore pants)? Or was it because I am a feminist and people often equate feminism with lesbianism?

Maybe someone told him I was gay. But why would he categorize me without direct information from me? Wasn't that somehow unethical? In fact, if I had been gay and didn't want anyone to know, his referral would have "outed" me.

The dean's assistant never called back, and I never said anything to the dean. I still wonder if I should have handled the situation differently. What would you have done? Why?

My story implies many issues related to sexuality. A private aspect of one's identity, sexuality, has become more public than it used to be. Not long ago, it would have been unthinkable for an employer to mention an employee's sexual orientation, and it's still taboo in many places. The student's difficulties reflect the reality that homosexual individuals often struggle with fitting into heterosexual contexts. Being both black and lesbian may have compounded her struggles, which reinforces the point that intersections of social identity matter. And, my initial reaction to deny that I was a lesbian stresses the stigma of homosexuality and the privileged status of heterosexuality in the United States. Related to that, my colleague and I had never discussed each other's sexuality; she assumed that I was straight. My second-guessing why the dean thought I was gay exemplifies how we "read" nonverbal cues to infer a person's sexuality.

In this chapter, we will explore these and other issues related to sexuality. I begin by defining sexuality and explaining why it matters. Next, I offer an overview of historical perspectives on sexuality in the United States and discuss how people acquire information about sexuality. Then I look at communicating sexuality in the workplace. Our journey into these matters shows sexuality as another significant aspect of social identity that reflects and reinforces dominant ideologies in the United States.

What Is Sexuality and Why Does It Matter?

Sexuality is a complex, contested, and controversial topic. How would you define sexuality? Here's a thorough definition:

> sexuality is the social expression of social relations to and social reference to bodily desire or desires, real or imagined, by or for others or for oneself, together with the related bodily states and experiences. . . . Others can be of the same or opposite sex, or even occasionally of indeterminate gender.[1]

I like this definition because it captures the complexities of sexuality: it portrays sexuality as social; it encompasses reality and fantasy; and it acknowledges biological aspects of sexuality. It also implies various physiological issues beyond sexual intercourse, such as puberty, menstruation, pregnancy, and menopause. The latter part of the definition reflects categories of sexuality currently used in society, which are heterosexual, homosexual (gays and lesbians), and bisexual. However, sexologist Alfred Kinsey and his coresearchers contended that sexuality ranges along a seven-point continuum, from "exclusively heterosexual" to "exclusively homosexual."[2]

Sexuality recently has received more public attention than ever in the United States, a country that has many sexual problems, including teen pregnancy, rape, sexual abuse, and sexual harassment.[3] Also, political agendas often focus on any number of sexuality issues, including abortion, sex education, censorship and pornography, gay and lesbian rights, U.S. military policy, HIV/AIDS, and welfare reform. Sometimes politicians conflate sexuality with race and class, as in exaggerated images of black "welfare queens," depicted as single women parenting several illegitimate children.

Sexual scandals about celebrities often headline the media. Politicians' sexual conduct is frequently a hot topic in the news media. Political candidates also have resorted to mudslinging about their opponents' sex lives. Occasionally, the media will report that a celebrity has "come out," or spread rumors that a famous person is gay. Sex also is rampant in other media, including feature films, music videos, magazines, television shows, and the

Internet (where "sex" is the most frequent search topic). Many teenagers and young adults are sending sexually explicit messages or photos via communication devices (primarily cell phones). This new behavior, known as "sexting," has raised concerns among parents, educators, and legislators.

Sexuality also matters because of the rise in political activism related to gay and lesbian rights. Various organizations, including federal and state governments, churches, corporations, and educational institutions, are dealing with issues such as gay adoption, partner benefits, and gay marriage. A strong and visible gay, lesbian, bisexual, transgendered, and queer (GLBTQ) community and their allies seek to ensure equal opportunity and treatment across many sectors of society.

Many organizations have responded positively to these demands. In 1996, IBM extended health benefits to partners of homosexual employees, and almost five hundred other companies, including Apple Computer, Ben and Jerry's, Fox Broadcasting, Xerox, AOL Time Warner, and Levi Strauss, currently offer similar benefits. According to Crooks and Baur, more than 8,000 companies offer domestic partner benefits.[4] Many universities have developed gay and lesbian studies departments, thereby creating a forum for education about sexuality issues. Some also have instituted GLBTQ student organizations. The Obama administration has introduced legislation to repeal the "Don't Ask, Don't Tell" policy that prevents gays and lesbians from serving openly in the U.S. armed forces.

However, an antigay movement also is growing, along with general negative attitudes toward homosexuals. Harassment of teens who are gay or perceived to be gay is widespread in public schools.[5] Furthermore, public school districts still need to do more to address the needs of lesbian, gay, and bisexual students.[6] The U.S. Supreme court ruled in June of 2000 that the Boy Scouts of America as a private organization has a First Amendment right to exclude gays. However, the Girl Scouts of America does not deny membership if someone discloses she is gay. This organization allows each local council to make its own decision about sexual orientation issues.[7]

Current concerns for gay rights center on parenting and marriage. Some states have developed antigay marriage legislation. In 1996, Congress passed the Defense of Marriage Act, which gives states the right not to recognize same-sex marriages performed in other states; many states followed with laws to prohibit legal recognition of same-sex marriages. In 2009, 36 states had statutes prohibiting same-sex marriages.

Finally, sexuality matters because it is an important aspect of everyone's identity and experiences:

> Sexuality has always been an obsessive human concern; it has often been the "real" subject of cultural, religious, and political discourse that did not dare to mention it or did not have the language for addressing it directly. We now possess both the language and the cultural temerity to discuss sexuality as straightforwardly as we like and with a frankness that would have shocked people a few decades ago.[8]

With these matters in mind, let's look at how sexuality has been constructed in the United States.

Constructing Sexuality in the United States

The history of sexuality in the United States represents a fascinating example of how we construct social identity through power relations.

Colonial Views on Sexuality

Sexuality was a major concern for Europeans in the New England colonies, particularly the Puritans and Pilgrims (separatists from the Church of England who wished to reform religion). Based on strict religious doctrine, these groups viewed the sex act solely as a means to an end: reproduction. In addition to concerns about adhering to religious dictates, they advocated procreative sex because they needed a critical mass of laborers for the growing society. Consequently, clergymen and lawmakers collaborated to develop and enforce religious doctrines and legal statutes to facilitate reproduction. They proclaimed that only married couples should engage in sex, strictly to procreate and not for pleasure.[9] These views of sex contrasted sharply with native people's norms.

Across the diverse communities of indigenous people, norms about sexuality varied. However, a universal theme of sexuality as a vital life force prevailed across all groups.[10] Similarly, Africans whom the colonialists enslaved, viewed sexuality as "powerful, pleasurable, and generative."[11] Because they believed humans should suppress their animal urges, colonialists thought these differences proved that African slaves and native people were subhuman. They used the newly developed printing press to create and circulate reports of indigenous people as wanton savages. They also disseminated "captivity" narratives describing rapes of white women and depicting natives as sexually dangerous.[12] This imagery helped colonialists justify seizing resources, destroying native culture, and coercing Indians to assimilate to European ways. It also helped them to rationalize slavery.

Statutes reinforced biblical bans on nonconjugal (unmarried) or nonprocreative sexual behavior such as fornication, rape, adultery, incest, and sodomy.[13] For instance, Massachusetts justified citing sodomy as a capital crime by quoting a verse from the Bible (Leviticus 20:13).[14] The penalty for adultery and sodomy in most of the new colonies was death, though lawmakers rarely enforced it. However, numerous individuals received public lashings. Other punishment included fines and banishment. Laws for adultery were gender biased, as a married man could be charged for adultery if he engaged in sex with an engaged or married woman, while a married woman could face charges regardless of the marital status of her male partner. In Boston, 18-year-old Mary Latham was hanged along with one of the twelve lovers with whom she confessed to having committed adultery.[15]

Stances on sexuality reflected other gender power dynamics. For instance, colonialists believed that men were seed sources of birth, while women were simply receptacles. Thus, it was sinful and wasteful for men to release their precious seed for purposes other than making babies. Therefore, sodomy and bestiality laws were developed along with legal sanctions against adultery.

Victorian Era–Early 1900s

Colonial views of sexuality evolved into views espoused in the *Victorian Era* in the United States (1820–1850). Named for Queen Victoria of Great Britain (1837 to 1897), this perspective dictated that women and men should practice sexual self-control and discipline, engaging in sex only as married persons seeking to reproduce. Upper- and middle-class white women were strongly encouraged to help men overcome their animal passions. Middle-class reformers formed voluntary groups like the Women's Christian Temperance Union to counter sexual activities such as prostitution and obscenity and to help men resist sexual temptation.[16] Religious authorities cautioned these women against excessive sex. Due to advances in publishing technology, authors wrote and disseminated sexual advice literature instructing women and men to channel sexual desires in procreative marital sexual activity.[17] These sources pushed women to be delicate and ladylike, to provide comfortable homes for their husbands, and to fulfill their families' spiritual needs. Many of these women constrained their bodies with corsets, hoops, and bustles.

In the eighteenth and nineteenth centuries, doctors and the general public viewed masturbation as a "deadly disease."[18] These attitudes fostered rumors that masturbation can cause blindness or insanity. Many antimasturbation pamphlets and books were printed and distributed. Manufacturers created devices to prevent young males from playing with their penises while they were in bed.[19] Inmates in asylums were forced to wear metal antimasturbation devices.

In 1873, thanks to zealous efforts by a political conservative named Anthony Comstock, Congress passed a series of bills known as the Comstock Laws, which banned the mailing of "obscene" material. The statutes were so ambiguous that physicians or other health practitioners could not mail information on contraception or on any personal reproductive matter without breaking the new laws. Over 3,600 persons were arrested, and 800,000 pictures were destroyed.[20] Comstock also helped to create the New York Society for the Suppression of Vice.

Despite conservative groups' efforts to curb citizens' exposure to and involvement in sexual activities, reformers continued to circulate information about sexuality (e.g., contraceptive methods and abortion techniques) through a variety of printed matter and public lectures. In addition, prostitution, the world's oldest profession, thrived. Among categories of sex workers, a class system prevailed: at the high end were mistresses or courtesans, whom a man would set up in private, separate quarters; next came brothel workers who lived in houses of ill repute, but were relatively safe from public exposure; at the lowest and most vulnerable level were streetwalkers.[21]

The medical profession rose in the late nineteenth century and began to influence thought and discourse about sexuality. The primary authority on sexuality was transferred from priests/religious leaders to medical men (few women were physicians then).[22] The medical community, including physicians and mental health professionals, studied a variety of issues related to sexuality, including genetic factors and hormones. Pathologies and norms of sexual health became popular topics of public discussion. The primary sexual "problems" of these times were hysteria, prostitution, and masturbation. However, knowledge about women's sexuality was limited due to the high percentage of male physicians and to prohibitions against certain medical procedures (including autopsies) on women.

Toward the end of the nineteenth century, the ideal of sexuality for procreation between women and men prevailed. This ideal, however, was challenged by an ethic of "different-sex pleasure," which acknowledged woman-to-man erotic desire as distinct from reproductive acts. These contrasting views of procreation and recreation underpin early notions of "heterosexuality," a term coined in 1892 by Dr. James G. Kiernan in an article entitled "Sexual Perversion." Kiernan denoted heterosexuality as a perversion, an abnormal manifestation of sexual appetite unrelated to reproducing the species. Thus, "this first exercise in heterosexual definition described an unequivocal pervert."[23]

Not too long afterward, Viennese psychiatrist Richard von Krafft-Ebing published an influential text on pathological sex that discussed "hetero-sexual" and "homo-sexual" eroticism. This marked a historic shift away from the age-old procreative norm. Krafft-Ebing designated heterosexuality as a naturally occurring eroticism related to procreation. However, sensual pleasure was judged as lowly, as something that humans should strive to overcome. Consequently, in 1901, *Dorland's Medical Dictionary* defined "heterosexuality" as nonprocreative, abnormal or perverted desire for the opposite sex.[24] In 1923, *Merriam-Webster's New International Dictionary* cited a similar definition with its debut of the word "heterosexuality."

Then came Sigmund Freud, "the master heterosexual norm builder."[25] Freud contended that libido (sex drive) was not limited to reproduction but also encompassed natural pleasure. Freud pronounced heterosexuality as positive and normal. He and British sexologist Havelock Ellis popularized the idea of sexuality as a facet of self-identity that should not be repressed.

This brief history of heterosexual discourse shows how we came to normalize sexual eroticism as separate from reproductive urges. As a result, society increasingly accepted the hetero pleasure principle, and heterosexuality "gradually came to refer to a normal other-sex sensuality free of any essential tie to procreation."[26] Thus, connotations and denotations of heterosexuality shifted from abnormal to normal, and they became normative in the twentieth century.

Sexual Revolutions

In the twentieth century, three sexual revolutions occurred within the United States, all after major wars: World War I, World War II, and the Vietnam War. The first major change in attitudes toward sexuality took place in the early 1900s. The famous Kinsey report stated that "the percentage of women born between 1900 and 1909 who had intercourse before marriage doubled from 25 percent to 50 percent."[27] However, sex conservatives adamantly fought to maintain the idea of sex as strictly procreative. To counter their efforts, many authors wrote explicitly about (hetero)sexual relations, in fiction as well as nonfiction. Sex educator Mary Ware Dennett was convicted of mailing an "obscene" essay that actually was a 21-page sex-education pamphlet. In 1912, Margaret Sanger, a nurse in New York City, wrote a series of articles on female sexuality. Concerned about health implications and complications for women who bore many children, she actively resisted efforts to suppress her quest to distribute birth control information to women. She published her own magazine, *The Woman Rebel*, and she wrote and distributed a pamphlet entitled *Family Limitation*. When Comstock charged her with violating the law, she fled to Europe. However, due to public outcry, the information was disseminated through a solidified movement for sexual education, and charges against Sanger were dropped. Birth control became more accepted, especially for middle-class women.[28] Sanger, concerned with women in poverty, opened an illegal clinic to distribute diaphragms shipped from Europe. She also promoted research on birth control hormones.

In the euphoria following the end of World War I, the Roaring Twenties were a time of celebration. Society became much more sexualized, and a new morality arose that "stressed instant gratification and fulfillment through consumption and leisure."[29] A body of "experts," including ministers, doctors, advertisers, marriage manual writers, and businessmen, circulated solutions and advice about sexuality. The rising hegemonic role of these experts "had enormous implications for the American sexual system. They encouraged sexual expression rather than repression in an ideal that represented the solid beginnings of a liberation of sexuality from Victorian rigors."[30] Marriage manuals explained "how to" have satisfying sex. The courts began to change their definitions of obscenity. And, the invention of automobiles enabled couples to spend time alone, sometimes on a "lovers' lane."

Moreover, due to educational reform, young people left home to attend school and participate in extracurricular activities, which gave them more private time to explore their sexuality. As women gained more rights, such as the right to vote with the passage of the Nineteenth Amendment in the 1920s, and as more women entered the workforce and attended college, they gained access to a world that was previously occupied mainly by men. Thus, women and men had more opportunities to interact with each other.

Due to an expanded emphasis on consumerism, this period also marked the beginning of using sex to sell "everything from cars to toothpaste."[31] In addition, motion pictures played a pivotal role in attitudes toward sex, as they freely portrayed sexual passions. In 1934, *Webster's* defined "heterosexuality" as "manifestation of sexual passion for one of the opposite sex; normal sexuality."[32] That same volume defined "homosexuality" as "eroticism for one of the same sex." Thus, heterosexuality and homosexuality had become normalized terms in the United States.

The second sexual revolution occurred in the middle of the twentieth century, following World War II: in 1953, Hugh Hefner published the first issue of *Playboy* magazine; similar to the 1920s, more women entered the workforce; the first birth control pills were distributed in 1960 in the United States, freeing women to make choices about having children. Birth control pills made it easier for women not to have children so they could enter the workforce and pursue careers. In 1965 the U.S. Supreme Court, in *Griswold v. Connecticut*, ruled that states could not prohibit the right to use contraceptives by married couples. However, women continued to confront the double standard that it is natural for men to be aggressive and sexually driven and for women to be submissive and chaste. In 1964, a group of concerned citizens developed a nonprofit voluntary health organization, known as the Sex Information and Education Council of the United States (SIECUS), which promotes comprehensive education about sexuality and advocates the right of individuals to make responsible sexual choices.

As the Vietnam War continued from the 1960s into the 1970s, many citizens criticized the government's involvement in the war. They also began to challenge societal norms about other aspects of life, such as religion and sexuality. Also at this time, debates continued about sex education in the schools. Conservative political and religious groups objected to any type of sex curriculum. In 1970, a "purity" movement opposed sex education, and several states passed antisexuality education mandates, while the American Association of Sex Educators and Counselors (now known as American Association of Sex Educators, Counselors, and Therapists), a nonprofit organization, was formed for professionals (including educators) interested in promoting understanding of human sexuality and healthy sexual behavior.[33]

In 1980, after the outbreak of Acquired Immune Deficiency Syndrome (AIDS) many states required or recommended AIDS education. More states have specific programs directed toward AIDS education than sex education in general.[34] Many nationally organized groups against sexuality programs currently exist, including Eagle Forum, Focus on the Family, American Family Association, and Citizens for Excellence in Education.

Concepts of Homosexuality

Concurrent with these historical developments related to heterosexuality, members of society confronted homosexuality. Freud's ideas about "heterosexual and homo-sexual offered the modern world two sex-differentiated eroticisms, one normal and good, one abnormal and bad, a division which would come to dominate our twentieth-century vision of the sexual universe."[35] This perspective portrays heterosexuals as more valuable because they can reproduce the species.

In the 1800s, medical specialists recommended and performed drastic treatments such as surgical procedures or castration to "cure" same-sex desire. Other procedures included aversion therapy, where technicians would administer shocks to homosexual men as they viewed erotic photographs of men. Doctors performed hysterectomies on lesbian women and lobotomies (a surgical procedure that severs nerve fibers in the frontal lobe of the brain) on gay men. They also administered hormone treatments for women and men.

In the 1940s, previously isolated homosexual individuals moved from rural communities to cities and began to meet others like themselves and to form social networks. In 1948, the now-famous Kinsey report uncovered a high incidence of men who reported having sex with men. In the 1950s, homosexuality was viewed as an individual problem, not as reflecting characteristics of a minority group. The medical community proclaimed homosexuality to be a mental disease, and religious groups called it a sin. Hundreds of gay men or men suspected to be gay were fired from government jobs or ousted from the armed services. To counter systematized oppression of gays, a ***homophile movement*** arose to celebrate homosexuality. In the 1950s, middle-class homosexuals formed groups such as the Mattachine Society (a national support network for gay men) and the Daughters of Bilitis (which supported lesbians).

In 1952, the first printing of the Diagnostic and Statistic Manual of Mental Disorders (DSM; the most recent version is DMS-IV-TR) of the American Psychiatric Association (APA) classified homosexuality as a "sociopathic personality disorder." As I noted in chapter 2, defining homosexuality as a mental disorder based on anecdotal evidence and cultural stereotypes and assumptions rather than clinical research represents a classic example of the power–knowledge relationship. Medical experts used their power to make an unsubstantiated claim that most of the public accepted as truth. Combined with societal stereotypes, the APA's "diagnosis" facilitated and legitimated oppressing homosexuals.

In the 1960s, with other groups clamoring for civil rights, groups of gays and lesbians began to challenge the stigma of homosexuality. During that time, police routinely harassed patrons in gay bars, especially in working-class neighborhoods. On June 27, 1969, gay, lesbian, and drag queen patrons, most of them people of color, of the Stonewall Inn in Greenwich Village in New York decided to fight back when the police raided the bar. The ensuing five days and nights of disturbances have been recorded as the first gay riot, known simply as "Stonewall." By the end of July, a large group of women and men in New York had formed the Gay Liberation Front. The following June, the Christopher Street Liberation Day March not only commemorated the first anniversary of the riot, but it also initiated the tradition of annual Gay Pride Day parades during the month of June in many U.S. cities.[36] Thus, the Stonewall conflict helped to construct a social identity group for homosexuals. The gay liberation movement sought to radically alter society's view of sexuality. One of their primary goals was to convince mental health professionals to reverse their stance on homosexuality.

In June 1968, Charles Socarides published his book *The Overt Homosexual* and became one of the most widely quoted authorities on the subject. He described homosexuality as "a dread dysfunction, malignant in character, which has risen to epidemic proportions."[37] To counter these claims, gays and lesbians and their allies mobilized to defuse antigay hostility. In a book entitled *Society and the Healthy Homosexual*, George Weinberg coined the term "homophobia" in 1972. In 1974, yielding to mounting pressure from gay activists and their allies, the American Psychiatric Association removed homosexuality from its designation as a mental disorder. Also in the 1970s, the term "sexual preference" was replaced with "sexual orientation," because "preference" implies choice. This distinction between preference and orientation leads us to an ongoing, controversial debate about sexuality.

Sexual Orientation

Theoretical debates about sexual orientation reveal the contested nature of the topic of sexuality. I can only begin to convey the basics of these complex and controversial discussions. Similar to other aspects of identity we are studying, the two primary perspectives on the origin of an individual's sexuality are essentialism and social constructionism. The ***essentialist*** viewpoint contends that one's sexual orientation is a historical, natural, and unchanging aspect of identity based on physiological sources (e.g., hormones, the brain, and genetics). In contrast, the ***social constructionist*** perspective classifies sexual identity as a product of sociohistorical conditions. According to this viewpoint, people become gay or lesbian due to family environment (specifically, their relationship with mother and father), seduction (a gay person "converts" them), or conscious choice.

Whereas members of other traditionally disenfranchised groups (e.g., women or people of color) tend to dispute essentialist rationale for their social identity, many members of the gay movement and their allies accept and advocate the idea that sexuality is innate. They want to be understood in essentialist terms.[38] This position against social constructionism matters because "if homosexuality is purely a social construction, then laws against it or laws protecting the rights of homosexuals might be absurd."[39] Moreover, the idea that sexuality is "real" may justify a struggle to achieve gay identity. Research in medicine, psychiatry, and psychology has contributed to this stance. Current scientific interest in the origins of sexuality tends to focus on homosexuality rather than heterosexuality. Some contemporary scientists hope to support gay and lesbian rights by proving that sexual orientation is biological and genetic. A poll found that 49 percent of the general population and 75 percent of gay persons think that homosexuality is something people are born with. Those who believe that homosexuality is innate tend to have more positive, accepting attitudes toward issues that involve equal rights in employment.[40]

Alternatively, some members of the GLBTQ community prefer the social construction perspective because "it suggests that people can change the boundaries of the construction and thereby change—or escape entirely—the social consequences of what it means to be gay."[41] They reason that although the essentialist position might encourage society to become more accepting, it also might tempt them to develop genetic engineering, or otherwise try to "cure" homosexuality. They might even abort embryos that have "the gay gene." And, society may view homosexuals negatively, as they often perceive persons with disabilities. Thus, some GLBTQ persons fear that the essentialist viewpoint may equate homosexuality to a biological defect.

In recent years, the ***queer movement*** has emerged to challenge essentialist or universalist notions of gay identity as either gay, lesbian, or bisexual. Members of this movement contend "that queers are different from the mainstream and that these differences should be celebrated, not silenced."[42] They intentionally refer to themselves as "queer" to connote varieties and complexities of sexuality, and they reject the notion that "queers should try to fit in with the mainstream by attempting to appear 'normal.'"[43]

According to contemporary research, sexual orientation may arise from multiple developmental pathways. For instance, sexual orientation seems to be at least partially determined through genetics.[44] Psychologists J. Michael Bailey and Richard Pillard conclude that since physical cues, such as those that are visual or olfactory, attract humans to one another, aspects of sexual orientation must be "more or less wired in."[45] Moreover, the social matrix in which an individual lives will influence how an individual experiences and enacts sexuality. Medical researcher William Byne concludes that research about genetic bases of sexuality is inconclusive. He asserts that "we should ask why we as a society are so emotionally invested" in the outcome of biological research on sexual orientation. He also asks, "Will it—or should it—make any difference in the way we perceive ourselves and others or in the way we live our lives and allow others to live theirs?"[46]

The origins of sexual orientation remain uncertain. However, members of society have constructed categories and roles of sexuality. Legal, religious, and medical-scientific discourses have moved from an emphasis on sexual behavior to sexual personhood, thereby classifying various forms of sexual identity. Although what we now label as "heterosexual" and "homosexual" feelings and behaviors seem always to have existed, consciousness about homosexual and heterosexual identity is a postmodern development. Moreover, attitudes toward sexuality correspond with changes in society, such as the influx of women into the workplace or the advent of HIV/AIDS.

Society has constructed heterosexuality as the normal and superior category of sexuality. Consequently, heterosexuals enjoy advantages that persons of other sexual orientations do not. To explore dynamics of heterosexual privilege, a group of straight-identified students at Earlham College developed a questionnaire similar to the one that Peggy McIntosh created about white privilege. Here are some statements that they *ask straight persons to consider:*

- If I pick up a magazine, watch TV, or play music, I can be certain my sexual orientation will be represented.
- I can be sure that my classes will require curricular materials that testify to the existence of people with my sexual orientation.
- People don't ask why I made my choice of sexual orientation.

- I do not have to fear revealing my sexual orientation to friends or family. It's assumed.
- I can easily find a religious community that will not exclude me for being heterosexual.
- I can count on finding a therapist or doctor willing and able to talk about my sexuality.
- I am guaranteed to find sex education literature for couples with my sexual orientation.
- I am not identified by my sexual orientation.
- I can be open about my sexual orientation without worrying about my job.
- If my day, week, or year is going badly, I need not ask of each negative episode or situation whether it has sexual orientation overtones.
- I can go for months without being called straight.

These statements imply dynamics of heterosexual privilege and indicate some of the challenges that confront lesbian, gay, bisexual, and queer-identified persons.

The preceding overview reveals that "like gender, sexuality is political. It is organized into systems of power, which reward and encourage some individuals and activities, while punishing and suppressing others. . . . The modern sexual system has been the object of political struggle since it emerged and as it has evolved."[47] Federal and state governments, the mass media, educational systems, and the church have exerted powerful influence on our perceptions and beliefs about various aspects of sexuality.

This brief history of the social construction of sexuality does not begin to illustrate complex varieties of sexual identities and their implications. Individuals confront and negotiate numerous issues related to their sexuality, depending on intersections of race, class, religiosity, age, ability, and sexual orientation. For instance, homosexuals comprise countless co-cultures, each of which enacts (or not) sexuality in distinct ways and encounters distinct challenges. Among rare research about sexuality that considers intersections of identity, findings show that GLBTQ persons of color may experience multiple external and internalized oppressions. A study about Asian American sexual minorities reported that they simultaneously deal with racism in white heterosexual and GLBTQ communities, heterosexism within their cultural communities, plus internalized racism and heterosexism.[48]

Some GLBTQ baby boomers will face unique challenges as they age. Although they have witnessed progress in gay rights, they also were in their late 30s during the Gay Pride movement. Therefore, they grew up in an era when society vilified gay people. Many of them have experienced blatant and subtle discrimination, and internalized negative attitudes about their sexuality. They may experience discrimination in various services designated for older persons, such as senior centers, nursing homes, and retirement communities. They also may face economic obstacles; for example, Social Security does not allow survivor benefits for same-sex couples. Given the history of activism among boomers in general, GLBTQ boomers are likely to "advocate for more responsive programs, services, organizations, and policies over the next 20 years."[49] In addition to implying complexity of issues related to sexuality, this overview of how we have constructed sexuality presents sexuality as a significant aspect of identity.

•••• Spotlight on Media ••••

Communicating Sexuality on Television

In the early days of television, married couples were portrayed as having separate beds, and you would never have heard them mentioning a sexual act, let alone engaging in one. Today, sex dominates most mainstream entertainment television. "The number of sexual scenes on standard network programs has nearly doubled since 1998 . . . Among the 20 most-watched shows by teens, 70 percent include sexual content (talking about sex, sexual innuendo), and 45 percent include sexual behavior."[50] Moreover, rates of sexual content have risen significantly over time. Soap opera characters engage in an average of six to ten sex acts per hour. And let's not forget daytime talk shows, which cover topics like "who's my baby's daddy," to incest, to "is it a woman, or is it a man?" contests. Almost every day you can witness the spectacle of people bringing relatives, friends, or acquaintances on national television to confess or confront each other about all sorts of sexual behaviors. Sexuality is even more explicit on cable and pay-per-view networks, with some dedicated to pornography. Since 1981, music videos have displayed progressively extreme views of females and their sexuality. We constantly view the rampant use of sex to sell anything from cars to cable TV, as well as drugs for erectile dysfunction.

Researchers assessed the sexual content of 25 prime-time television shows popular among adolescents in 2001–2002.[51] They sought to analyze relationships between how adolescents process television content and how they develop sexually. They found that television enacted a Heterosexual Script, which serves as a blueprint for societal norms for romantic and sexual relationships. This script reproduces heteronormative and patriarchal ideologies about gender roles and sexuality. For example, the shows tended to depict sexuality as a defining component of masculinity by showing males as preoccupied with female bodies, and consumed by sexual thoughts, fantasies, and urges. The centrality of sexuality in males' lives was consistent across characters' age, race, and family roles. In contrast, the shows portrayed females as denying or devaluing their own sexual desire, seeking to please males, and trading their sexuality as a commodity. The shows also showed differences between how women and men view romance and sex: women want/need relationships (especially boyfriends or husbands); men want/need independence (they prefer sexual fulfillment over relational intimacy). The researchers concluded that "television offers mutually impoverished constructs of male and female sexuality, which may ultimately preclude boys' ability to say no to sex and girls' ability to say yes."[52]

Acquiring Information about Sexuality

Throughout our lives, numerous sources socialize us about sexuality. Adolescents receive most information about sex from informal sources, mainly their peers (especially same-sex friends). They also learn from dating partners, different-sex friends, the media, and reading on their own. According to a large-scale study, teens acquire the least amount of sex information from their mothers and teachers, and even less from their fathers.[53] The mass media that adolescents favor rarely include accurate information about sexual health. An analysis of the rare sexual health content in four media (television, magazines, music, and movies) popular among adolescents revealed ambiguous and/or inaccurate content. These media reinforced traditional gender stereotypes of males as obsessed with sex and sexual performance, and females being responsible for protection against pregnancy.[54] Basically, the media are not providing much sexual health content for their adolescent audiences. In terms of formal sex education, in 1996 the federal government provided funding to states whose schools taught abstinence-only in their sex education programs. In 1996, 49 out of 50 states adopted the program and took the funds; today, only 33 states receive this funding. Many schools have found the abstinence-only approach to be ineffective and have chosen instead to teach students about protection from pregnancy and disease, should they decide to engage in sexual relations.[55]

While heterosexual teens tend to turn to their peers, young people who realize that their sexuality may not fit societal norms often consult the Internet. The Internet provides a level of security and anonymity that allows them to explore their sexuality. They can construct and interact with a virtual community of similar adolescents, and they can come out safely online before they disclose their sexuality to anyone in person.[56]

Communicating Sexuality in Organizations

Sexuality infuses organizations, as members engage in a variety of sexual relationships, ranging from flirtations to short-term affairs, to committed partnerships.[57] The organization is a logical and relatively safe place to meet a prospective romantic and/or sexual partner. Employees meet prospective mates or spouses, have affairs with one another, and sometimes break up at work. In most organizational settings, employees routinely engage in such behaviors as sexual banter, jokes, teasing, gossip, and flirting. Basically, the workplace is a fertile site for performing sexuality.

How people express or repress sexuality depends on the type of organization. For instance, sociologists Jeff Hearn and Wendy Parkin differentiate sexploitation organizations from those that do not foreground sexuality.[58] The former include any type of organization that trades on sexuality, including the pornography industry, "escort" services, strip clubs, and sexual aids manufacturers and retailers. The latter encompass most other workplaces.

Hearn and Parkin also discuss distinct sexuality matters that confront members of total (or closed) organizations—institutions such as prisons, asylums, the military, or boarding schools—where members spend all of their time.[59] In those places, authorities often engage in obtrusive control and surveillance mechanisms for staff as well as residents.

The sexual makeup of the institution can complicate sexuality policies. For example, members of single-sex organizations may be concerned about homosexual activity. The extent to which such organizations develop and enforce policies hinges on their primary attitude toward sexuality. Prisons for adults probably have different attitudes and rules than the military, and both are likely to differ from boarding schools for girls or boys.

When I went to college in 1968, I lived in a girls' dormitory. If a male visited me, he had to sign in at the front desk, and I had to keep my door open. He also had to leave by 10:30 PM. The housemother monitored these visits, and any girl who broke the rules could be evicted. Not only does my dormitory experience illustrate how total institutions might implement policies about sexuality, it also shows, once again, the importance of context. When I went to graduate school in the mid-1970s, I resided in a coeducational dormitory where everyone came and went freely, with no monitoring by the resident assistant.

Even when people in organizations do not refer directly to sexuality, sexuality always is an absent presence. An awareness of sexual harassment policies may dictate and discipline our behaviors. Or, norms or policies about appearance may control how we dress, and whether we should act or dress in a more or less sexual manner, depending on our role. We may not act on sexual attraction to a superior, subordinate, coworker, client, or student because of formal or informal policies.

Aware of potential consequences, many people carefully choose words and monitor their actions. Some professionals fear that cross-sex mentoring may evolve into sexual relationships, or that other people may infer such relationships. Gay and lesbian workers also may limit mentoring interactions with others of the same sex for fear that people may think they're coming on to them.

Expressing Sexuality at Work

How people express sexuality at work varies according to context. Blue-collar workers tend to use more explicit sexual language and generally are permitted (expected?) to be more vulgar than white-collar workers. For some working-class men, sexualizing the workplace may signify a form of resistance against the rigors and repetition of their work. Unfortunately, these acts also may be patriarchal, and they may reinforce women's subordination.

Different control mechanisms seem to exist regarding sexuality, depending on whether one primarily uses one's mind or one's body at work. I consciously downplay my sexuality when I dress for work. My awareness of my sexuality stems not only from being a woman, but also from being a black woman. I do not want to personify stereotypes about black women as sexually loose. Furthermore, I think it is especially important to counter the stereotype that blacks in general lack intellectual capability.

Particular issues related to sexuality confront women due to pregnancy, menstruation, menopause, or lactation. Some women may help to reinforce heteronormativity by adhering to heterosexual norms. For instance, a study on makeup at work concluded that some heterosexual women wear makeup as a conscious mark of heterosexuality. Some of the women in this study said they wore makeup to avoid being labeled as lesbian or as someone who doesn't want to attract men. The researchers concluded that women who wear makeup might help reproduce inequality at work because they follow workplace norms about appearance. However, those women also may be "seeking empowerment and pleasure," and wearing makeup may be an act of resistance to being asexualized.[60] Some lesbians in this study reported wearing makeup to "pass" as heterosexual, one of many strategies that gays and lesbians may employ to conceal their sexuality.

In an article entitled "The Price of Passing: A Lesbian Perspective on Authenticity in Organizations," communication scholar Anna Spradlin reports "continuous conversational moves from the standpoint of a lesbian who has lived the 'don't tell' side of the [don't ask, don't tell] equation."[61] Spradlin offers six specific communication strategies that lesbians and gays may use at work. (1) Distancing includes avoiding informal contexts such as company picnics or standing around the water cooler, and conversations. (2) Dissociating encompasses "minimizing public interaction with gay or lesbian persons."[62] (3) Dodging means shifting or avoiding topics to steer clear of anything that might expose gay issues, such as "what did you do this weekend?" (4) Distracting includes cultivating heterosexual aspects of identity. For instance, Spradlin would tell people that she was divorced. (5) Denial includes withholding information about one's primary relationship status. (6) Deceiving consists of "intentionally constructing dishonest messages to indicate a heterosexual rather than a gay identity."[63] As Spradlin observes, constant performance of these strategies can take its toll on lesbian and gay employees: "The price I paid for passing was the prevention of authentic, healthy relationship development within the workplace, the erosion of self-esteem and integrity, excessive tension within my own primary relationship, and the sheer drain of professional and personal energy."[64]

Spradlin's struggles imply issues that some lesbian, gay, and bisexual persons may confront as they decide whether or not to disclose their sexuality to their coworkers. Employees may decide to come out at work because they want to be honest and demonstrate integrity at a personal level, to obtain benefits of building open relationships, and to educate others about sexual minorities.[65] However, they must weigh potential negative consequences. They also must decide whom to tell, when, and how. Some people drop hints or display evidence such as photos with partners. One of my coworkers invited me to lunch to disclose that she is lesbian. Another e-mailed me while she was away on travel for the job. Thus, there are numerous complex issues related to using communication to construct and perform sexuality. For example, most GLBTQ persons must repeatedly negotiate coming out processes, and they may live double lives that can negatively impact their self-esteem as well as their workplace relationships. Many of them deal with challenges that heterosexual persons do not even have to consider.

Romantic Relationships

Romantic relationships include those between two people in which welcomed, mutual elements of sexuality or physical intimacy exist. Surveys show that romance abounds in office settings. According to some sources, close to half of all romantic relationships begin at work.[66] Romance at work is more likely to occur now than ever due to: longer, more intense work hours spent with coworkers who share common interests, such as work or career goals; increased numbers of women at work (often in equal or higher-level positions than men); and relaxed sexual mores in our society.[67]

Romantic relationships can affect workplace dynamics. Liaisons may result in lessened productivity, work motivation, and work participation on the part of the persons in the relationship. In addition, a couple's romance may elicit favoritism or claims of favoritism, which in turn might affect employee morale. Coworkers may think that members of a couple will be more loyal to themselves than to their coworkers or the organization. The lovers also may become the topic of workplace gossip. Moreover, romances gone sour may precipitate claims of sexual harassment from the spurned individual. On the other hand, the partners may become more productive and motivated because their personal needs are being satisfied.[68] This may contribute to an improved workplace climate. However, research indicates that negative consequences tend to outweigh positive ones.[69]

Coworkers' attitudes toward peers' romantic relationships can vary according to the nature of the relationship. In one study, coworkers reported less trust for peers in relationships with superiors than peers involved with peers.[70] Marital status and sexual orientation also matter. Historically, a double standard has operated when workplace romances bloom. If heterosexual relationships were exposed, organizations would usually relocate or terminate the woman rather than the man.[71] Some organizations are known to have rigid policies. For instance, the military bans sexual involvement among soldiers. Their "don't ask, don't tell" policy refers to heterosexual as well as homosexual liaisons. In contrast, many organizations do not have firm policies in place. According to a study of human resources professionals, an effective office romance policy should:

1. recognize that office relationships exist;
2. establish a mechanism whereby relationships and problems are to be reported confidentially;
3. employ mediation to solve relationship problems, but still reserve the use of warnings and extreme discipline measures;

4. separate romance from sexual harassment, but retain the discipline measures for unreasonable or serious noncompliance;
5. rely on seminars to counsel workers on the pluses and minuses of workplace romances, including the company's climate and its procedures;
6. create a general environment of trust and support for employees.[72]

Sexual Harassment

Most research about organizations and sexuality focuses on ***sexual harassment,*** defined as "any unwanted sexual behavior" that creates an intimidating, hostile, or offensive working environment.[73] Also, formal discourse about sexuality in organizations tends to refer to sexual harassment, categorized as: (1) ***quid pro quo***—incidents when the harasser has power or authority over the victim. A harassment incident can include offensive sexual innuendoes and jokes, physical contact, sexual requests or remarks, demands for sexual favors in exchange for job retention or promotion; and (2) ***hostile environment***—sexually offensive conduct by coworkers that makes doing the job difficult for the victim. Both forms of sexual harassment are prosecutable under Title VII of the Civil Rights Act of 1964.

Statistics indicate that 50–75 percent of women working outside of the home experience sexual harassment in their jobs. Women in female-dominated jobs are more likely to experience quid pro quo sexual harassment by a boss or a person in a position of authority who uses that power to coerce sexual activities. Women in male-dominated jobs are more likely to experience a hostile environment, that is, unwelcome remarks or behavior from coworkers.[74] In those cases, some males may attempt to maintain their territory because they do not believe a woman belongs in the role. Although most discourse about sexual harassment concentrates on heterosexual men harassing heterosexual women, the reverse can occur, as well as same-sex harassment. Concentrating primarily on male to female harassment can perpetuate ***heteronormativity,*** the assumption that heterosexuality is the norm.

Dominant notions of masculinity can influence women's and men's responses to sexual harassment. For example, women may consider behavior that could be defined as sexual harassment merely to reflect the old saying, "boys will be boys." A research project revealed that women self-identified with dominant organizational interests by categorizing unwanted sexual attention as an everyday, sedimented practice, or concluding that the act was isolated and unusual. Women who do not confront the harasser or complain to others who can address the unwanted behavior are in effect enabling the behavior. Women in this project seemed unaware that they were helping to reproduce domination and patriarchal perspectives.[75] Men who experience behaviors that could be sexual harassment also may respond based on norms of masculinity and heteronormativity. They may not report what happened because they fear that others might question their masculinity, whether the alleged harasser is female ("why would a 'real' man turn down an opportunity for sex?") or male ("are you gay?").

Women of color may experience sexual harassment at the intersection of gender and race due to the "dual categories of oppression."[76] A study of Hispanic and African American women found that they grappled with various issues related to their racial and gender identities.[77] For instance, some of them hesitated to report incidents because they did not want to fulfill stereotypes about being too emotional, or being an angry woman of color. Some of them said that they probably would not report someone of their own race. The researchers concluded that victims of sexual harassment must "navigate sexual harassment experiences while coping with various social constructions [in addition to gender and race], including class, sexual orientation, and so forth."[78]

Most organizations have implemented policies and procedures related to sexual harassment. Their efforts may be paying off, as the number of grievances filed with the EEOC has gradually decreased over the last decade. In 1997, close to 16,000 charges were filed.[79] In fiscal year 2008, this number dropped to 13,867, of which 15.9 percent were filed by men.[80]

Although sexual harassment definitely merits attention, focusing only on sexual harassment can help to produce and reproduce Victorian views of men as sex predators and women as passive, asexual victims. Thus, emphasizing sexual harassment can have negative implications. Some men may avoid interacting with women for fear of being accused of sexual harassment. They may not include women in networks or mentoring activities, which might affect women's chances for advancement. In addition, an emphasis on sexual harassment fails to acknowledge the reality of sex as pleasure for women and men of varying sexual orientations; it reinforces taboos on "sexuality as pleasure"; and it reflects the ideology of rationality, in opposition to emotionality. Because organizations usually expect an employee to be impersonal and objective, she or he cannot also be sexual, unless that is part of the occupational role. Moreover, dominant discourse about sexual harassment constrains women by objectifying them as potential victims, and by marking them as subject to scrutiny. This discourse can help discipline women to desexualize themselves. This unspoken perspective on sexuality in organizations reveals how some organizations seek to repress sexuality at work.

Conclusion

Sexuality is a primary, primal part of human identity. Across the history of the United States, constructions of sexuality reflect changing attitudes toward reproduction, pleasure, and hetero- versus homosexuality. Currently, ideologies of heteronormativity infuse dominant institutions of society, as GLBTQ groups and their advocates seek equality. Moreover, a double bind persists as heterosexual women generally are expected to be chaste, while heterosexual men tend to be socialized to perform aggressive sexuality as a marker of masculinity: "The Victorian sexual philosophy in America is part of a traditional approach to life in which male dominance is accepted and the inequality between women and men is considered proper."[81] And, attitudes and behaviors vary depending on other aspects of identity such as gender, ethnicity, race, religion, and age. Although advertisements, television programs, movies, and Internet pornography bombard us with explicit and implicit sexual behaviors and lifestyles, we "continue to harbor remnants of an overall degrading and fearful view of sexuality."[82]

• • • • • ID Check • • • • •

1. What is your sexual orientation?
2. How important is your sexual orientation to you? Explain.
3. What primary sources have taught you about your sexual orientation?
4. How, if at all, do you express your sexual orientation (e.g., through language, communication style, dress, accessories, music, and so forth)?
5. Does your awareness of your sexual orientation ever help you communicate with others? Explain.
6. Does your awareness of your sexual orientation ever hinder how you communicate with others? Explain.
7. What situations, if any, do you avoid because of concerns related to your sexual orientation?
8. What situations, if any, do you seek because of your sexual orientation?
9. What advantages, if any, do you enjoy based on your sexual orientation?
10. Do you know of any stereotypes about your sexual orientation? If so, list them.
11. Are you ever aware of stereotypes about your sexual orientation as you interact with others? Explain.
12. How do the media tend to depict your sexual orientation? Do media depictions correspond with your sense of your sexual orientation? Explain.
13. Do you think your attitudes toward sexual orientation intersect with any other facets of your social identity, for instance: your gender? your race? your age? your religion?

Reflection Matters

1. What, if anything, did you find intriguing in this chapter? Why?
2. According to the sociohistorical overview, what are examples of how people used communication to construct sexuality throughout the history of the United States?

3. Do any current news stories involve issues that this chapter covers? If yes, what points do they exemplify?
4. What are examples of power relations in the construction of sexuality in the United States?
5. What were/are your main sources of learning about sexuality? How knowledgeable to you feel about sexuality?
6. Have you ever seen, participated in, or heard about a romantic relationship in the workplace? Describe the relationship, and relate your story to issues raised in the chapter.
7. Do you think that workplaces should have policies regarding romantic relationships? Explain.
8. What experiences do you have, if any, with talk about sex at work (e.g., jokes, sexual innuendoes)?
9. What impact do you think media representations of sexuality have on young persons' attitudes and behaviors?
10. Do you agree or disagree with the statement: We "continue to harbor remnants of an overall degrading and fearful view of sexuality"? Explain your position.
11. Do you believe that sexual identity is innate or socially constructed or both? Explain.
12. What do you think of the idea of a high school for GLBTQ students? What might be advantages and disadvantages for the students?

Chapter 7

Ability Matters

When I was in elementary school, kids in the projects whom we called "retarded" rode off in a bus that took them to a different school than the rest of us. In junior high, those children went to the same school as the rest of us, but they still rode a bus, while we walked. And, they had classes in a separate part of the school. Sometimes, as their bus passed us, my friends and I would snicker and cackle, "Escape, escape." I saw a comedy on television where the audience laughed loudly when a kid who had been diagnosed as dyslexic told his dad that he didn't want to "ride the short bus to school."

A few years ago, for the first time in over twenty years of teaching, I taught a student with a visible physical disability. "Antoine" was a young black male who used a wheelchair. When I first saw him, I wondered if he had been shot. Recognizing the ever-potent power of media images of young black men, I quickly dismissed that thought. Early in the semester, Antoine told me that he had muscular dystrophy. I tried to treat him as I would any other student, even as I respected his condition. I joked with him like I did with other students, and I gave him constructive feedback. Whenever he talked with me after class, I sat down beside him so that we would be on eye level (I learned this tip during my research for this chapter). We agreed that I would periodically look at him so he could nod when he wanted to speak during class, because he couldn't raise his hand. The course entailed group projects that required students to meet outside of class. Antoine felt that students in his group didn't always include him, and they sometimes seemed patronizing. Unfortunately, this experience was not new to him. He once lamented, "People judge me for what I *can't* do instead of what I *can* do."

The following semester, another student told me he no longer informed his professors that he had a learning disability. Based on previous experience, he believed they would treat him differently, that they would patronize him. Therefore, he was not taking advantage of the services the university provides for students with learning disabilities, because students have to disclose and document their impairment to qualify for services. One student said that after she trusted a professor enough to reveal her disability, the professor challenged whether or not her condition qualified as a disability. The student was devastated. Yet another student confided that when he told a faculty member that he has Asperger's Syndrome (often viewed as a high functioning form of autism[1]), the professor replied, "Oh. I just thought you were coming to class high [on drugs or alcohol]." These types of interactions can lead students with learning disabilities (and other "invisible" disabilities) not to tell their professors, even though our university has policies to facilitate learning for students with learning disabilities. For instance, students may request extended time for exams or a quiet environment in which to take a test.

While walking on campus, I saw a young man in a wheelchair struggling to get up an incline. As I considered offering to help, another young guy came behind the chair and said, "Let me help you, man." While he pushed the chair, they chatted easily with one another.

During a course I taught on difference matters, a student divulged his learning disability to his classmates and me after wrestling with whether or not he should tell us. Aware of his presumed privileged status as a white male, he did not want to seem to be whining. Here we can see the impact of intersections of identity as well as related complexities of privileged and disadvantaged social identity categories.

My experiences illustrate a few of the issues I address in this chapter. The fact that I rarely have (knowingly) taught students with disabilities shows that persons with disabilities often are not part of mainstream society. However, since I'm seeing an increase in students with learning disabilities, perhaps that's changing. In addition, some disabilities are visible, while others are not. Consequently, some people like the students with learning disabilities can "pass" as nondisabled, while others who are wheelchair users like Antoine do not have that option. For all I know, other students in my classes may have had disabilities. I regret that I hadn't actively considered this possibility until recently.

Students' reluctance to reveal their learning impairments demonstrates that some persons with disabilities are apprehensive about being stigmatized. Employees with unapparent disabilities also opt sometimes to conceal their condition, even if they are entitled to accommodations for their disability. These concerns illustrate that—similar to the other categories we've studied—although governmental legislation attempts to remove barriers for persons with disabilities, psychological and social barriers persist.

We will explore these and other issues related to ability as a socially constructed aspect of identity arising from a dominant ideology of normality in the United States.[2] I begin by explaining why ability matters, after which I define key terminology related to disability. Next, I offer a sociohistorical overview of ability and disability in the United States, after which I discuss contemporary communication issues. Then, I discuss disability and work. I conclude by describing positive approaches to supporting and valuing persons with disabilities.

Why Ability Matters

From birth to death, ability is a salient and significant aspect of identity. Due to modern technology, ability matters even before birth, as parents can learn whether or not their baby has a congenital defect. And, sometimes they will decide to abort. When a baby is born, people want to know if the child is healthy. A common ritual is counting the newborn's fingers and toes. These concerns are understandable in a society that places a high value on being able-bodied. Individuals perceived to be abnormal or disabled are likely to be labeled in ways that can stigmatize them for the rest of their lives. Thus, ability matters because our society emphasizes being "normal," which can lead to dire consequences for persons with disabilities and their families.

Ability also matters because of demographics. An estimated 20 percent of the population aged five or older is living with some type of disability, thus comprising the largest minority group in the United States.[3] Among those, the highest percentage has physical disabilities. Numbers of persons with disabilities have increased and may continue to rise because of medical advances that allow people to remain alive who previously might not have survived, including premature babies, persons with spinal injuries, older people with debilitating illnesses, and wounded members of the armed services.

My increasing experiences with students with disabilities probably occurred because more students with disabilities are entering higher education in the United States than in previous years. The increase may be due in part to positive effects of policies for educating K–12 students with disabilities. The numbers and diversity of these students are likely to continue to rise due to recent legislation for students with disabilities as well as expanded benefits for members and veterans of the military who served on or after September 11, 2001, many of whom may have acquired varying disabilities.[4] However, because policies require students with disabilities to voluntarily disclose their condition in order to qualify for accommodations, similar to the students I described earlier, these students will continue to face the recurring and often agonizing decision of whether or not to inform their professors. Moreover, universities will need to improve resources and services for this growing group of students, and they will need to better inform students with disabilities as well as faculty about legal requirements.[5]

Census data reveal that differences in age, gender, race, and ethnicity matter to persons with disabilities.[6] According to the 2000 census, disability rates rose with age for females and males, but were higher for women than men aged 65 and older, and lower for women under 65 years old. Disability rates also varied across racial and ethnic groups. Asians had the lowest overall disability rate. Whites also had a low overall rate, even though they also had a higher median age. Blacks and American Indian and Alaska natives had the highest disability rate among all racial and ethnic groups. A higher proportion of people with disabilities (17.6 percent) were poorer than persons without disabilities (10.6 percent). Thus, once again, we see the impact of intersecting nondominant social identity categories.

Ability matters so much that various advocacy groups continually struggle to gain civil rights for persons with disabilities. Persons with disabilities have been segregated, isolated, and excluded throughout the history of the United

States. Although types of disabilities vary, persons with disabilities endure "a common set of stigmatizing social values and debilitating socially constructed hazards."[7] Many persons with disabilities have recurring experiences of "cultural devaluation and socially imposed restriction, of personal and collective struggles for self-definition and self-determination."[8] As groups sought to change these conditions, one major outcome is an interdisciplinary academic area known as Disability Studies, which became an organized area of scholarship in the 1980s. Disability Studies emerged from political science and sociology as those disciplines conducted research on reforming public policies. This field has evolved to encompass many areas of study. Disability Studies scholars advocate approaches to disability that incorporate social, political, and cultural perspectives, and that recognize persons with disabilities as a minority group entitled to civil rights.

Another related outcome of organized resistance to mistreatment of persons with disabilities is the landmark 1990 Americans with Disabilities Act (ADA), a civil rights law to protect persons with disabilities from economic and social discrimination. The ADA created a new category of protected minorities in the United States.

Thus, ability matters just like other social identity groups: due to changing demographics and an increasing focus on the civil rights of nondominant group members. In addition, the history of how people in the United States have dealt with human ability parallels other aspects of identity. For instance, media portrayals affect our perceptions of persons with disabilities, and stereotypes abound about persons with disabilities.

Also similar to other social identity groups we've studied, these changes mean that persons with and without disabilities will interact with one another more frequently than ever, across and within various contexts. Moreover, persons with disabilities now have a wide variety of options for communicating, thanks to wonderful advances in assistive technology devices, such as voice recognition and output technology; electronic pointing devices that can control cursors with eye movements, brain waves, nerve signals, and ultrasound; computer screen magnifiers; sip and puff systems (activated by inhaling or exhaling); Braille embossers; text-to-speech synthesizers; and touch screens.

However, the matter of ability also differs significantly from other aspects of social identity. The concept of ability is much more complex. Numerous categories and classifications of physical and mental disability exist, with widely ranging consequences and implications. Also, the nature and extent of types of impairments vary greatly. For instance, wheelchair users like Antoine can have differing degrees of use of their limbs, and they may or may not have other impairments. Some persons with disabilities may be in constant or recurrent physical discomfort or pain, while others may not. Furthermore, unlike other minority groups in the United States, persons with disabilities "have had fewer opportunities to develop a collective consciousness, identity or culture, let alone interrogate cultures of ableism."[9]

Ability also differs from other social identity categories because our ability status can change drastically in the blink of an eye. Ability may change in minor to major ways, with the potential to reverse or not. Moreover, "everyone is a little bit able-bodied and a little bit disabled. The degree to which we are one or the other shifts throughout life."[10] These perspectives probably affect how nondisabled persons interact with persons with disabilities. When they encounter someone with a disability, they may be more aware of their own vulnerability. As disability activist Paul Hunt observes: "For the able-bodied, normal world, we [persons with disabilities] are representatives of many of the things they most fear—tragedy, loss, dark and the unknown."[11]

In addition, most of our lives will be touched by ability issues, whether for self, loved one(s), coworkers, or others. My only sister has bipolar disorder (previously known as manic depression), and she lived for years in a mental institution. One of my cousins was developmentally disabled at birth. She is living on her own after years of excellent special education, thanks to the generosity of the wealthy family her parents worked for. An older cousin of mine was born deaf. She lived independently during the 1950s and 1960s. When I was a little girl, I was fascinated that she lived alone.

Ability also matters because "the *concept* of disability has been used to justify discrimination against other groups by attributing disability to them."[12] In fact, "it may well be that all social hierarchies have drawn on culturally constructed and socially sanctioned notions of disability."[13] As disability studies historian Douglas Baynton explains:

> Disability was a significant factor in the three great citizenship debates of the nineteenth and early twentieth centuries: women's suffrage, African-American freedom and civil rights, and the restriction of immigration. When categories of citizenship were questioned, challenged, and disrupted, disability was called on to clarify and define who deserved, and who was deservedly excluded from, citizenship. Opponents of political and social equality for women cited their supposed physical, intellectual, and psychological flaws, deficits, and deviations from the male norm. These flaws—irrationality, excessive emotionality, physical weakness—are in essence mental, emotional, and physical disabilities, although they are rarely discussed or examined as such. Arguments for racial inequality and immigration restrictions invoked supposed tendencies to feeblemindedness, mental illness, deafness, blindness, and other disabilities in particular races and ethnic groups.[14]

Groups accused of such disabilities vigorously denied these characteristics, therefore reinforcing negative notions about disability. Thus, disability has functioned as a sign of inferiority for other groups that have been assigned to the lower levels of society. In sum, ability matters because it is a powerful and prevalent principle for judging social worth in the United States.

What Is Disability?

Legal definitions of disability use three key words to characterize ability status: disability, impairment, and handicap. As stated by the ADA, "an individual with a ***disability*** [emphasis added] is defined . . . as a person who has a physical or mental impairment that substantially limits one or more major life activities, a person who has a history or record of such an impairment, or a person who is perceived by others as having such an impairment. The ADA does not specifically name all of the impairments that are covered."[15] According to the World Health Organization (WHO), ***impairment*** includes "any temporary or permanent loss or abnormality of a body structure or function, whether physiological or psychological. An impairment is a disturbance affecting functions that are essentially mental (memory, consciousness) or sensory, internal organs (heart, kidney), the head, the trunk or the limbs. [A ***handicap***] is the result of an impairment or disability that limits or prevents the fulfillment of a role that is normal, depending on age, sex, and social and cultural factors."[16] Please note that some people view "handicap" as a pejorative term.

Disability and handicap imply distinct relationships between persons with disabilities and society at large. Although the terms are sometimes used interchangeably, they have different meanings: "A disability becomes a *handicap* when the physical or social environment interacts with it to impede a person in some aspect of his or her life."[17] For instance, a person with paraplegia who can function in the physical environment using a wheelchair, ramps, and curb cuts may be handicapped by buildings or public transportation that are not accessible to wheelchair users.[18]

Impairments and disabilities have been categorized in numerous ways. One scheme cites six categories: physical conditions, mental conditions, sensory impairments, learning disabilities, neurological conditions, and addictive disorders.[19] However, these categories do not begin to convey the fact that ability "is not simply located in the bodies of individuals. It is a socially and culturally constructed identity. Public policy, professional practices, societal arrangements, and cultural values all shape its meaning."[20] Disability scholars concur with this sociocultural perspective on disability:

> Disability is a broad term, within which cluster ideological categories as varied as sick, deformed, ugly, old, maimed, afflicted, abnormal, or debilitated—all of which disadvantage people by devaluing bodies that do not conform to cultural standards. Thus, disability functions to preserve and validate such privileged designations as beautiful, healthy, normal, fit, competent, intelligent—all of which provide cultural capital to those who can claim such status.[21]

Consequently, "we are all, regardless of our subject positions, shaped and formed by the politics of ***ableism*** [emphasis added],"[22] which refers to "a network of beliefs, processes and practices that produces a particular kind of self and body (the corporeal standard) that is projected as the perfect, species-typical and therefore essential and fully human."[23]

Constructing Disability in the United States

As historians Paul Longmore and Lauri Umansky observe, "Disability has always been central to life in America."[24] Attitudes toward disability and persons with disabilities have varied over recorded time, depending on economic conditions, intellectual thought, cultural preferences, and religious tenets. In preindustrial society, religion and superstition dominated attitudes and beliefs. Persons with family and kin networks took care of persons with disabilities. They viewed disabilities as natural occurrences, based on God's will, or as evidence of sin and evil.

Industrial Revolution

Disability gained prominence as a social issue in the mid-nineteenth century, due to the Industrial Revolution. The rigors of new, mechanistic employment environments called for able-bodied employees. Since work organizations were structured on the premise of ability, they excluded persons not perceived to be able. Workers' bodies became viewed as extensions of machines. This relationship between machine and body contributed to the idea that the body should be mechanically perfect.[25]

The environment created by industrialization helped generate the concept of disability. When pressing demands of the labor force increased the need for workers, the government enlisted physicians to differentiate persons with actual impairments from those who were exploiting public aid programs and avoiding work.[26] These developments led to the social construction of disability as a medical problem of an individual. In addition to demands for physical fitness, the Industrial Revolution also required a higher educational level of workers. Anyone unable to attain about a third-grade education was labeled "feebleminded." This label encompassed not only those with mental impairments but also those with mobility challenges or anyone with a communication impairment, such as a hearing or speech impediment.

Thus, due to industrialization, persons with disabilities were further marginalized because they weren't seen as fit to participate in the new labor force. Public sentiment toward persons with disabilities became increasingly negative. In some cities, statutes known as "ugly laws" proclaimed that "no person who is diseased, maimed, mutilated or in any way deformed, so as to be an unsightly or disgusting object, is to be allowed in or on the public ways or other public places."[27]

The Census Bureau began to collect information about disability status in the 1830 Census. In 1849, Massachusetts allocated funds for the Massachusetts School for Idiotic Children and Youth. The stage was thus set for identifying persons with disabilities and segregating them in dehumanizing institutions. Deeply held fears and prejudices produced strong custodial measures due to the perception that someone with a disability was a menace who needed to be locked away, a burden who needed to be sterilized or exterminated, or a vulnerable being who needed to be protected.[28] An asylum movement arose to place the "feebleminded" into institutions maintained by private religious groups, charitable groups, and the state. Some institutions were educational facilities, some were rehabilitative, and many were merely custodial.

In 1890, institutions, referred to as "hospital schools," and vocational programs sought to train "cripples." The word "cripple" referred to individuals who had mobility impairments, such as amputees and paraplegics. The word "cripple" also implied economic dependency and reliance on charity. Cripples symbolized the antithesis of United States citizenship, which required that one be gainfully employed. "Crippledom" was viewed as a serious social and economic problem, and cripples were viewed as parasites.

The medical field developed a concept known as "rehabilitation" to eliminate the dependency of cripples. The purpose of rehabilitation was to enable persons with disabilities and assimilate them into work organizations. Rehabilitationists believed that a cripple's worst problem was being rejected from the workplace. This problem was especially hard for males, because every male was obligated to work, to provide for his family. Thus, programs sought to "cure" male cripples so that they could get jobs. Most rehabilitation efforts focused on getting the individual to fit with socially constructed expectations of "able-bodiedness" rather than on getting other members and institutions of society to make adjustments to meet the needs of the individual.[29]

By the turn of the twentieth century, the responsibility of caring for persons with disabilities had shifted from families to local governmental authorities.[30] Citizens had moved from the protestant ideology of familial obligation to persons with disabilities to more worldly notions. The government used disciplinary power to develop institutions to contain and control persons with disabilities. Government programs placed many persons with disabilities under professional supervision, "either to mend them into fit citizens or to sequester them permanently for society's safety."[31] This approach shaped the lives of many persons with disabilities throughout the twentieth century.

Eugenics

A primary source for the rehabilitation or rejection approach to dealing with persons with disabilities was the eugenics movement, which took place during the first three decades of the twentieth century. ***Eugenics*** is a science of social engineering that seeks to improve hereditary qualities of human beings through careful selection of parents. "Positive" eugenics stresses improving genetic characteristics, while "negative" eugenics focuses on wiping out undesirable family lines. The eugenics movement emerged from complex circumstances, including declining birthrates among the wealthy, an influx of immigrants, economic turmoil, urban growth as people migrated from farms, and a growing belief in the powers of science.[32]

During those times (the early 1900s), "progressive reformers had a strong faith in science as the cure-all that would herald in a new era of rational control of both nature and human society."[33] Eugenicists contended that sterilization of one "defective" could save society thousands of dollars in state care. Supporters of eugenics pronounced persons with mental retardation as evil, poisonous, "reproductive menaces." As a result of the eugenics movement, widespread legislation allowed states to involuntarily sterilize individuals thought to be biological transmitters of socially undesirable traits, such as mental retardation. Legislation also tried to prevent marriage for these persons.

The eugenics ideology of normality and abnormality became entrenched in U.S. society. Groups such as the Carnegie Institution for Experimental Evolution and the Race Betterment Foundation and their wealthy backers, including steel industry leader Andrew Carnegie and cereal magnate J. H. Kellogg, helped to popularize themes of selective breeding. Biology textbooks included chapters on eugenics that endorsed sterilizing "unfit" people, restricting immigration, and segregating races. State fairs included Fitter Families exhibits, where attendees could get a genetic evaluation and compete in a "Fitter Family" contest to try to win a medal that proclaimed, "Yea I Have a Goodly Heritage."[34]

In a well-known case against Carrie Buck, a poor white woman labeled as feebleminded, the Supreme Court upheld eugenics sterilization laws. In the 1927 Court decision, Chief Justice Oliver Wendell Holmes wrote: "Three generations of imbeciles are enough."[35] Due to the 1922 sterilization law (for persons perceived as feebleminded, insane, criminal, epileptic, inebriate, diseased, blind, deaf, deformed, and dependent—orphans, homeless, tramps, and paupers), over 65,000 persons were sterilized involuntarily for a so-called "genetically related reason," between 1921 and 1964.[36]

However, many persons, including noted geneticists, openly criticized the eugenics movement. According to some sources, Adolph Hitler relied on information from eugenics studies to mount his campaign of racial purity.[37] Due to heightened criticism of unscientific methods as well as the negative implications of the eugenics-based activities of Nazis, the eugenics movement expired in the late 1930s.

Medical Model of Disability

Eugenics perspectives on normality and fitness were based on the ***medical model of disability,*** which personalizes disability by placing it in the individual, viewing it as a medical problem the individual faces, rather than examining social structures and addressing the social marginalization and economic deprivation of many people with disabilities. This model lends scientific credibility to the idea that physical and mental abnormalities form the root of all problems that confront persons with disabilities. This model presents disability as "pathological rather than political, clinical and not cultural, fundamentally different from race, class, and gender."[38] This medical model not only ignores sociological and psychological aspects of disability, it also denies or disregards how society excludes persons with disabilities. Thus, the medical model (de)legitimates an individual based on her/his loss or inabilities and needs. As a result, a person with a disability may become the condition: for example, "a person becomes a 'paraplegic' who then becomes part of a grouping of 'paraplegics' with homogeneous characteristics assumed."[39]

Within the medical model rests an ***ideology of normality,*** which contends that the normal state of being is to be in good health; therefore sickness is a deviation from normality.[40] Persons in power have emphasized this concept of normality to measure, categorize, and manage populations. They invoke "normal" as an ideal to exclude anyone defined as below average, according to whatever form of assessment or measurement is in vogue. For instance, some teachers who worked with deaf students did not want them to use sign language because they believed it was more savage than "normal" ways of communicating.[41]

Concerns about normality often sparked the federal and state government to develop and administer public policy. These policies "have defined who may work and who may receive public subsidies if they do not work; who may attend school and what services they will receive when they get to school."[42] They also determine accessibility to public transportation and private telecommunication systems. The medical perspective dominated policy making, professional practice, and societal arrangements, as governmental initiatives usually focused more on "curing" persons with disabilities than ensuring their civil rights.

Social Model of Disability

To contest the medical model, scholars developed a ***social model of disability*** that acknowledges cultural, social, and political factors that contribute to the construction of disability. This perspective contends that disability is not the problem of an individual; rather, it is a social and environmental issue arising from society. A condition does not disable an individual; external restraints do. The social model implicates a wide variety of organizations and institutions, including school systems, health care and health financing systems, public transportation, hotel services, and other services. The social model "attributes the creation of disability to the dominant socio-cultural environment . . . which views disability as deviance, damage, dependence—the so-called 'sick' role—and perpetuates labels and stereotypes which stigmatize, disempower, deskill and marginalize disabled people."[43] The significant shift in perspectives on disability from a medical model to a social model resulted primarily from disability rights activism.

Disability Movements

The disability movement arose as persons with disabilities and their advocates responded to persistent abuses and conditions by demanding their rightful place in society. This heterogeneous group lobbied extensively and often engaged in public demonstrations. The first recorded civil protest took place in 1935, when the League for the Physically Handicapped conducted sit-ins and marched in picket lines to demand government-funded Works Progress Administration jobs. Initial stages of the movement also occurred as parents demanded rights for their children with diseases. The American Federation for the Blind was established after World War I by veterans and other adults with vision impairments who refused to become dependent and make brooms and cane chairs for the rest of their lives.[44]

Although disability rights activism branches back through U.S. history, it became particularly dynamic during the last third of the twentieth century. In 1960, a group who called themselves the "Rolling Quads" (most of them had polio) initiated The Center for Independent Living at the University of California, Berkeley.[45] This led to the Independent Living Movement, developed in 1971. Currently, more than 400 centers for independent living exist across the United States and the world.[46]

Between 1968 and 1990, Congress passed fifty acts related to a wide range of issues affecting persons with disabilities, including education, transportation, employment, and access to facilities, buildings, and services. In 1973, the government passed the Rehabilitation Act—the first civil rights law for people with disabilities. This act applied only to programs receiving federal funding. Section 504 of the act formed the basis for programs for persons with disabilities at institutions of higher education, as it "made it illegal for a federal agency, public university, defense or other federal contractor to discriminate against anyone solely by reason of handicap."[47]

In 1975, President Gerald Ford signed the Education for All Handicapped Children Act, which mandated a free and appropriate education for all children 6–21 years of age. This act also mandated Individualized Education Plans for children with disabilities and required providing them opportunities to be educated along side their nondisabled peers.

On January 8, 1974, the People First movement began in Salem, Oregon. Modeled after similar initiatives in Sweden, England, and Canada, this advocacy group sought to organize a convention where people with developmental disabilities could network. As they discussed what to call themselves, someone said, "I'm tired of being called retarded—we are people first."[48] Thus, the group was named People First. This self-advocacy movement has expanded internationally to 43 countries, with over 17,000 members. Over 800 such groups exist in the United States.

In 1977, during the White House Conference on Handicapped Individuals, 3,000 persons with disabilities came to Washington, D.C. That same year, groups of persons with disabilities and their advocates conducted sit-ins in ten cities to demand full implementation of Section 504. In San Francisco, 200 persons locked themselves in the Federal Building for 28 days. In March 1988, students at Gallaudet University, founded in Washington, D.C., in 1864 for deaf and hard-of-hearing persons, engaged in a five-day "Deaf President Now" protest. Their efforts culminated in the hiring of Dr. I. King Jordan, the first deaf president of the university. In 1990, during the Wheels of Justice march, 475 people in wheelchairs assembled in front of the White House, while 250 persons in wheelchairs sat the base of the Capitol. Some members of American Disabled for Attendant Programs Today (ADAPT) chanted, "Access is our civil right," as they crawled up the 83 marble steps of the Capitol. Each of them carried a miniature scroll inscribed with words from the Declaration of Independence.[49]

In July 1990, after concerted, persistent effort by many activist groups, Congress passed the watershed Americans with Disabilities Act to increase access to education, jobs, and other types of services and institutions for individuals with disabilities and to provide equal opportunities for employment:

> The ADA prohibits discrimination in all employment practices, including job application procedures, hiring, firing, advancement, compensation, training, and other terms, conditions, and privileges of employment. It applies to recruitment, advertising, tenure, layoff, leave, fringe benefits, and all other employment-related activities.[50]

The ADA also specifies providing reasonable accommodation for persons with disabilities, including:

> acquiring or modifying equipment or devices, job restructuring, part-time or modified work schedules, reassignment to a vacant position, adjusting or modifying examinations, training materials or policies, providing readers and interpreters and making the workplace readily accessible to and usable by people with disabilities.[51]

Although the ADA has helped to accomplish significant change, backlash has occurred from many institutions as employers deal with ambiguity of terminology and policy related to reasonable accommodation. Even as employers may be confused, some of them enact power relations to discourage employees from asking for accommodations. They may perceive such requests as threats to organizational hierarchy and authority. In response, they may deny a need for accommodations, withhold information about legal rights, and use fear to induce compliance.[52] Employers' reticence to provide accommodations may reflect an ideology of hierarchy that nondisabled persons are more valuable than persons with disabilities, which means that persons with disabilities don't deserve accommodations. Since the ADA was enacted, numerous lawsuits have tested the waters, with contradicting outcomes.

In the wake of the ADA, disability social movements persist as groups strive to allow persons with disabilities to live "normal" lives, for instance by gaining greater access to mainstream social life. Some activists also view and value disability as an alternative identity, as constituting a culture.[53] They seek radical transformation of attitudes toward disability based on the premise that disability is simply a normal variation of human difference. They want to redefine the identity of persons with disabilities as *around* their disability rather than *in spite of* it.

For example, some deaf activists refer to their culture with a capital "D." Members of the Deaf community fervently oppose the medical model of disability and its impetus to "cure." This social identity group arose in the mid-1980s as residential schools attracted deaf people who had been geographically dispersed.[54] They formed social networks and then a community. Those who identify with the Deaf culture believe that deafness is more social than physiological. They define themselves as a linguistic minority rather than a disabled minority. They view attempts to cure deafness as cultural genocide, and they label those who wish to cure deafness (including hearing parents of deaf children) as "audists."[55]

Similarly, since the late 1990s, members of the Asperger's/autistic community have advocated a difference perspective instead of a deficit model. Australian disability activist Judy Singer coined the term "neurodiversity" to conceptualize atypical neurological development and related conditions as normal human differences.[56]

In conclusion, approaches to understanding disability range from a biological model to perspectives that acknowledge social construction and power dynamics. Furthermore, "thinking about disability required major shifts of consciousness—from charity to civil rights, from sentimentality to a recognition of a wide spectrum of human possibilities—before laws could even be thought about."[57] Currently, many activist attitudes toward disability endorse accepting persons with disabilities as different rather than rejecting them as defective.

Communicating Ability

As you have seen, communication plays a central role in retaining and revising perceptions of disability. Because language matters, persons with disabilities and their advocates have challenged offensive labels and created new ones. One disability activist explains: "Keep in mind that some phrases are no longer used in polite conversation. We never, ever use the terms *mentally retarded* or *crippled* for any reason whatsoever. In the evolution of our language, those terms have become derogatory and should never be used."[58] Tool #5 on page 153 provides additional examples for how to communicate humanely about persons with disabilities. In addition, at the end of this section, I provide a set of guidelines for communicating with persons with disabilities.

Research on communication and disability concentrates on psychological and sociological variables related to ***interability communication,*** interactions between persons with disabilities and nondisabled people.[59] During these interactions, nondisabled persons may rely on group stereotypes about people with disabilities, rather than view the person with a disability as an individual. In contrast to ***intrability communication***—communication between nondisabled persons—interability communication tends to take less time, with increased physical distance between communicators, less eye contact (but more staring), and less smiling. Interability interactions also tend to be more anxious and more inhibited. Basically, communication between nondisabled people and persons with disabilities is often awkward.

Author Andrew Potok describes some of the challenges of interability communication:

> When I talk to nondisabled people, they mostly identify me according to their learned and largely unthought-about attitudes and definitions. My physical disability, blindness, dominates and skews the ablebodied person's process of sorting out perceptions and forming a reaction. The rela-

• • • • Spotlight on Media • • • •

Communicating Disability in Movies

Media portrayals of persons with disabilities have tended to be infrequent and stereotypical. A study of over 300 films from the late 1890s to the early 1990s identified 10 persistent disability stereotypes, none of which resembled actual experiences of most persons with disabilities.[60] Two stereotypical images that dominate film and television portrayals of persons with disabilities are "Tiny Tim" and "Super Crip."[61] Tiny Tim refers to the frequent depiction of a person with disability as a victim, a burden on friends, family, or society. Super Crip alludes to the person who against all odds overcomes her or his infirmity. Movies also often depict a person with a disability as someone who lashes out at society and/or is part of an unsuccessful relationship.

The number of movies portraying one or more persons with disabilities has steadily increased since the 1970s. In addition, portrayals gradually are becoming more realistic and positive, due in part to activists who worked to raise public awareness of these issues, as well as collaborative efforts between film producers and persons with disabilities. For instance, Neal Jimenez wrote and co-directed *The Waterdance* (1992), a critically acclaimed film about a group of men who were newly disabled who met at a rehabilitation center.[62] Jimenez based the film partly on his own experiences with paraplegia.

A recent study analyzed 18 feature films produced between 1975 and 2004 that portrayed individuals with physical disabilities, and reported promising findings.[63] In general, the films "no longer portray characters with disabilities as comic figures or beasts."[64] They also portray persons with disabilities as sexual beings, whereas early films showed them as asexual or as dangerous sexual monsters. In addition, films are portraying characters with more depth, and revealing more of their human qualities.

However, movies continue to portray superhuman heroism and courage, focusing on some great obstacle the person overcame. Moreover, they tend to show characters with disabilities enmeshed in self-pity and engaging in self-destructive behaviors, such as rejecting help from caregivers. Many films depicted persons with disabilities as unable to lead successful lives, often implying that they would be better off dead. Films neglected to show persons with disabilities integrated into communities or workplaces, or living independent lives. These recurring images send the strong message that a life with a disability is horrific and that persons with disabilities are burdens to others. Often when movies portray disability as an individual characteristic and problem, they neglect to delve into societal issues such as challenging stigma and social discrimination against persons with disabilities.

Overall, feature filmmakers are making notable progress away from ableist images of individuals with disabilities. These changes matter because more realistic and humane portrayals of persons with disabilities influence viewers to perceive persons with disabilities in a more positive way.[65] They also can help to construct a healthy self-image for persons with disabilities.

> tionship is often strained because of fear, pity, fascination, revulsion or merely surprise, none of which is easily expressed within the constraints of social protocol. Should the nondisabled person offer assistance? Acknowledge the disability? What language or expectation should he use or avoid? For my part, am I only or mostly my disability? Are other attributes worth checking out? Should I attempt charm or deference or humor? It's a stressful situation for both parties.[66]

As Potok implies, attitudes, behaviors, and experiences during interability interactions usually are different for persons with disabilities as contrasted with nondisabled persons.

A group of researchers asked persons with spinal cord dysfunction to write about their experience of living with a disability.[67] Among their responses were frustrations related to communication processes. For example, one person stated: "My companion has been addressed rather than myself even when I have engaged in the conversation. I have been spoken down to as if my comprehension level is affected by my eye level."[68] Several participants reported getting unwanted attention; one person said, "I can't get used to how people look and stare at me all the time, and ask questions about what happened to me."[69]

Some persons with disabilities have developed a repertoire of responses for relatively predictable interability interactions. They may employ proactive strategies to control interactions to minimize differences. For instance, a wheelchair user might ask a person to sit down when they are interacting, so they can communicate "eye-to-eye."[70] Those who have invisible disabilities may delay disclosing their condition to try to seem "normal."[71] Persons with visible disabilities report that they would like to "get the discomfort 'out of the way,' and they want the nondisabled person to treat them as a 'person like anyone else' rather than focus solely on their disability."[72] They often try to divert attention from the disability for fear that "once they have disclosed, the disability may become the basis for all future interactions."[73]

Some persons with disabilities try not to "make waves." They may feel pressured to be nice and understanding and to tolerate what they perceive to be abusive, discriminatory treatment: "People with disabilities have a certain obligation to be docile, unprovocative, undemanding. If an ablebodied person crosses over into the disability space, [she or] he expects a warm welcome."[74] These types of responses may be easier when the person with a disability does not mind, or welcomes, patronizing behaviors. However, patronizing, stereotypical responses can make persons with disabilities feel sad, angry, and irritated. Furthermore, when a person with a disability feels that someone has been insulting or a threat to positive self-identity, she or he may struggle with whether to be assertive and confrontational or to accept the behavior.

Communication scholar Dawn O. Braithwaite asked individuals with physical disabilities to discuss times when nondisabled persons ask probing personal questions.[75] Many of the respondents felt that most nondisabled people were simply curious. Whether or not they felt comfortable disclosing information about their disability depended on their relationship with the person; that is, they were more likely to disclose if they knew the person, if they felt comfortable with the person, or if they were likely to interact again. They also were more likely to disclose information if the disclosure seemed relevant and appropriate. And, they tried to figure out why the person was asking the questions to see if the curiosity seemed healthy or morbid. Some of the participants tend to respond favorably to children because they hope to help children acquire more positive attitudes about disabilities. Persons with disabilities will disclose information depending on their personal characteristics, including mood and feelings of comfort or discomfort. Also, some persons with disabilities are shy. Or, like most people, sometimes they just do not want to be bothered, while at other times, talking about themselves is not a problem.

Participants in Braithwaite's study reported that their usual strategy is to talk about "normal" topics in order to appear normal and to downplay their disability. Sometimes they acknowledge or communicate information about their disability, which might reduce others' discomfort, clarify norms, and facilitate communication. When someone asks an inappropriate question, persons with disabilities choose from a few strategies, including switching topics, ignoring the question or the questioner, withdrawing, or directly asking the offender to leave them alone. Sometimes persons with disabilities will mask negative, angry responses to stupid, annoying questions. Or, they may bluntly tell the other person that it's none of their business. They often suppress anger and use humor or sarcasm. When one wheelchair user who has no motor function below her neck notices someone looking at her legs or hands to discern if she has any movement, she might ask them to hand her something and explain that she has limited use. As Braithwaite's study and related projects reveal, "persons with disabilities live in a world of reduced privacy."[76] Potok describes a time when he was trying to work out at a gym while listening to a book, when a man continuously interrupted him to ask questions about his guide dog.[77]

Nondisabled people tend to react predictably to persons with disabilities, depending on the context. For instance, the more unattractive a disability seems to be, the more negative the reaction. Similarly, the more visible the disability, the more negative the initial reaction tends to be. Origin of the disability is another issue, as persons often try to understand the degree to which the person seems responsible for her or his condition, whether the condition is contagious, or if it is temporary or permanent.[78] The effectiveness of interability communication also depends on whether or not a disability affects physical aspects of communication. Disabilities that disrupt the flow of communication, such as stuttering, are more likely to elicit anxiety and frustration.[79]

Nondisabled people often are uncertain about how to treat individuals with disabilities, as well as about how a person with a disability might perceive them. This uncertainty can stem from not knowing what persons with disabilities can and cannot do or from conflicting social norms. Persons without disabilities may simultaneously feel a variety of responses to a person

Tool No. 5

"People First" Language

Similar to the other social identity groups we're studying, people with disabilities and their allies have developed guidelines for preferred terminology known as People First Language (PFL).[80] PFL provides an objective way to acknowledge, communicate, and report on disabilities by stressing each person's individuality. It *acknowledges that individuals with disabilities are not their diagnoses or disabilities. They are—first and foremost—people.*[81] By focusing on the person rather than a disability, PFL seeks to promote understanding, respect, and dignity and to decrease generalizations, assumptions and stereotypes.

People First Language invites us to refer to the individual first and the disability second. So, you would say "a child who is autistic" instead of "the autistic child." Use People First Language to tell what a person HAS, not what a person IS. One author explains: "I have multiple sclerosis but that's not what I want to be known for. I hate it when a person first meets me and all they want to talk about is my wheelchair or my multiple sclerosis. That's not who I am." She elaborates: "Know me first as a person with my own thoughts, opinions, beliefs, experiences, career, dreams, and political associations."[82]

People First Language emphasizes abilities instead of limitations. For example, say "a man walks with crutches," not "he is crippled." Also, do not refer to a person as bound to or confined to a wheelchair. After all, wheelchairs liberate people with disabilities by making them mobile. Here are a few other examples of People First Language:

People First Language

Say this:	*Instead of this:*
People with disabilities	The disabled; the handicapped
Person with a mental disability	Retard; psycho; lunatic
James has bipolar disorder	James is a manic depressive
Pat has a learning disability	Pat is learning disabled

As you consider what terms to use regarding someone with a disability, consider this advice from a disability activist: "Keep in mind that some phrases are no longer used in polite conversation. We never, ever use the terms mentally retarded or crippled for any reason whatsoever. In the evolution of our language, those terms have become derogatory and should never be used."[83]

Also ask yourself if you even need to mention a disability when referring to someone. Is it relevant? Furthermore, note that, similar to other groups, persons with disabilities have varying opinions about how others refer to them. The author quoted earlier says: "I don't care if someone calls me a 'disabled person.' It doesn't bother me. Others care very much."[84] I'd rather err on the side of seeming to be politically correct than insulting someone. What about you?

with a disability, including fear, sympathy, revulsion, or prejudice, that may make them feel guilty. They may view a person with a disability as either a nonentity or as an object of pity.[85] They also may be afraid they will say the wrong thing. As a result, they may avoid or shorten interability interactions rather than face what they anticipate to be an unsettling situation.[86] In addition, they may want to project a positive image, "not only as a fully functioning person *without* a disability but also as a helpful and charitable person *toward* people with disabilities."[87] Thus, persons without disabilities may use accommodating speech intended to be nurturing and considerate that comes across as overly patronizing.

In early phases of interability relationships, nondisabled persons often exhibit curiosity about the other person's condition, especially when the disability is visible. They bring up personal topics like sexual activity, eating, driving, and so forth, that they usually would not discuss with nondisabled people, especially strangers or new acquaintances. One person who has had polio reported:

> Well, I've had people walk up to me on the street and say, "Oh isn't it wonderful that you get out of the house?" and people ask me, "Well, how do you get dressed in the morning?" Perfect strangers walk to me off the street and ask me, "Can you cook," or, you know, "do you have any feeling in your legs?"[88]

The preceding discussion shows that nondisabled people tend to behave in predictable ways based on perceiving a person with a disability as a member of a stigmatized group rather than as an individual. They often enact ideologies of normalcy based on the high value our society places on mental and physical ability. And, they tend to rely on stereotypes and assumptions to guide their behaviors and attitudes.

To conclude, interability interactions can be awkward and strained for persons with and without disabilities. However, although nondisabled persons often feel uncertain, persons with disabilities usually can anticipate predictable interactions. Moreover,

> a central feature of the disability "insider" experience is a persistent and disquieting sense of mistaken identity. Across a range of situations and interpersonal relationships, persons with disabilities find that the identities they forge and present to the world are commonly dismissed by others in favor of stereotypical identity ascriptions.[89]

People with disabilities often believe they "must submerge their spontaneous reactions and authentic feelings to smooth over relations with others, from strangers to family members to the personal assistants they rely on to maneuver through each day."[90] These challenges may be even harder for persons with impairments that affect communication because they have limited ways to express their identity or disprove stereotypes. And those persons whose abilities are not visible must contend with "the omnipresent dilemma of deciding when and how much to reveal about their socially 'discreditable' status."[91] In essence, they struggle with challenges—similar to those experienced by members of other nondominant groups—to decide whether or not to "pass" as a member of the dominant group. Moreover, "passing" as able-bodied comes with the price of disavowing an aspect of one's self. These challenges can be especially daunting in traditional power relationships such as doctor–patient, employer–employee, and teacher–student when the person with a disability is in the power-down position.

However, all persons with disabilities do not accept or enact a stigmatized identity. Some of them "relinquish or redefine unattainable comparative-status standards, such as normality, that no longer have meaning, and they adopt new goals that fit their lives."[92] Increasingly, persons with disabilities from various backgrounds are learning to think about disability as a social justice issue rather than as a category of individual deficiency. They view themselves as members of a disability community that is socially oppressed. This shift in perspective can have an emancipatory impact on self-image, and can encourage persons with disabilities to reject stigmatized or tragic victimhood status.

As I noted earlier, a central communication goal of many persons with disabilities is to be accepted and treated as "persons first." They want others to perceive them as a human being rather than as an objectified disability.[93] Ironically, however, persons with disabilities "who achieve 'people first' status are not achieving full normative status but are only legitimizing an able-bodied resemblance through their desire for normality."[94] This paradox demonstrates the complexity of ability matters.

It seems appropriate to conclude this section with the Ten Commandments of Etiquette for Communicating with People with Disabilities.[95]

1. When talking with a person with a disability, speak directly to that person rather than through a companion or sign language interpreter.
2. When introduced to a person with a disability, it is appropriate to offer to shake hands. People with limited hand use or who wear an artificial limb can usually shake hands. (Shaking hands with the left hand is an acceptable greeting.)
3. When meeting a person who is visually impaired, always identify yourself and others who may be with you. When conversing in a group, remember to identify the person to whom you are speaking.
4. If you offer assistance, wait until the offer is accepted. Then listen to or ask for instructions.
5. Treat adults as adults. Address people who have disabilities by their first names only when extending the same familiarity to all others. (Never patronize people who use wheelchairs by patting them on the head or shoulder.)
6. Leaning on or hanging on to a person's wheelchair is similar to leaning on hanging on to a person and is generally considered annoying. The chair is part of the personal body space of the person who uses it.

7. Listen attentively when you're talking with a person who has difficulty speaking. Be patient and wait for the person to finish, rather than correcting or speaking for the person. If necessary, ask short questions that require short answers, a nod or shake of the head. Never pretend to understand if you are having difficulty doing so. Instead, repeat what you have understood and allow the person to respond. The response will clue you in and guide your understanding.
8. When speaking with a person who uses a wheelchair or a person who uses crutches, place yourself at eye level in front of the person to facilitate the conversation.
9. To get the attention of a person who is deaf, tap the person on the shoulder or wave your hand. Look directly at the person and speak clearly, slowly, and expressively to determine if the person can read your lips. Not all people who are deaf can read lips. For those who do lip read, be sensitive to their needs by placing yourself so that you face the light source and keep hands, cigarettes, and food away from your mouth when speaking.
10. Relax. Don't be embarrassed if you happen to use accepted, common expressions such as "See you later," or "Did you hear about that?" that seem to relate to a person's disability. Don't be afraid to ask questions when you're unsure of what to do.

Interability Interactions at Work

A primary element of identity for adults in the United States is whether or not they work, as well as the type of work they do. In many social contexts, one of the first questions a person asks another is, "What do you do?" For many persons with disabilities, employment holds a special meaning, because they may wish to demonstrate their value by being gainfully employed. Like most other people, they buy into the ideology of autonomy and independence that dominates U.S. society. Since the Industrial Revolution, ableness is the normative standard of work, and persons with disabilities often are not seen as competent and capable. Consequently, others may treat persons with disabilities differently throughout employment processes, from recruitment, to hiring, to everyday interactions, to being promoted, to being terminated.

Potential employers often have false assumptions about persons with disabilities' job-related abilities, performance levels, absenteeism, turnover rates, and costs of accommodation.

> An accommodation is a modification to the work environment that enables a qualified individual with a disability to participate in the job application process, or perform the essential functions of a job, or equally benefit from the same employment opportunities and rights afforded similarly situated individuals without disabilities.[96]

Yet, average direct costs of accommodation are $400 or less, and those outweigh benefits gained when employees receive accommodation.[97] As a result of these and other misgivings, employers may not even consider persons with disabilities for employment. However, persons with disabilities tend to perform as well as nondisabled workers; they have equal or lower absenteeism or turnover rates; and they tend to have better safety records than nondisabled persons.[98] They also often work harder than nondisabled employees because they foresee challenges in landing another job.

When persons with disabilities do get to apply for jobs, they may have different interview experiences: interviewers tend to place more physical distance between them, conclude the interview more quickly, behave more formally, and rate the persons either more negatively or overly positively than they do interviewees who do not (seem to) have disabilities.[99]

Applicants with disabilities have to decide how much to disclose about their disability as well as any needs for accommodation. Those with unapparent disabilities may postpone disclosing their condition until and if they need accommodations.[100] They do not want interviewers to stigmatize them, yet if they don't disclose their condition, the interviewer may not trust them if they learn later about the condition. Although research about self-disclosure in interviews by persons with disabilities is inconsistent, it mainly shows negative repercussions.[101]

Once hired, persons with disabilities and their coworkers often experience the types of interability communication challenges I discussed earlier. In addition, persons with disabilities may compensate for their disability by working longer hours, coming to work sick and in pain, or decreasing their medicine to lessen side effects.[102] Although persons with disabilities may confront many obstacles at work and in other contexts, many organizations and institutions are making substantive efforts to include and value them.

Promising Practices

Almost three-quarters of the top industries are hiring persons with disabilities. Technology-based industries are leading the way, followed by manufacturing and communications. These companies develop communication strategies to address various disabilities, and employees with disabilities educate their coworkers and supervisors about their disabilities. IBM implemented five strategies: (1) commitment from top management; (2) respect for the person with a disability; (3) a focus on abilities; (4) providing full access to all aspects of employment; and (5) making accessibility a way of life.[103] They established a communication plan to help eliminate false stereotypes and negative attitudes.

Another positive example is Passion Works Studio in Athens, Ohio, which supports collaborations between artists with and without developmental disabilities.[104] Since 1998, the studio has created a successful product line of unique art pieces by translating artwork into jewelry, ornaments, flowers, greeting cards, and other items. The project has created employment for artist participants, while raising understanding and respect. It also has generated a renewable funding stream to continue arts programming in a rural Appalachian community where income and support for the arts have been below state and national medians. Passion Works "provides a model for how other service providers (e.g., directors of homeless shelters, or rape and abuse crisis centers) can position art as a form of knowledge construction and sustainable economic and social growth."[105]

According to a recent report on disability in higher education, many colleges and universities are going above and beyond their legal responsibility to offer reasonable accommodations and to ensure physical access for students with disabilities.[106] One school offers a Learning Service program to facilitate students' transitioning from high school to college. The Disability Services office at another university hired a financial aid liaison to work specifically with students with disabilities, who often incur expenses related to their disability such as testing to document their condition, assistive equipment, and medical devices. Some schools reach out to students with disabilities and their parents, and others offer training and orientation to help students develop self-advocacy skills. In addition, many schools have established assistive technology labs equipped with a variety of tools that can facilitate learning. Some Disability Services offices are forging partnerships with veterans groups to develop strategies for supporting veterans with disabilities on their campuses. Finally, many institutions are conducting training sessions for faculty and staff to educate them about legal issues as well as provide resources to help them interact effectively and humanely with students with disabilities.

Conclusion

Disability is a complex, socially constructed aspect of social identity based on hierarchies of a wide variety of mental and physical capabilities. Members of U.S. society refer to an ideology of normality to evaluate and stratify these capabilities. Attitudes toward, and treatment of, persons with disabilities have varied depending on sociocultural, political, religious, and economic conditions. Although a social model has partially replaced the medical model of disability, persons with disabilities continue to endure discriminatory treatment in a society that places premium value on ability and fitness. The ideology of normality often constrains interability communication, which can hinder productive and enjoyable interactions between persons with and without disabilities. However, disability activism has generated impressive and continued progress toward including, valuing, and empowering persons with disabilities within and across numerous sectors of society.

• • • • *ID Check* • • • •

1. What is your ability status (i.e., do you have a disability, or are you nondisabled)?
2. How important is your ability status to you? Explain.
3. What primary sources have taught you about your ability status?
4. How, if at all, do you express your ability status (e.g., through language, communication style, dress, accessories, music, and so forth)?
5. Does your awareness of your ability status ever help you communicate with others? Explain.
6. Does your awareness of your ability status ever hinder how you communicate with others? Explain.
7. What situations, if any, do you avoid because of concerns related to your ability status?
8. What situations, if any, do you seek because of your ability status?
9. What advantages, if any, do you enjoy based on your ability status?
10. Do you know of any stereotypes about your ability status? If so, list them.
11. Are you ever aware of stereotypes about your ability status as you interact with others? Explain.
12. How do the media tend to depict your ability status? Do media depictions correspond with your sense of your ability status? Explain.
13. Do you think your attitudes toward ability intersect with any other facets of your social identity, for instance: your gender? your age? your social class? your sexual orientation?

Reflection Matters

1. What did you find intriguing or interesting in this chapter? Why?
2. Do any current news stories involve issues that this chapter covers? If yes, what points do they exemplify?
3. According to the sociohistorical overview, what are examples of how people used communication to construct ability and disability throughout the history of the United States?
4. What are examples of power relations in the construction of ability and disability in the United States?
5. What do you think of the disability activist perspective that "disability is simply a normal variation of human diversity"? Related to this, how do you feel about the Deaf community's belief that they represent a linguistic minority?

6. Locate a Web site related to disability. For instance, you can focus on a specific disability (e.g., dyslexia, HIV/AIDS, blindness, paraplegia, quadriplegia, deafness, developmental disability, Alzheimer's, learning disability, muscular dystrophy, ADHD), a disability activist group or organization, or a related topic (e.g., eugenics), an online magazine or newsletter devoted to persons with disabilities, or a site on assistive technology. Describe and critique the Web site. Include the following: Cite the Web site address. What is the purpose of the Web site? Who developed it? Who is the intended audience? Is the Web site useful/informative? How could the Web site be improved? What did you learn from this Web site?
7. Have you had any experiences with interability interactions? If so, describe and critique them.
8. Why do you think many employers are challenged by the concept, "reasonable accommodations" for persons with disabilities?
9. If you are affiliated with a university, what types of services does it provide for students with disabilities? How about faculty and staff with disabilities? How comprehensive and effective do these services seem to be?

Chapter 8

Age Matters

Now that I've stopped dyeing my hair to show my natural silver, more people call me "ma'am." Plus, more salespeople are asking if I'm eligible for a senior citizen discount (and sometimes I am). After I stopped coloring my hair several years ago, people stopped telling me I looked young for my age. I have mixed feelings about these interactions. I don't want to care what others think about my age. Yet, I also don't want them to think I am "old," since being old in our society is undesirable, especially for a woman. Sometimes people call a man with gray hair "distinguished," but they rarely say that about a woman. Then again, some people think that gray hair represents wisdom, which certainly is true in my case! Fortunately, being gray probably doesn't hurt my credibility as a professor. It may even work to my advantage. One of my friends recently told me I'd probably look ten years younger if I colored my hair.

Can you remember a time when you could not wait to reach a certain age? Why was that number so important? I've known many college students who were eager to turn 21. I wonder why [smile]? I remember anxiously waiting to be 13, a teenager! Because I was born in 1950, I relished the idea that I would be a half-century old at the turn of the century. When I was younger, 50 seemed almost ancient. The closer I got to that milestone, and now that I am beyond it, 50 does not seem that old.

My reflections about age foreshadow some of the issues I illuminate in this chapter. Categories related to numerical age, such as "senior citizen" or "teenager," can influence self-esteem, attitudes, and expectations. In addition, our society has developed laws, policies, and procedures based on age categories. Rights to vote, to drive, and to drink are tied to age minimums. Many businesses offer discounts to "senior citizens," a category created around 1938. The social identity of teenager (created in the 1920s) holds significant meaning for individuals, organizations, and institutions, including educators, legislators, advertisers, employers, entertainment companies, and clothing manufacturers.

My conflict about my gray, oops, I mean silver, hair demonstrates the power of societal discourse about aging. My use of "silver" instead of "gray" shows how word choice conveys meaning. "Gray" connotes dull and gloomy, while "silver" means shine and luster. "Silver" also refers to a valuable metal.

In our society, we tend to value youthfulness and to devalue growing old. Some professions, such as newscaster, athlete, or actor, are less forgiving of signs of aging than being a professor. Attitudes toward aging in certain professions also may vary according to gender; we tend to be more critical of women than men. Evidence of negative attitudes toward growing and being old include incessant ads for products to make you look and feel young, and the saying, "You can't teach an old dog new tricks." Ironically, however, dominant discourses also seem to malign the younger generation (persons between fifteen and thirty). Film and television portrayals of these groups tend to be one-dimensional, stereotypical, and unflattering.

Thus, age definitely matters in contemporary U.S. society. *Merriam-Webster's Dictionary* defines ***age*** as "the time of life at which some particular qualification, power, or capacity arises or rests."[1] This definition previews the point of this chapter: age is a socially constructed aspect of identity based on dominant ideologies that dictate which categories in the life span we tend to privilege or penalize. First, I discuss different aspects of age. Next, I elaborate on why age matters, after which I provide an overview of how we have constructed age in the United States. Then, I describe communication issues related to age and aging.

What Is Age?

Age basically refers to the length of a person's existence since birth. We usually measure age in years, except that children anxious to grow older often indicate their age in half- and even quarter-years. However, age is more complex than simple increments based on the calendar.

Have you ever heard the saying, "Age ain't nothin' but a number"? Well, age may be just a number, but that number counts. For instance, how old are you? In which age group do you fall: young, middle-aged, or old? What, if anything, does that category mean to you? What privileges, if any, do you have that someone in a different age group might not? What constraints, if any, are associated with your age group? Are you aware of any stereotypes about your age group? Although our experiences with aging can vary depending on other aspects of social identity, such as gender and race, each of us will encounter predictable perks and penalties based on where we're located on the life span.

An age-based social hierarchy helps to organize social and economic life. Age permits entry into, and exit from, certain status positions. For instance, infants have relatively little power, which changes as they move from one age status to another. In contrast, most adults have control over their lives, at least until some of them become elderly. Age can determine whether or not we are permitted to be gainfully employed, as well as how much we can earn, and how many hours we can work.

Typically, we use chronological age to categorize and therefore distinguish people. We classify ourselves and others into age groups that signify a variety of meanings, all of which are socially constructed. Each of us is socialized to behave according to our age, as seen in comments like "act your age," "grow up," or "you're too old to . . ." and we usually expect others to do the same.

We also learn age-related norms about certain life events, including the maximum age when children should go to college, move out of their parents' home, get married, have children of their own, and so forth. Although these norms can vary according to ethnicity and religious background, when individuals do not meet an expectation based on age, others may compare them to that norm, in favorable or unfavorable ways.[2]

Why Age Matters

The United States is an age-conscious society. One of the first things we teach children is to tell their age. I cannot count how many times I have engaged in the ritual of asking a child, "How old are you?" Up to a certain age, children value being older—as seen in the tendency to proudly declare their age in half years ("I'm eight AND A HALF"). In addition, we socialize them to look forward to specific ages such as 13, 16, 18, and 21.

From the 20s through middle age, people rarely mention their age, except at certain milestones such as every ten years. Some women never tell their age, probably because we socialize each other not to ask a woman her age, which demonstrates the sex bias in negative connotations of aging. In contrast, people over 70 often disclose their age without being asked.[3] For instance, in response to the everyday query "How are you?" an older person might reply, "Well, I'm fine for an 80-year-old." The listener usually takes the bait and responds with praise or disbelief: "Really? You don't look 80," or "That's great." Have you ever experienced that?

Marking a particular age sometimes intersects with other aspects of social identity, such as religion, gender, or ethnicity. Some Latino families celebrate their daughter's fifteenth birthday with a ritual known as *quinceañera.* When they turn thirteen, some Jewish youth engage in bat mitzvah (girls) and bar mitzvah (boys) ceremonies. Many teenaged girls have "sweet sixteen" parties. These rituals illustrate the significance of age in our society.

Similar to other social identity categories, demographics about age matter. Sheer numbers paint an unprecedented age landscape that matters for all ages. The percentage of older adults in the United States has tripled since 1900; in the history of the world, two-thirds of all people who ever lived past the age of 65 are alive today.[4] As baby boomers (those born between 1946 and 1964) like me assume senior citizen status, more elderly persons than ever will populate the United States. We will witness an exponential increase in numbers of growth of older persons, giving new meaning to the phrase, "Seniors Rule!"

Not only are older folks in the United States greater in number, they are living much longer. In 1900, the average life expectancy was 49; in 2001, it was 76. The age 85-and-over population has grown 31 times larger since the beginning of the twentieth century. As of November 2008, the Census Bureau recorded 96,000 people who were 100 years or older. If that trend continues, the centenarian population may reach 600,000 by 2050.[5]

As longevity has increased, so has the health and vitality of the elderly (persons 60 years of age or older).[6] Only about 5 percent of elderly persons reside in hospitals or require nursing home care. Most older people will continue to work, due to economic concerns such as maintaining their household and caring for aging parents and/or adult children, but also because of a strong work ethic. Potential policy and program effects of the aging of 76 million baby boomers are attracting the interest of both public and private sectors. Baby boomers may affect retirement and transform what it means to be old in the U.S. Baby boomers are likely to differ from current older adults by being more willing to advocate for programs, policies, and services.[7]

Matters of age differ according to other aspects of identity such as race, gender, and sexuality. Demographers have predicted dramatic increases in the number of minority elderly, the fastest growing segment of older Americans. In the 2000 census, racial-ethnic minorities comprised 16.4 percent of persons 65 or older; by 2050, over 35 percent of persons 65 or older will be people of color.[8] In 2006, racial minorities accounted for nearly one-half of children under 5 years of age.[9] Consequently, by 2030, a new type of generation gap will occur as most young persons will be people of color, and most elderly persons will be white. This divide will occur in part because of relatively high immigration rates among Hispanics and Asians of child-bearing age. All of these projections have implications for policy as well as how we interact with one another.

Women account for four out of five people 100 years of age and older. Women are more likely to experience chronic illnesses and disabilities because of their longer lives. They are more likely than men to be single, live alone, and be poor in their older years.[10] As I noted in the chapter on sexuality, gay baby boomers will experience different challenges than heterosexual members of this cohort. GLBTQ seniors are twice as likely to live alone, and more than four times as likely to have no children. The bottom line is the older American population of the twenty-first century will look vastly different from the profile of older Americans at the turn of the last century.

These age distinctions matter because members of social identity groups who have been privileged throughout their lives tend to continue to reap benefits as they age, just as those who have been oppressed usually continue to suffer. In 1994, a retired man received $785.24 in social security benefits, while a retired woman received $602.26; similar distinctions occur in race-gender breakdowns, with white men at the top of the earnings chart, and women of color at the bottom.[11] Currently, women are less likely to receive pensions than men. Cumulative effects of disadvantage across life include chronic health problems, suffering from results of poor nutrition, living in substandard conditions, and chronic stress. These and other developments can affect public policies related to aging, including public health concerns as well as employment policies and retirement benefits.

Another growing concern is ***ageism,*** "the systematic stereotyping and discrimination against people because they are old."[12] Ageism in the workplace has become more visible as members of the bulk of the workforce grow older. (The Bureau of Labor Statistics classifies workers as "older" when they turn 55.) However, age bias tends to be much more subtle than other -isms. Some people may not even realize that they are enacting age ideology. Age discrimination may well become the major civil rights issue during the early part of the twenty-first century. Workers filed a record number of age bias claims in 2008, up 30 percent from the previous year.[13] Following the lead of other disenfranchised groups, some older people and their allies have created advocacy groups, such as the Gray Panthers and the American Association of Retired Persons (AARP), "a nonprofit membership organization dedicated to addressing the needs and interests of persons 50 and older."[14]

As numbers of older persons increase, the pool of younger persons is shrinking due to a drop in birthrate after the baby boom. Thus, the demand for older workers has increased as numbers of new labor force entrants decrease. Generation X (persons born between 1960 and 1980) will be the primary source of labor in the United States for the next 10 years. This group represents the smallest population in history, and the smallest number of entry-level workers. Thus, it is highly likely that intergenerational interactions will occur in workplaces. Some analysts believe that this situation borders on a crisis as members of different generations tend to have varying values and ideals related to work. Conflicting needs, as well as wary attitudes toward one another, may generate opposition between groups.

Children in elementary school today have the potential of living longer than any previous generation. To help prepare them for longevity, we need more formal education programs that focus on aging. Although we often hear about population trends and the increased life span, schools and colleges rarely educate or even orient students to prepare them for a long life.[15] Indeed, "most young people still reach adulthood with little preparation for their own aging. Nor do they recognize the enormous implications of population aging as the longevity revolution of the twentieth century spills over into the twenty-first."[16] When they reach their seventies, they may be seen as the "young-old" if we reach predicted numbers of centenarians.

In addition to changes in demographics and their potential consequences, age matters because we all confront its effects. Unlike the other categories of social identity we are exploring, which remain relatively fixed (except for ability, which can change in the blink of an eye), age identity changes across our life span. And, we are likely to deal with age-related issues for our loved ones. Each one of us can potentially become part of an age group and benefit or suffer accordingly. Therefore, age clearly matters for everyone.

Constructing Age in the United States

Although we take age as a category of identity for granted, "the significance of age as a number is relatively new."[17] The history of the United States from the fifteenth century until the new millennium illuminates interesting contrasts in perspectives on age. How we have constructed age echoes patterns in other aspects of social identity because humans have used medical or scientific "knowledge" to justify a hierarchy based on human physiology and the decline of bodily functions due to aging.

The colonial United States consisted of communities that were controlled economically and politically by white, male elders who owned shops that sold a variety of hand-crafted goods and who were involved in the governance of the community. However, in the nineteenth century, large industries replaced the craft shops that older men had operated. Younger workers and immigrants, who were willing to work for lower wages, were hired by these manufacturing companies. By the middle of the nineteenth century, older workers were replaced by younger ones, and citizens demonstrated a growing social aversion toward old age.

Concepts and Attitudes about Old Age

Negative attitudes toward getting old arose due to "scientific" information about aging. Toward the end of the nineteenth century, physicians believed that all elderly persons required constant medical care. This ***deficit model of aging*** characterizes old age as a pathological condition in which individuals undergo physical and mental decline.[18] This conception stemmed from limited experiences with healthy elders, as physicians treated only those who were sick and dying. They concluded that disease and decline are inevitable among older people.

Along with medical models of aging as decline, early social science scholarship depicted old age as an undesirable condition, a social problem connected to poverty and diminishing health. Consequently, due to a perception that aging causes dependency, a discourse of old age as a "second childhood" arose. As society became more industrialized and focused on productivity, elderly persons were seen as unnecessary. This logic justified casting older people aside or placing them in the poorhouse.

By the end of the nineteenth century, old age was deemed a social problem. Most people accepted this stereotype and began to exclude the elderly from social life. This marked the beginning of age-segregated programs like senior citizen centers, nursing homes, and retirement villages. However, the desire for and access to these services varied according to race, social class, economic, and cultural traditions. For instance, some Native American families did not want to separate their elders from their family, and different generations of family members lived under the same roof.[19]

After World War II, ***gerontology,*** the study of aging, developed standards and measures to evaluate how people adjusted to the aging process. During the twentieth century, the government initiated several legislative measures related to aging, including the Social Security Act of 1935, a federal program of mandatory old-age retirement benefits, and the Older Americans Act (OAA) of 1965, which funds state agencies on aging to provide social services programs, senior centers, volunteer programs, nutritional services, and health care. The OAA developed the Administration on Aging (AoA), an agency of the United States Department of Health and Human Services. The OAA is best known for its nutrition, transportation, and long-term care ombudsman programs. The act established the nationwide Aging Network composed of 57 state and 655 local agencies on aging, 225 Native American Indian tribal organizations representing more than 300 tribes, more than 2,000 senior centers, and 27,000 providers of services for older people and their families in communities all across the United States.[20] Medicare, which provides health care for older persons, was also established in 1965, and the Age Discrimination and Employment Act (ADEA) was passed in 1967 for workers 40 and older.

These governmental initiatives were political responses to cultural constructions of older people as frail, dependent, and a collective burden on the country. Singling out older people as medically vulnerable marks a significant difference between the United States and other Western nations, where government-subsidized health care is considered a basic need for citizens of all ages.

Gerontology emerged as a major research topic in the 1970s, when the government funded studies of government spending on programs for the elderly. Most of the influential research framed old age as a "problem" for policy makers and for elders themselves.[21] Current policy initiatives include the Social Security Retirement Trust Fund, developed due to concern that mass numbers of baby boomers would stress the social security system when they retired. National policy makers in the executive and legislative branches of the government are crafting and advancing proposals to modernize, redirect, and secure entitlement programs for older Americans, including social security, the Medicare program, and the Older Americans Act.

Concepts and Attitudes about Children

As U.S. society developed attitudes, policies, and laws related to older people and aging, it also focused on children and younger adults. During the early days of colonization, the government struggled with whether or not to assist white indigent families with child care. After the Revolutionary War, the government established laws to remove poor white children from their families.[22] However, from early settlement until late in the nineteenth century, families were interdependent units where most children actively engaged in household duties, farm work, or household industries, and children were integral to the family's economic standing. Societal attitudes toward children during those times differed drastically from current sentiments: "For most of our history, until the twentieth century, the social worth of children was understood primarily in terms of economic rather than emotional value."[23] Nonslave children without fathers or those born out of wedlock were considered orphans; they were contracted out as apprentices to masters who took them into their households. Children born into slavery were under the control of masters of households. In 1776, one in every five children was a slave. Not only did these children work at hard labor from an early age, but also they were considered legal chattel that could be bought and sold.

Most children in working-class families during the industrial revolution held some type of job, often engaging in monotonous, sometimes dangerous work. Productivity increased because of machinery, and many factories hired children because they were agile and quick. Children as young as 5 years of age worked in textile industries. One in every five children 10–15 years of age worked in permanent jobs. In 1820, nearly one-half of the textile mill workers were children working 10-hour days in appalling conditions. Many children in urban areas worked in "tenement trades"; in cramped conditions in their homes, children produced thousands of items such as artificial flowers, beads, bedding, and cigars (the children often performed the final act of licking the cigar paper to seal the cigar). Many of them did "junking" work, which entailed picking through trash and scavenging for items like scrap metal. By 1900, the United States was the industrial leader of the world, and the "nimble fingers" of young persons were invaluable tools. With the advent of labor unions, many employers hired children to avoid adult strikes.

In the late 1800s, children began to shift from being "economically useful" to "economically useless," but "emotionally priceless." This change occurred due to a child labor movement and compulsory education. Society invested in institutions to extend for children the period of "leisured growth and development, especially schools and institutions that emphasized play."[24] In the twentieth century, concerned citizens began to pay attention to child labor. Child labor reformers asserted that childhood should be a time of natural development.

However, a sharp class distinction troubled changes related to child labor. Working-class families who needed children's income fought against economically privileged reformers, accusing them of trying to impose their philosophy of parenting.[25] This concern was especially significant for immigrant families whose cultural traditions taught that children should contribute to the economic well-being of the family. During those times, the ***culture of poverty*** ideology blamed parents as defective and took children from families to protect them.[26] Children who had no parents or who were from poor families were placed in institutions, primarily orphanages. Some were assigned to work on farms. Children of former slaves shared with their parents the hard life of sharecropping.

Close to a century ago, no federal laws existed to restrict or control child labor (although some states had passed their own laws.) The U.S. Children's Bureau was established in 1912 to develop programs that "provide for the safety, permanency, and well-being of children."[27] In 1938, thanks to the efforts of Secretary of Labor Frances Perkins and the support of President Franklin Roosevelt, Congress passed the Fair Labor Standards Act (FLSA).[28]

Developed mainly for vulnerable workers such as sweatshop employees and children, the FLSA restricts the ages, hours, and working conditions of school-age workers. However, the act exempts certain occupations such as child actors, migrant farm workers, and newspaper deliverers. Children who work for their parents are exempt if they are not employed in hazardous occupations such as mining or manufacturing.[29]

Due to these considerable changes in conceptions of childhood, the twentieth century is known as the era of youth.[30] Childhood became marked as a distinctive period in the life span. Shifts in thinking about childhood had far-reaching implications for law, education, manufacturing, labor, marketing, and entertainment. Thus, according to psychologist Ken Dychtwald, young people have enjoyed a type of "age power" because of their influence on society. However, he contends that the twenty-first century will belong to the "new old" because of projected demographics as well as the increasing economic and political power of aging baby boomers. Dychtwald believes that the United States will once again become a gerontocracy (rule by elders), as it was in colonial times.[31] However, he believes that women will wield much more power in the future than they did in the past.

Birth Cohorts

In the twentieth century, the ***birth cohort,*** a grouping of people born during a specific span of years, became a significant social construction related to age. Labels for cohorts (or generations) include traditionalists or veterans (1922–1945); baby boomers (1946–1964); Generation Xers (1964–1980), also known as twentysomethings, post-boomers, baby busters, slackers, and the thirteenth generation; and Nexters (1980–2000), also known as Generation Y, millennials, echo boom, and generation next.[32]

Members of a birth cohort tend to share experiences and circumstances such as war, an economic depression or boom, catastrophic events such as 9/11 and the *Challenger* explosion (or more recently the *Columbia* disaster), social movements, popularity of certain entertainers, or birth of a music genre. These "reference points" can affect attitudes and behaviors. For instance, "members of a cohort who come of age in lean times or war years think and act differently than those born and raised to their majority in peace and plenty."[33] Members of different cohorts thus have different reference points.

The size of birth cohorts varies. By the end of the nineteenth century, the population of the United States had begun to decline. Early in the twentieth century, birth rates began to rise as a flood of immigration occurred due to hard times in Europe. In addition, prosperity in the United States sparked unprecedented birth rates. However, the depression dampened birth rates. As the United States enjoyed significant economic growth and prosperity after World War II, the population boomed again. Then, the postwar boom waned, in part because of birth control pills, an invention that began to affect population.[34]

Cohorts also vary according to other aspects of social identity such as gender, race, and class. Among women who lived through the depression era who are now elderly, women of higher social class report stronger feelings of mastery and assertiveness than women who were working class, who report more feelings of helplessness and passivity.[35] A comparative study of Navajo and Anglo elders revealed distinct differences in attitudes toward health and health care. For example, "while Anglos are likely to view illness as impersonal and as caused by germs, Navajos view health and illness as related to one's interpersonal relationships, tradition, and religion."[36] The size of cohorts matters to aspects of economic and social life such as employment, retirement, social security benefits, education, and so forth.

Does Aging Mean Decline?

When I worked in the research division of the National Center on Black Aged in the 1970s, I transcribed audiotaped oral life history interviews of elderly black people who were raised in the South. Although most of them were poor and had done hard physical labor for most of their lives, their attitudes toward life were remarkably positive. Those interviews correspond with research findings that older blacks tend to express more contentment with their lives than their white peers. Their feelings may stem from a reverence for aging that exists in some black communities, strong social networks, and a sense of having beaten the odds.[37]

Across the history of the United States, the ideology of aging as a process of physiological and mental decline motivated many governmental initiatives and societal perceptions. However, current medical information concludes that aging does not necessarily lead to decline. Numerous studies refute myths about aging, such as diminishing capacity to learn. The old saying "you can't teach an old dog new tricks" may be true, but you can teach an older person. Some believe that older people are unwilling to learn. Yet, many older persons have a heightened curiosity about acquiring information and learning new things. In fact, the capacity to learn extends into the 70s and beyond. Moreover, lifelong learning contributes to a sense of vitality. While older persons usually experience some physiological decline, such as slower physical reactions and loss of visual acuity or hearing, these problems are not as extreme as typically presented.[38]

Despite increasing longevity and growing evidence that aging does not necessarily mean decline, societal discourse continues to repeat a master narrative of decline. Numerous sources teach us "early and well to dread aging and to be on the look out for any signs of decay and decline."[39] This recurring plot implies that we reach a peak at a point in our youth, after which it's all downhill. Media and other sources bombard us with products and methods to rejuvenate ourselves or to repress the aging process. Ads proclaim that we can defy age; we can have youthful skin. This narrative suggests that individuals are responsible for warding off age and its inevitable dire consequences. It encourages a consumption mentality that feeds a multimillion-dollar cosmetic products industry as well as cosmetic surgery and other body-altering industries.

Not all women or men enact roles that the master narrative of aging dictates. Some of us script alternative stories for ourselves, even as we comply to a certain extent. As I said earlier, I no longer dye my hair. However, I carefully select my wardrobe to not look old-fashioned. And, especially because I work with younger people, I try to keep a fresh, updated image.

To challenge negative perspectives on aging, some educators have developed curricula from a social constructionist approach. They propose four concepts for aging education: "Aging is a natural and lifelong process of growing and developing; older people are valuable and contributing members of society; people need to plan for becoming older; people have much control over the older person they become."[40] Thus, they hope to give younger persons who might live longer than ever a more positive outlook on aging, while also socializing them to value older persons in their lives.[41]

In summary, age is a social construction that encompasses categories such as "elderly," "middle aged," and "young," or "baby boomer." These relatively new constructions helped to create a new consciousness. Moreover, increases in discourse about generations seem to have prompted more generational consciousness that arises from unprecedented and rapid changes in areas such as technology, media, education, and health care.[42] Although attitudes toward age groups have fluctuated across history, a dominant ideology of aging as decline persists. And, because of numerous economic and social changes in the past two centuries, age cohorts increasingly are segregating themselves. Beyond their immediate family, most people in the United States tend to "associate with and value their contemporaries to the exclusion of other age groups."[43] Combined with the ideology of aging as decline, this tendency holds significant implications for communication.

Communicating Age

Intergenerational Communication

Most research about communication and aging focuses on adult intergenerational interactions, with an emphasis on how communicators interact with older persons. Scholars often analyze attitudes and behaviors by applying ***communication accommodation theory,*** which describes and explains how "people modify their speech and conversational strategies according to situational, personal, or even interactional variables."[44] Communication accommodation theory contends that people will tend to attune more to people who are in their in-group than their out-group. ***Accommodation*** refers to ways a person adapts or adjusts a speech response to (actual and perceived) features of another person. For example, if you think an older person is hard of hearing, you might speak louder than usual.

Positive accommodation strategies include convergence or high attuning, when a person mirrors the other person's speaking styles. Convergence often signals in-group solidarity or personal affiliation.[45] Negative strategies include divergence (counterattuning), underaccommodation, and overaccommodation. Divergence refers to moving away from the other's speech style: "we diverge or counterattune our speech patterns away from others when we wish to indicate out-group membership or distance ourselves personally."[46] Speakers also may diverge to communicate disapproval for the other social identity group.

Underaccommodation occurs when someone seems insensitive to the other person's viewpoint, for instance by using dismissive or excessively authoritarian communication styles.[47] ***Overaccommodation strategies*** include simplifying, (speaking in short sentences or using childlike vocabulary); clarifying, (loud speech, repetition, slow speech, and careful articulation); using diminutives like "sweetie" or "honey"; and speaking in a demeaning emotional tone.[48] This mode of speaking seems to presume that a person has limited communication competence. For instance, a person might assume that

Communicating Age in Magazine Ads

Magazine advertisements are an important media source for socializing us about social identity groups. Magazine ads can reproduce dominant ideas about aging through how they portray older adults and adolescents. A comparison of magazine advertisements in India and the U.S. found that they tended to underrepresent older persons in proportion to their numbers in both countries. They also tended to advertise products related to "stereotypes that intimately connect older adulthood and ill health,"[49] based on persistent negative ideas about old age. In addition, the ads more frequently featured older women in health-related advertising. These depictions may perpetuate the ideology of aging as decline, as well as the idea that women should strive more than men to appear youthful.

Gender differences also exist in ads in teen magazines, an important socializing force for young females and males.[50] Researchers analyzed full-page advertisements in four popular teen magazines (2005–2006) to see how they portrayed women and young girls.[51] The ads prominently featured thin-ideal images, through conspicuously thin models (most of whom were white). Ads to sell clothing featured underweight models, while ads for beauty enhancing products depicted average-sized models. These ads may be telling teenaged girls that they need to be thin to look good in trendy clothes, and that average-sized girls need to use products to improve their beauty. On a positive note, ads in these magazines showed young women in a variety of settings, as contrasted with ads in magazines for older women, which often placed them in more domestic contexts (aligning with the idea that a woman's place is in the home). The researchers concluded that today's teen magazine ads may endorse "a more progressive, empowered concept of the female role."[52]

an older person is feeble minded. Speakers who perceive or expect older persons to have limited cognitive or sensory abilities often will overaccommodate them through patronizing speech, which also is called secondary baby talk or elderspeak.[53]

Most communication research focuses on overaccommodation. In certain circumstances, overaccommodation strategies may be appropriate, and some elderly persons may not mind them. Older people who live in institutions tend to evaluate such behaviors more positively than those who do not.[54] However, although such behaviors are usually motivated by good intentions, they can backfire. Older people may feel disrespected and depersonalized, or their self-esteem and well-being may be diminished. They also may restrict how much they interact with others. And, repeated patronizing responses may result in self-fulfilling prophecy. As elderly people develop expected characteristics and exhibit cues that elicit behaviors from others, a vicious cycle can result. In the long run, it may become difficult for an older person to constantly resist inappropriate communication behaviors from other people.

People often interact with older persons based on intergroup characterization rather than individual characteristics. In other words, people often rely on strong stereotypes of aging and older people to direct their communication behaviors, instead of considering each older person as a unique individual.[55] Stereotypes related to the ideology of physical and mental decline inundate Western society, particularly in the media. Recurring depictions of old people tend to be negative, often portraying them as absent minded, egocentric, incompetent, irritable, grouchy, frail, dependent, verbose, nagging, or hard of hearing.[56] Although positive stereotypes such as "perfect grandparent, golden ager, and elder statesman" exist, we rarely see them.[57]

Images and language forms that treat older persons as members of a devalued social category contribute to ageist behaviors and attitudes. Most words used to describe older persons are derogatory. Can you think of four or five such words? Jokes and humor about older people frequently portray physical and mental losses, as well as diminished sexual attractiveness and sexuality. These stereotypes often equate growing older with diminishing communicative competence. These and other perceptions may affect how others interact with an older person as they process cues of old age such as bent posture, vocal quality, clothing style, hearing aids, canes, and gray hair. Rather than view the person as an individual, people may respond to the stereotyped persona of "elderly communicator."[58]

These and other negative perceptions of aging form the basis of the Communication Predicament of Aging (CPA) model. The initial version of this model presumed that old-age cues invoke only negative stereotypes.[59] However, the model was extended to include positive stereotypes. The model asserts that people will interact differently with older persons according to whether they view them with positive or negative stereotypes. When younger adults' communication seems overly accommodative, older persons may experience communicative challenges that affect how they interact with others.[60] Persistent overaccomodative interactions can become a downward spiral that impacts older persons' sense of control and self-esteem. One group of research participants evaluated communication skills such as hearing and vocabulary of a positively stereotyped elderly person more favorably than they did for a negatively stereotyped person. In a hypothetical interaction with an elderly person, participants tended to speak more slowly to the negatively stereotyped person. They also exhibited differences in other vocal characteristics such as intonation, volume, and emphasis.[61]

This stereotype-sensitive version of the CPA model not only considers the impact of types of stereotypes, but it also acknowledges other factors. Research shows that older people exhibit more complex perceptions than younger people of relationships between aging and communication abilities. And, middle-aged to elderly persons are less likely than much younger persons to engage in patronizing speech with older adults. Context also seems to matter during intergenerational interactions. Meeting an older person in a health context such as a hospital or a nursing home may invoke different stereotypes and responses than meeting the same person in a university setting.[62]

Researchers also have studied national cultural differences in intergenerational communication. Although they reveal some differences between cultures, they found that younger adults across a wide variety of cultures tend to judge communicating with older people as difficult, involving nonaccommodation and obligatory politeness.[63] A study of intergenerational experiences in the U.S., Japan, and the Philippines found that younger adults tended to perceive communicating with their peers more positively than communicating with older adults, whom they rated as more nonaccommodating and requiring more respect-obligation. Younger adults from all groups also reported avoiding elderly people more than people in their age group.[64] Differences between the groups included young people from the U.S. feeling less obligated to show respect than Japanese and Filipino respondents. Young adults from the U.S. also were less likely to avoid older people than young people from Japan and the Philippines. The researchers concluded that "accommodative practices can, cumulatively, have significant *long-term* effects even on an individual's health status."[65]

Although research tends to focus on how individuals perceive and interact with older persons, one project sought to understand younger persons' perceptions of how older people interact with them. An in-depth analysis of a group of young white adults' retrospective accounts of conversations with older people revealed aspects of satisfying and dissatisfying interactions. The largest category of responses related to unsatisfying interactions that encompassed underaccommodative behaviors. These include instances when the younger person perceived that the older person was "either not listening, interrupting, inattentive, or unable to align with the younger person's communicative needs."[66] Other examples of underaccommodation include condescending comments such as "when I was your age. . . ." Participants also reported feeling frustrated when older people offered painful self-disclosure (PSD) about topics such as medical problems, accidents, and family losses. Some of them felt obligated to be polite or bite their tongue out of respect for older people. They also said that some older people stereotyped them, for example, as being party animals or irresponsible. The young persons often felt defensive.

Young participants reported that satisfying encounters with older persons included accommodative behaviors, such as socioemotional support. Younger people felt gratified when older persons seemed to attune to their communicative needs and did not "go too far with advice or being overly parental."[67] Another satisfying category was narratives, when old and young persons told interesting stories. Younger persons viewed these narratives as satisfying because they provided firsthand knowledge of past events, they were entertaining, or they facilitated conversations. Another feature of satisfying interactions was mutuality or common ground.

Participants also reported surprising instances when older persons did not meet their expectations of how older people behave. For example, one person said, "They are both retired and are very much in love (they even hold hands!)."[68] When younger participants perceived an older person as defying a stereotype, they viewed the person as exceptionally different from other older people. Thus, their stereotypical perceptions of older people in general probably remained intact. The researchers concluded that satisfying conversations tend to be accommodative while dissatisfying interactions tend to be characterized by nonaccommodation. However, stereotypes of older persons occurred in both types of conversations:

> In reports of dissatisfying conversations, stereotyping was much more explicit and ageist; for example, attributions of "grumpiness," "complaining," and "senility" were commonly linked to age. In satisfying reports, stereotyping was more often implicit and couched positively, as in "like a grandmother," or in benevolent terms; for example, older people were labeled "cute" and "sweet."[69]

These responses imply that young people tend to patronize older people. Moreover, the results generally suggest that young people tend to categorize older people as belonging to an out-group—"the elderly." In addition, stereotypes may impede intergenerational interaction. As the researchers note, "being characterized like a 'perfect grandmother' may be positive but may also be as personally and socially restricting as being characterized as a 'good wife.'"[70]

A group of scholars developed the Communication Enhancement of Aging (CEA) model to focus on the need for personalized intergenerational interaction.[71] They endorse educational programs to help people understand normal aging processes and how to communicate more effectively. The model encourages communicators to assess others based on individuals instead of groups, to adjust their communication behaviors only as needed. In essence, this model seeks to counter ageism. Attempts to understand and improve intergenerational communication can yield useful insight for members of all generations as we interact in a variety of contexts. This information will be especially relevant to the workplace, the main context where generations interact with one another.

Communicating Age in Organizations

Did you know that four generations of adults comprise the U.S. workforce? Common labels for these groups are veterans, baby boomers, Generation X, and Generation Y. Baby boomers comprise the largest percentage, and this isn't likely to change soon. This unprecedented configuration of the workforce has occurred because more older persons than ever before are working, people are working and living longer, and the proportion of baby boomers to Generation Xers has increased. In addition, a large number of people who purchase and consume goods and services are and will be old. Human resources professionals and consultants are trying to figure out how to respond to this scenario. Sometimes they seek advice from experts who usually cite traits of various generations and their implications for employee relations. For instance, some claim that your birth cohort is related to what motivates you and what you value most as rewards.

Hierarchies and Age Roles

Multiple generations working together is not a new phenomenon. In early days of industrialization, at least three age cohorts were employed in manufacturing worksites. The circumstances were different, though. Employees were usually segregated due to position and hierarchy. Older, senior employees (mainly white males) worked at the head office, in top positions; middle-aged employees tended to occupy middle management jobs; and the youngest employees either worked on the factory floor or in trainee or "junior" slots. Most employees interacted primarily with people in their own birth cohort. When intergenerational communication occurred, the older person usually held the dominant position.

In today's postindustrial, information-centered society, generational mixing is more frequent: "The old pecking order, hierarchy, and shorter life spans that de facto kept a given generational cohort isolated from others no longer exist, or they exist in a much less rigid, more permeable manner."[72] In addition, older workers no longer have most of the power:

> The once "natural" flow of resources, power, and responsibilities from older to younger arms has been dislocated by changes in life expectancy, increases in longevity and health, and disruption of a century-old trend toward negative population growth, as well as changes in lifestyle, technology, and knowledge base.[73]

Because some younger workers will have essential credentials and expertise, such as technological skills and knowledge for twenty-first-century organizations, traditional age-role profiles may not be as common: many younger persons are assuming senior managerial positions while older persons are reentering the workforce in subordinate roles. This trend is notably evident in high-tech, banking, and consultancy sectors where younger people play key roles in delivering products or services. Younger persons may be charged with managing or supervising older ones. They may assume even more prestigious leadership positions, such as owner or CEO.

In addition, due to technological advances, many businesses have eliminated middle-management positions, leading to more horizontal organizational charts as fewer levels separate workers at the bottom of the hierarchy from the bosses at the top. Simultaneously, the workplace is changing due to technology, globalization, downsizing, and reengineering. The four generations may navigate these changes in different ways, due to "differences in values and views, and ways of working, talking and thinking."[74] These differences may lead to generational conflict in the workplace:

> Oldsters holding fast to their decades of gains are increasingly being pitted for organizational survival against youngsters hungering for their own advancement and security. That they have closed ranks against one another is natural—even when those age group alliances are unspoken and informal and masked by generational name calling and categorization.[75]

Age Discrimination

Employers may discriminate against older applicants by not even considering them for employment. In one research project, a consulting firm sent over 30 offices two virtually identical resumes except for the applicants' age: one was 36, the other 54.[76] All but two queries yielded requests to interview the 36 year old. No one asked to interview the person over 50. Some companies engage in ageism by euphemism; they use terms such as "energetic, vigorous, up on the latest trends, and able to relate to our demographic" to describe preferred qualifications.[77]

Stereotypes of older workers include that they are more costly and less productive than younger ones, they are technologically incompetent and computer-phobic, and they are unwilling to make changes and difficult to train. Employers perceive older workers as more costly due to the perception that their health care benefits cost more. Yet, research suggests that employees with school-age children tend to cost more. When children are sick, one of the parents needs to stay home from work to care for them. Thus, workers with children may be more likely to be absent from work, which is an expense for the company.

Companies sometimes use reengineering or downsizing as an excuse to get rid of older workers. These organizations unreflectively let older workers go first, based on the high salaries of more tenured employees. However, analysts contend that the costs may be more expensive than anticipated, as employers need to train a new employee while forfeiting the older worker's experience, loyalty, and maturity. Also, retaining an employee on the payroll may postpone payout of pensions. Employers often pass over older workers when assigning training and career development opportunities. This may evoke a self-fulfilling prophecy. Some employers figure that they should not invest training money in employees over 45 because it is a waste of resources. Employers believe they can get more for their money when they hire younger persons, who tend to be more flexible, adaptable, accepting of new technology, and better at learning new skills. Also, younger workers tend to be more willing to work longer hours.

Older workers also confront the myth that they will lose motivation. However, some of them wish to continue to work as a matter of self-worth and/or a pressing economic need as retirement funds may not cover their living expenses. Many older people become depressed after they retire and would prefer to contribute somehow to society. Older people often accept and internalize stereotypical ideas about age, especially less-educated older people, which may result in learned helplessness.[78] Others resist age stereotyping and ageism. Many who believe that they have suffered age discrimination take their cases to court. The number of age discrimination cases filed with the EEOC rose from 16,585 in 2005 to 24,582 in 2008.[79] However, age discrimination cases can be hard to prove (only 60 percent of people who filed cases have won), and many never make it to trial. Also, the process takes a long time. However, juries tend to award higher amounts in age discrimination cases than in other discrimination cases (e.g., sex, race, or disability).[80] Among age-bias lawsuits, approximately one-fourth are filed by persons in their 40s. One woman's boss commented, "It's nice to see that someone over 40 can do something." Fired at the age of 42, she successfully sued the company.

Positive Aspects of Intergenerational Mixing

Intergenerational mixing can stimulate creativity and productivity. Practical approaches to maximizing positive aspects of age differences at work and creating a successful intergenerational workforce include anticipating and allowing generational conflicts and potential differences to surface in order to address them efficiently and effectively. In addition, managers should tactically use employees with different backgrounds, experiences, skills, and viewpoints. They also should value cohort differences and view them as strengths; one way to do this is with mutual mentoring, where persons from different age cohorts share resources and insight.

I once worked as a video instructor for a CD-ROM textbook company whose principals were two Generation Xers and a baby boomer. The younger woman and man conceived the idea based on their sense of their cohort's preferred ways of learning. The older man brought to the partnership a strong track record in the traditional publishing industry. Their employee base was a mix of generations. As I developed materials for the CD-ROM product, and during filming, I worked with employees from various age cohorts. The camera operator, sound man, and assistant director were probably under 20 years old; the director was in her 30s; and the producers' ages probably ranged from twenty-something to middle age. The star (me!) was 53. Our collaboration was a phenomenal example of how to invite and respect intergenerational perspectives.

Some organizations are implementing intergenerational programming, which AARP defines as the "purposeful bringing together of different generations in ongoing mutually beneficial planned activities designed to achieve specified program goals."[81] These programs help young and old persons share their talents and resources, and support each other in mutually beneficial relationships for them and their community. An intergenerational service learning project linked a class of preschoolers with at-risk fifth graders from an elementary school and senior citizens from a community center. They ate lunch and read books together. This program "enhanced preschool cognitive, social, emotional, and physical development while enriching the lives of neighboring senior citizens and school-age children alike."[82]

Conclusion

Our final social identity category, age, resembles the other categories we have studied. Age is socially constructed. Attitudes toward age have varied across history. Attitudes toward age reflect dominant ideologies (specifically, the ideology of aging as decline). A hierarchy of age dictates who tends to be privileged and who tends to be disadvantaged. However, age differs from the other categories because everyone is subject to both the privileges and penalties of age, depending on our location on the life span.

Due to increasing longevity, we are witnessing an unprecedented pattern of age cohorts in the United States. As numbers of older persons rise, so will the needs to ensure quality of life for them. Moreover, due to economic necessity as well as personal preference, more people are remaining at work beyond retirement years. Consequently, members of various generations will need to interact with one another in many types of organizational contexts. They will need to change negative patterns of communication that often characterize intergenerational interactions. Sometimes, traditional roles will be reversed, as younger persons assume managerial and leadership positions. Combined with projections about demographic changes related to gender, race, ability, and sexual orientation, these developments indicate that age will be an extremely important matter in the twenty-first century. However, the generation gap doesn't have to be a communication gap!

1. What is your age?
2. How important is your age to you? Explain.
3. What primary sources have taught you about your age?
4. How, if at all, do you express your age (e.g., through language, communication style, dress, accessories, music, and so forth)?
5. Does your awareness of your age ever help you communicate with others? Explain.
6. Does your awareness of your age ever hinder how you communicate with others? Explain.
7. What situations, if any, do you avoid because of concerns related to your age?
8. What situations, if any, do you seek because of your age?
9. What advantages, if any, do you enjoy based on your age?
10. Do you know of any stereotypes about your age? If so, list them.
11. Are you ever aware of stereotypes about your age as you interact with others? Explain.
12. How do the media tend to depict your age? Do media depictions correspond with your sense of your age? Explain.
13. Do you think your attitudes toward age intersect with any other facets of your social identity, for instance: your gender? your social class? your race?

Reflection Matters

1. What did you find intriguing about this chapter?
2. Do any current news stories involve issues that this chapter covers? If yes, what points do they exemplify?
3. According to the sociohistorical overview, what are examples of how people used communication to construct age throughout the history of the United States?
4. What are examples of power relations in the construction of age in the United States?
5. What birth cohort do you belong to? What are distinguishing events, interests, and characteristics of your birth cohort? Do those characteristics affect your sense of yourself? Explain.
6. If you are younger than 55, write an essay about turning 65. Begin by discussing how you feel today about growing older. Then write a hypothetical description of your 65th birthday, from the moment you

awaken until you go to bed that night. Examples of issues you might cover include: How will you feel? What will you be doing at that time in your life? How will you look? With whom will you celebrate? How will you celebrate? What will you be planning to do for the rest of your life? How will the world be different than it is today? If you are 55 or older, write an essay about turning 90, and follow the instructions above.

7. Have you ever learned about aging during formal school curricula? Explain.
8. How well do you tend to interact with people 20-or-more years older than you? Or, with people 10-or-more years younger?
9. Have you ever worked with someone from a different age group than yours? How was the experience? Did age matter?
10. Do you socialize mainly with people your age? Explain.
11. Have you ever over- or underaccommodated while interacting with someone older than you? With someone younger? Explain.

Chapter 9

Communicating Social Identity

"So why are you telling us this?" asked a colleague who read a draft of this book. "What am I as a reader to do with this? How am I to use it?" she wondered. Her questions helped me figure out how to conclude the book. The purpose of this chapter is to summarize key points we have covered. I briefly discuss four primary premises of the book, and I recommend several ways to apply what you have learned.

Difference Matters

My first response to the question, "So why are you telling us this?" is simple: I want you to understand that difference matters. Although all humans differ somehow from one another, some categories of difference make a difference. Our study of sociohistorical developments show that humans perceive and treat one another differently depending on the social identity categories they embody. We focused on gender, race, class, ability, sexuality, and age because these categories are significant in contemporary U.S. society. These differences matter for many reasons, including demographic changes, concerns about civil rights, equal opportunity legislation, increased emphases on diversity, and backlash against change efforts. Therefore, encountering difference not only is inevitable, but it also may be challenging or controversial.

Some people believe that difference does *not* matter because they think our society has solved problems of inequalities and injustices. However, research repeatedly reveals that differences in social identity continue to matter in the United States. To challenge ideologies (belief systems) that perpetuate inequalities and injustices, we have to acknowledge that difference matters.

If you agree that difference matters, you may need to revise your attitude toward difference. I invite you to think of difference as "a starting point for understanding the richness of life," as "unique manifestations of the possibilities of humankind."[1] In other words, try to appreciate and value difference. An appreciative stance can help us reap benefits of difference for society in general, for organizations where we interact with one another, and for our own personal growth and development.

Social Identities Are Social Constructions

Humans organize groups of people based on characteristics such as skin color and perceived ability. We classify social identity categories that we may assume to be natural and permanent. However, social identity categories are artificial and subject to change. As you have seen, meanings of gender, race, class, ability, sexuality, and age have varied historically. Thus, labels and hierarchies of social identity groups always are products of their times. Humans engage in social processes to manufacture differences; they refer to dominant belief systems to conclude that some differences are more important than others; and they assign value-based meanings to those differences.[2]

However, we do not have to accept traditional notions that social identity groups are natural and unchangeable. We can change our beliefs and behaviors regarding social identity groups. We can imagine and perform alternative meanings of our own social identities. Basically, we can affirm our "humanity as free agents with a capacity to create, to construct, to wonder, and to venture."[3]

It seems ironic that although we define the United States as an individualist culture, people rarely seem to behave as individuals. Even though we are relatively free to choose how we enact identity, we usually are predictable. We tend to choose friendships, clothing, food, music, recreational activities, careers, and so forth, based on the social identity groups to which we "belong." Plus, we often seem to make decisions based on group identity rather than considering our multiple options.

I encourage you to make more mindful choices about how you're living rather than be a puppet or a parrot. Snip the invisible strings that control your behaviors. Rewrite the scripts that tell you how to be in certain situations. Resist the pressure to conform to societal expectations about your social identity groups. Remember that your attitudes and actions help to create who you are.

Power Matters

Across history, humans have enacted power relations to make, maintain, and modify meaning about social identity. Powerful sources such as science, politics, medicine, religion, the media, and so forth use dominant belief systems to create and circulate hierarchies of human differences. Socialization processes related to these hierarchies are powerful and persistent; they teach us to believe dominant ideas about matters of difference. As a result, most people take for granted these hierarchies and the ideologies on which they are based. Persons in positions of privilege tend to reap benefits from these hierarchies, while people placed in lower levels are more likely to be disadvantaged.

Thankfully, throughout the history of the United States, some members of nondominant and dominant groups have challenged belief systems that discriminate against certain groups and favor others. Dominant groups often have used their power for good. Advocates for change have resisted hegemony by initiating social movements, campaigning for laws, developing social and economic programs, and engaging in other actions to challenge the status quo. Countless individuals have worked hard separately or in groups to achieve freedom and equality. You can do the same. Regardless of your positions of privilege and disadvantage based on your various social identities, you can resist and transform power dynamics that compel us to comply with unjust belief systems.

Communication Rules!

Communication can help or hinder progress toward equal opportunity for life, liberty, and the pursuit of happiness. Through various means and modes, we communicate to produce, interpret, and share meaning about diverse groups of people. We develop and disseminate classifications and hierarchies of gender, race, class, sexuality, ability, and age. We create labels, ascribe meaning to them, and use them to refer to one another. And, we co-create and re-create our identities as we interact with one another. Our families, peers, the media, teachers, religious leaders, and other sources socialize us about in-groups and out-groups, and we tend to accept the meanings they teach us as truth. We use communication to create and consume media reports about social identity groups and media portrayals (factual and fictitious) of social identity groups. Many, if not most, of these reports and portrayals reinforce dominant ideologies and stereotypes.

Even as communication reinforces dominant meanings of difference, communication facilitates social change. The media sometimes offer alternative narratives, depictions, and information that challenge mainstream conceptions of social identity groups. Advocacy groups use communication to develop and distribute information, engage in marches and rallies, and construct symbols to represent and advance their causes. Organizations develop and enforce policies; bystanders speak up when they witness inequities. Therefore, communication is central to applying what you have learned.

To summarize, I encourage you to appreciate and value difference, to contest and re-imagine conceptions of social identities, to realize the power of power and to empower yourself, and to acknowledge and use the power of communication. I refer to these ideas in the following recommendations.

Recommendations

As you read and reflect on the recommendations below, please understand that this list is not exhaustive. To be thorough, I would need to write another book. After all, processes of communicating social identity are complex and contextual. Numerous factors affect how we construct, reproduce, interpret, or share meaning about social identity. Therefore, instead of prescribing a particular path, I provide possible steps to apply what you have learned. I refer to some of the tools that I presented in previous chapters plus a few more ideas. To clarify what I recommend, I share a few more personal stories. Although I present them simply, these stories actually are multifaceted. I feel like I'm showing you a few photographs from a video documentary of my life. I can't even begin to capture complexities of contexts, characters, and conflicts that these stories represent. However, I hope the snapshots guide you for how to communicate social identity.

Be Mindful

I hope you've already begun to use Tool #1 (from chapter 1): mindfulness. If so, I also hope that you've begun to see how useful this tool can be. If you have responded to the Reflection Matters and ID Check questions throughout the book, you already are more mindful about difference matters. Continue that process by delving into your inner world to deepen self-awareness and heighten your consciousness. Observe yourself in the process of thinking. Think about what you're thinking about. Also notice your feelings.

As you monitor your thoughts, attitudes, and feelings, look for evidence of dominant belief systems. Ask yourself if you are relying on stereotypes or making assumptions about social identity groups. Notice when you have negative or emotional responses to images, phrases, words, and objects related to social identity groups. Track how you routinely respond to certain differences. Mark moments when you feel uncomfortable while interacting with members of other social identity groups, or when you judge individuals or assume things about them based on group stereotypes. Also be aware of when you judge people who belong to the same groups as you.

As you are being mindful, be honest. Mentally record your observations and decide what to try to stop doing, what to keep, or what to change. When you note something you'd like to change, acknowledge any negative feelings, such as guilt or shame, and be patient and loving with yourself.

When I observe my thoughts and feelings about difference, I am amazed by the power and persistence of mainstream belief systems, which frequently surface in my everyday life. Therefore, I try to detect when I am Thinking Under the Influence (TUI) of prejudices, stereotypes, and dominant ideologies. For instance, I try to notice when I feel surprised by someone "different," because my feelings often signify a negative assumption or stereotype.

A panelist on a program I attended was a wheelchair user who also was hearing impaired. When she made several witty comments, I noticed that her sense of humor amazed me. As I processed my feelings, I realized that I assumed she would have a gloomy outlook on life because of her disabilities. Aha! I was TUI of the prejudicial notion that disability is a state of being doomed.

An elderly man slowly boarded a bus I was riding on. After he sat down, he began to talk with another older man. As I eavesdropped on their conversation, I was impressed with how articulate they were, especially after the first man said he was 90 years old. I had assumed that both men would have limited communication competence. Aha! I was TUI of the dominant ideology of aging as decline. As the two of them joked and laughed, I wondered if other people write them off as "over the hill." I also lamented that others who are TUI might miss rich opportunities to interact with someone "different" because of stereotypes about being old.

TUI is not limited to perceptions of out-groups, especially for members of nondominant groups who may have internalized negative attitudes about their own groups. That's why I encourage you to focus on how you respond to people in your own social identity categories. For example, socialization sources have done a great job indoctrinating me about language. At an early age, I learned the stereotype that people who do not speak "proper" English were not intelligent. I am especially critical of black people who do not speak mainstream English. When my nieces and nephew were young, I would be so busy correcting their speech that I often missed what they were saying. Given dominant expectations about language standards, I was justifiably concerned that other people would harshly judge my family members. However, I probably could have helped them understand possible negative reactions to their communication style without negating their talk. I also could have encouraged them to develop a variety of ways of communicating to apply across different contexts, and to choose when to use them. Not long ago, as I watched a televised interview of a black male athlete, I was impressed with how well he used standard English. And, I usually wince when I hear black male athletes use nonstandard English. In both cases, I was TUI of mainstream beliefs about race, language, and intelligence.

Now when I catch myself TUI of stereotypes and dominant ideologies about language and speech, I remind myself that there is no right or wrong way to communicate, that the goal of communication is to share meaning. I'm still working on my bad habit of mentally judging and editing what people say. I try to focus more on *what* people say than on their language or communication style. I try to appreciate the beauty and variety of human expression. Basically, I try to reframe my negative attitudes about language and communication styles.

Communication scholar Gust Yep offers a great example of reframing: "I used to be concerned about the accent in my speech, but in recent years I have adopted a different attitude: My accent might simply be an indication that I probably speak more languages than my conversational partner."[4] Yep's perspective on language is more affirming and appreciative than demeaning of oneself and one's group. Of course, his viewpoint also applies to how we respond to members of other groups. I often think about this while talking with someone who speaks English as a second language.

In addition to being mindful of stereotypes and assumptions, try to identify how you are privileged according to social identity—regardless of your social identity profile. As I've said before, most of us embody both privileged and nonprivileged social identity groups. Locating privilege in your life may be difficult, because privilege can be hard to recognize. It's like telling a fish to detect water (what water?), or to describe how its gills function (what gills?). Sometimes persons who have not experienced discrimination and prejudice cannot comprehend or even believe that other people routinely encounter or expect to encounter negative treatment based on their social identity. Although some people struggle to see what they take for granted, our society will not achieve liberty and justice for all unless persons who are privileged recognize how privilege operates in their lives.

As I discussed in the sexuality chapter, after a friend of mine told me she was a lesbian and described challenges she faces, I became conscious of my heterosexual privilege. Confronting my heterosexual privilege helped me to see how whites may not perceive their privilege: just as some whites seem oblivious to race issues, I had been unaware of sexuality issues. Once I realized my heterosexual privilege, I became more sympathetic to gay/lesbian/bisexual/transgender/queer people and their allies. As a result of my raised consciousness, I now notice instances of heterosexism and stereotypes about homosexuality that I previously would not have seen. And, as I discuss later, I have become proactive about helping others understand the prevalence and consequences of heteronormative attitudes in our society.

I also have become increasingly aware of my social class and ability privilege, both of which allow me lots of latitude that I hadn't thought that much about. Becoming aware of these and other ways that I'm privileged help me to be empathetic with persons who do not enjoy such privilege, and—as I have done with sexuality—to identify ways that I might use my positions of privilege to help others.

In addition to tracking your thoughts while observing others and interacting with them, stay mindful of TUI while consuming media, such as newspapers, television, the Internet, music, and films. Recall my example of assuming that a group of Latinos in a newspaper photo had committed a crime. In that case, I was TUI of the stereotype that men of color are criminals.

As you monitor your thoughts and feelings, also check out your behaviors. While discussing privilege and power, a white heterosexual male explained how he became mindful of how he enacted male dominance: he found himself interrupting and dominating conversations, avoiding admitting he was wrong about anything, and assuming he had the right to occupy as much space as he needed in public places.[5] After learning that teachers often unconsciously treat female and male students differently, I monitored myself. I was dismayed to discover that I was guilty of many behaviors that researchers cited. I would call on males more often than females, and I would give males more positive feedback. Now, I pay attention while I'm teaching, and I try to treat students more equitably.

To conclude, one way to apply what you have learned about difference matters is to be mindful of your thoughts, feelings, and behaviors related to social identity. To help you become more mindful, consider the following questions whenever you are going to interact with someone.[6]

- What preconceived notions do I have about this person based on social identity characteristics (differences and similarities)?
- Are those notions positive, negative, or neutral?
- What might be the source(s) of those preconceptions?
- Will my preconceptions facilitate or impede communication?
- Am I open to learning about this person *and* myself during this interaction? Why or why not?
- Am I willing to be changed as a result of this interaction or experience?
- What communication tools can I use to try to create genuine communication?

Reflecting honestly on these questions will help raise your self-awareness. Although being mindful requires vigilance and commitment, the process can be rewarding because you might become more open-minded about difference matters. You also might identify areas to improve your attitudes and behaviors, which leads us to the second recommendation.

Be Proactive

A second way to apply what you have learned is to be proactive, which means taking "the initiative and the responsibility to make things happen,"[7] and "acting in anticipation of future problems, needs, or changes."[8] As leadership expert Stephen Covey explains, being proactive requires you to be "response-able," or capable of responding appropriately.[9] To become more response-able about difference matters and communicating social identity, refer to information from the book as well as insight you gain from being mindful. I especially encourage you to focus on privilege and power, and to learn more about various groups, including your own.

Focus on Power and Privilege. Once you've figured out how you're privileged through being mindful, decide how to use your privileged status to help other people. Sociologist Allan Johnson (a white heterosexual male) encourages privileged persons to "feel obligated to make the problem of privilege their problem and to do something about it."[10] He explains:

> For me, it means I have to take the initiative to find out how privilege operates in the world, how it affects people, and what all that has to do with me. It means I have to think the unthinkable, speak the unspeakable, break the silence, acknowledge the elephant [of privilege and oppression], and then take my share of responsibility for what comes next. . . . The fact that it's so easy for me and other people in dominant groups not to do this is the single most powerful barrier to change.[11]

In his book entitled *Privilege, Power, and Difference*, Johnson offers compelling ideas for how members of dominant groups can become proactive about their privilege and use it for social change.

As you consider becoming proactive about privilege, think about areas where you have power (Stephen Covey refers to these as "spheres of influence"), and how you can use that power for good. When I was the only faculty member of color in a university department, I could have felt disempowered as a woman and as a black person. However, I also was director of graduate assistants who taught an introductory course in organizational communication. That role authorized me to select teaching materials and develop assignments. After my friend and colleague Anna Spradlin wrote her article, "The Price of 'Passing,'"[12] I required teaching assistants to assign it in their classes. These assignments expanded the curriculum to delve more deeply into difference matters. And, some of those graduate assistants have become professors and are continuing to refer to Dr. Spradlin's work and related materials on sexuality. Two more examples: when I became a department chair, I asked faculty to put copies of their assigned textbooks on reserve in the library because some students may not be able to buy their books at the beginning of a term, or ever. Now that I am an Associate Dean and Chair of our college's Diversity Council, I am leading an initiative for students with disabilities. The council recently held a festival to increase awareness of disability, and we are developing resources for faculty and students. Also, students in my graduate class on research methods are completing projects about disability in higher education to develop recommendations that I will submit to faculty members and to the Office of Disability Services.

An additional approach to being proactive about power is to imagine how you might enact power relations differently. If you are a primary source of socialization, such as a teacher, manager, parent, or guardian, take seriously your role in shaping other persons' social identities. To help those for whom you are responsible, provide information, guidance, and experiences that encourage them to value differences. An abundance of resources exists to assist you with this suggestion.[13]

In asymmetrical power relationships (such as student–teacher, patient–physician, employee–manager, child–parent, interviewee–interviewer), you can alter scripted roles to challenge dominant ways of communicating. When a physician recommended a treatment program for me, I offered alternative information based on my medical history as well as on published research about black women. I told her I would prefer a holistic approach, and I explained why. After hearing my views, she agreed. I was proactive: I was prepared to discuss my health with her rather than simply accept her recommendations because she was the authority figure. However, I entered the conversation willing to listen to and respect her opinions. And, I appreciated her willingness to improvise her role.

As the authority figure in teacher–student relationships, I try to be flexible in my role. I invite students' opinions and ideas, and I am willing to change course policies and procedures based on their input. I also am receptive to unsolicited ideas or requests related to course material or assignments. I recently learned about critical communication pedagogy, an approach to teaching that focuses on studies of relationships between power and communication in educational contexts.[14] Critical communication pedagogy provides ways to analyze and transform educational contexts by applying principles of critical theory. It defines power as a processual, shared, and reciprocal element of classroom interactions. Thus, for example, it invites teachers to be self-reflexive regarding power dynamics of how they "manage" their classrooms. Critical communication pedagogy depicts teachers as agents of change, and it portrays the classroom as a significant site of social influence where actors engage in social construction of their and others' identities. Furthermore, critical communication pedagogy hinges on the basic premise that humans communicatively constitute power relations through social interaction, and therefore we can use social interaction in teaching to change those relations. I was gratified to see that I already enact some of the tenets of this approach, and I've become more committed and conscientious about applying them to my teaching.[15]

You also can rewrite scripts in symmetrical power relationships. On a televised public service announcement, a black male handed a white male a resume. After the black male left, the other man crumpled the resume and threw it into a wastebasket. "I think we already have enough color around here," he smirked to a white male colleague. The coworker retrieved the resume, smoothed it, and replied, "I don't think we do."

Another idea for being proactive is to be ready to respond to behaviors that seem discriminatory or otherwise inappropriate, like the preceding example. We can enact power relations to disrupt everyday moments of oppression, such as when people we know are laughing at jokes that target members of nondominant groups. During those moments, dominant group members can refuse to play their prescribed/expected role, which is going along with whatever happens when others engage in "ist" (e.g., racist, sexist, ageist, heterosexist) talk or behavior. Similar to the man in the public service announcement described above, dominant group members can decide that they will speak up when they encounter such behavior. Rather than comply with expectations such as laughing at a joke, a person can remain conspicuously silent, or speak up. Your response can be as simple as "I don't think that's funny."

Nondominant group members also can be proactive in situations like these. One challenge I often face is when someone uses "they/them" and "we/us" language. I experience this when women refer to men, blacks refer to whites or other racial-ethnic groups, middle-aged people refer to younger or older persons, straight persons refer to gay people or lesbians, and U.S. citizens refer to people from other countries. My responses vary according to the situation. In a group of black friends, I might point out that their remarks about members of other nonmajority groups resemble the negative stereotypes that other groups often level against blacks. Or, sometimes I quietly ask a person "Do you really believe ALL _________ are like that?"

The goal of speaking up in these situations is not to shame others or make them feel uncomfortable. Johnson explains:

> Systems shape the choices people make primarily by providing paths of least resistance. Whenever we openly choose a different path, however, we make it possible for others to see both the path of least resistance they're following and the possibility of choosing something else. . . . When people know that alternatives exist and witness other people choosing them, things become possible that weren't before.[16]

In essence, we can be role models, and "by our example, we can contradict basic assumptions and their legitimacy over and over again."[17] We might facilitate the process of choosing alternative paths or writing new scripts. Our actions might be especially salient for people who are open to change, but who don't know how to change.

To decide whether and how to respond to perceived discriminatory behavior, assess the situation before drawing a conclusion. Some years ago, I went with a group of black students to a restaurant where all of the other diners were white. One of the students complained that service was slow and asserted that the waitress was racist. Several other students nodded in agreement. The students' concerns were legitimate, given documented evidence that racism continues to occur in restaurants as well as other public places in the United States. However, I pointed out that the woman was the only server, and she seemed to be trying to get to each table in turn. After the students watched her for a few moments, they agreed with me.

To be proactive in situations like these, prepare yourself to respond rather than react. Reacting means acting without reflection, as in "knee-jerk reaction." In contrast, responding requires careful thought. Act only after you analyze a situation and decide what to do. A Chicana friend of mine was at a party with colleagues when an elderly white man (whom she had just met) put his arm around her, and said, "This is my little squaw." Although she is a vocal advocate of Chicana rights, my friend chose not to say anything. She assessed the situation and concluded that saying something to the man was not worth the potential consequences. If she had been in a different context, like her workplace, she might have responded differently.

You also can be proactive by investigating organizations that matter to you to learn how they deal with difference matters. For instance, what's their track record regarding diversity? Do they have an active, effective recruitment program for identifying diverse employees or members? What services or accommodations do they offer persons with disabilities? Do they provide diversity awareness training that encompasses a variety of social identity groups? Are training initiatives effective? Are accountability systems in place? Do they offer general and specific recourses for persons who feel they have been discriminated against? Do they have clear policies regarding harassment? How about mentoring programs or other career development opportunities?

Do they provide financial subsidies to cover expenses for required items such as uniforms or equipment? Does networking often take place at elite locations such as country clubs that require membership or invitations from members? What is the organization's record in terms of charitable giving?

What types of charities does the organization support? Also, "does your company have different rules, or application of rules, for employees at higher levels in the organization? What perks are offered only at certain levels? Do certain employees use one restroom or dining facility while all the rest have to use another?"[18] Do schools that you or your children attend have multicultural curricula? What about critical thinking classes, or media literacy programs?

Answers to these and similar questions can help you decide how to become proactive. Focus on issues that might require concerted, sustained efforts, or identify challenges that you can readily remedy, as I did for students who may not be able to afford textbooks, and as I'm working on for students with disabilities. Within organizations that matter to you, such as work, school, or place of worship, identify allies for social change and forge relationships with them. However, do research prior to joining a group or agreeing to serve on a task force or committee. Develop a set of criteria for evaluating whether or not you should become involved. For instance, I prefer to work with groups that clearly seem to have the power to make a difference. If they do not seem to have economic and political resources to implement any change the group recommends, I usually won't become involved. I also seek groups that are inclusive of various perspectives and people and that seem receptive to me and my ideas. I usually will not participate if I feel like I am just a token.

To become more proactive about power and privilege, volunteer your services, or share your expertise. I conduct free communication workshops for a variety of audiences. I frequently present empowerment workshops for women's groups. Once I worked with young, single mothers in a welfare-to-work program. I shared ideas and strategies related to self-empowerment and communication. I also taught them about social capital, and I advised them to establish networks (see Tool #4 in chapter 5) with a variety of people.

Speaking of networking, if you tend to be uncomfortable in certain co-cultural interactions, such as company-sponsored social events, strategize about how to overcome your apprehension. For instance, arrange to go to an event with a friendly coworker and stay for at least twenty minutes. Participating in such activities might help you gain information or form relationships that not only can help you advance your career but can also help others. You also can help others and yourself by becoming involved in mentoring programs, as a mentor or as a protégé. I recently accepted an appointment as Master Mentor at my university. You know I couldn't pass up an opportunity to be called a "master!" Mentor–protégé relationships can be empowering for both parties. Some individuals think they cannot be mentors because they are too young and/or inexperienced. I tell them they surely have *something* to share with others. For instance, college undergraduates can help high school students, or high school students can tutor or become role models for middle school students. In workplaces, persons at various levels of the hierarchy can mentor one another. You do not have to be a top-level manager or have an advanced degree to offer guidance.

Learn about Social Identity Groups and Other Cultures. I have gained so much from learning about other social identity groups, and I want you to benefit, too. You can find many kinds of books at local libraries about groups we have studied. And, numerous video media (available in public libraries or college media centers) cover related topics. The Public Broadcasting Corporation and the History Channel frequently air instructive, enlightening programs on television. Many universities and nonprofit organizations offer Intergroup Dialogue Programs that provide opportunities for members of varying social identities to share their experiences. For example, the University of Wisconsin-Madison offers a program developed by Peggy McIntosh (who originated the concept of white privilege) called SEED (Seeking Educational Equity and Diversity). Students, faculty, administrators, community members, and others engage in yearlong seminars to explore various issues related to identity, inclusion, and social justice.[19]

Currently, I am learning about the history of Latinos and Latinas in the United States, and I am improving my Spanish (I took a couple of courses decades ago in college). I'm making my way through a workbook, and I often listen to a Spanish-language radio station while I'm driving. I'm fortunate to live in an area rich with Latino culture, and I don't want to miss an opportunity to become more knowledgeable. I also intend to learn about Judaism because although I have Jewish friends and acquaintances, I recently realized that I know very little about their religion.

In addition to learning about other social identity groups, study your own. I have felt empowered and validated by reading about black women's history in the United States. Acquiring information about one's heritage is crucial to groups whose stories the media tend to negate, dilute, or omit. Until school curricula and mainstream media provide more inclusive and accurate information and portrayals, members of disenfranchised groups should take the initiative to learn about themselves to help them imagine and create more positive identities. Becoming more informed about your own group(s) can help you to identify and resist internalized oppression.

These are a few ideas for how to be more proactive, "take the initiative and the responsibility to make things happen."[20] In addition, a great resource for ideas for being proactive is *Positive Impact: Tools for Respecting Differences,* which lists 101 ways to make a positive impact in your community.[21] A final way to be more response-able about difference matters is to develop your communication skills, as I discuss next.

Fill Your Communication Toolbox

I've already shared a few tools for your communication toolbox throughout the book, and I hope you've begun to use them. In addition to these, you also can refer to communication theories I discussed to get ideas about how monitor your thoughts and feelings, interpret data, and express yourself. For instance, co-cultural theory,[22] accommodation theory,[23] and the Communication Enhancement of Aging model[24] offer options for communicating with others. In addition to collecting concepts from this book, you can search the discipline of communication for other tools. For instance, Jack Gibb's model for supportive communication provides guidance for how to offer feedback to someone.[25] To illustrate this approach, here's a story about a co-cultural interaction: During a work-related meeting where I was the only person of color in a group of ten employees, the group's leader repeatedly did not call on me when I raised my hand. He did acknowledge others who raised their hands. He also did not mention my contributions to a major project, although he cited everyone else. In addition, he credited one of my coworkers for an idea I had offered during the meeting. I felt marginalized, and I began to get irritated. At one point, one of my colleagues corrected the leader by acknowledging my input. In a private conversation with me after the meeting, that colleague expressed dismay at the leader's behaviors toward me.

After the meeting, I reviewed what had happened. Frustrated with second-guessing about whether the leader was behaving in a racist or sexist way, I decided to express my perceptions and feelings to him. I did not want to go into another group meeting dreading what might occur. I e-mailed him about my concerns: I described his behaviors by stating the facts (e.g., "you did not acknowledge my contributions to the project," "you gave X credit for my idea," "you did not call on me when I raised my hand"). I told him I felt ignored and ostracized because of his behaviors. I also said I was beginning to withdraw because I felt he did not value my contributions. He scheduled a meeting with me, and I restated my concerns. He apologized, and said he did not mean to ignore me. He also told me I was a valuable member of the group. In subsequent meetings, he was more inclusive.

This descriptive approach to offering feedback can help you communicate your concerns. Describe what happened rather than use evaluative or accusatory language, such as "you are disrespectful," or "you are racist (or sexist)." Also, indicate how you felt as a result of what happened. And, consider offering feasible suggestions for future interactions. In addition, be open to engaging in dialogue where you actively listen and respond to the other person.

This technique, like any other, is not guaranteed to elicit a positive response or a productive outcome. The other person might become defensive and dismiss or deny your perceptions. Or, the person might accuse you of being oversensitive. The relationship could be damaged. Therefore, you should analyze the situation and consider potential consequences. Regardless of outcomes, I almost always feel better when I have voiced my concerns, especially in situations that matter to me.

As you think about how to respond in situations like these, be mindful of the difference between intent and impact. The distinction between intent and impact is commonly used "in harassment-prevention and diversity training workshops to explain the importance of attending not only to what someone 'meant' in an interaction but also to the effect of that interaction on other parties."[26] According to sexual harassment training, impact takes precedent over intent when someone says or does something related to sexuality that has a harmful effect on another person.

When their behaviors negatively affect someone else, similar to my colleague, people sometimes say, "I didn't mean it." In situations like these, it is important to acknowledge that regardless of intentions, one's behaviors can have a negative impact. However, getting someone to see the importance of impact may be difficult because people sometimes "seem to think that if they don't *mean* it, then it didn't happen, as if their conscious intent is the only thing that connects them to the consequences of what they do or don't do."[27] Furthermore, saying "I didn't mean it" can impede dialogue about what happened, as well as honest reflection about if behavior change is needed and how to go about it.

I could easily have dismissed my behavior in classes where I treated females less equitably than males, by saying "I didn't mean it." However, to change systemic patterns of hegemony, we must acknowledge ways that we help reinforce dominant belief systems. To become proactive, I had to recognize how my behaviors reinforced patriarchy, and I had to change my communication patterns.

Because "I didn't mean it" often means a person was not thinking or just did not know any better, engaging in dialogue about intent and impact can facilitate understanding and change. Person A, whose behavior had a negative impact, must be open to understanding how that behavior impacted Person B. Simultaneously, Person B should be willing to understand that Person A may have meant no harm. Person B also should be willing to analyze why certain behaviors have an impact. For instance, members of social identity groups may be conditioned to react negatively to certain words and actions without considering context. Both parties might grow from processing the experience and deciding whether to and how to change their attitudes and behaviors.

Other areas of the discipline to consult include intercultural communication scholarship, which contains rich insight and information about social identity categories, including nationality and religion. Feminist studies and gender studies of communication also include viable concepts and perspectives. You also can refer to concepts and theories that are not explicitly related to social identity but that still facilitate communicating social identity. Examples include invitational rhetoric,[28] appreciative inquiry, [29] and dialogic theory.[30] Furthermore, you could acquire tools to build basic communication skills, such as listening.[31] For example, the man I mentioned earlier, who recognized his habit of dominating conversations, described how he became proactive: "With some effort, I've tried out new ways of listening more and talking less . . . such as telling myself to shut up for a while or even counting slowly to ten (or more) to give others a chance to step into the space afforded by silence."[32]

Two excellent resources that give specific advice for communicating about difference matters are: (1) *Speak Up! Responding to Everyday Bigotry,*[33] which refers to numerous real-life stories about interactions in numerous contexts where someone made offensive comments, and suggests how to respond to such comments, and (2) *Navigating Diversity,*[34] which refers to 50 actual incidents to provide a systematic approach for responding to offensive comments. I also encourage you to hone your critical thinking skills. Marlys Mayfield's book, *Thinking for Yourself,* is a wonderful resource.[35]

As you collect tools, use them! Don't let them rust. Also, share your tools with others.

Conclusion

Three general ideas for applying what you have learned from this book are to be mindful, be proactive, and fill your communication toolbox (and use the tools!). To follow these, you will need to be committed, vigilant, and persistent. I realize that some of my ideas may seem overwhelming. So, I encourage you to start small, and do what you can. But do something—and then do something else. I hope that finishing this book marks for you the beginning of a lifelong commitment to difference matters. Peace.

Reflection Matters

1. If you had to share *one* point from this book with someone you care about, what would you share? Why?
2. Have a conversation with someone you care about in which you actually share the point that you cited in question #1. Write a brief essay about the conversation.
3. What does it mean to you to appreciate and value difference? How have you appreciated and valued difference? What else might you do?
4. What additional ideas would you offer regarding how to apply what you have learned?
5. Choose at least one of your ideas (or one of mine) about how to apply what you have learned and create an action plan for accomplishing that idea. After you have developed a plan, implement it. Best wishes always.

Chapter Endnotes

Chapter 1

[1] Not his real name.

[2] I use the terms African American and black interchangeably.

[3] Lott, B., & Saxon, S. (2002). The influence of ethnicity, social class, and context on judgments about U.S. women. *The Journal of Social Psychology, 142*(4), 481–499, p. 482.

[4] Allen, B. J. (2000). Sapphire and Sappho: Allies in authenticity. In A. Gonzales, M. Houston, & V. Chen, *Our voices: Essays in culture, ethnicity, and communication* (3rd ed.). Los Angeles: Roxbury.

[5] Jennifer Simpson, personal correspondence.

[6] Ellis, D. Becoming a master student. (1997). http://www.accd.edu/sac/history/keller/ACCDitg/SSCT.htm (retrieved October 27, 2009).

[7] West, C. (1994). *Race matters.* New York: Vintage; William K. Rawlins (1992) uses the same reasoning in an earlier book entitled *Friendship matters: Communication, dialectics, and the life course.* New York: Aldine de Gruyter.

[8] "Difference" is a significant, complex construct about social identities. See, for example, Warren, J. (2008). Performing difference: Repetition in context. *Journal of International & Intercultural Communication, 1*(4), 290–308.

[9] Jenkins, R. (1996). *Social identity.* London; New York: Routledge, pp. 3–4.

[10] Jenkins, p. 4.

[11] Lindsley, S. L. (1998). Communicating prejudice in organizations. In M. L. Hecht (Ed.), *Communicating prejudice* (pp. 187–205). Thousand Oaks, CA: Sage.

[12] Encarta dictionary: "relating to or supporting the use of language or conduct that deliberately avoids giving offense, e.g., on the basis of ethnic origin or sexual orientation." http://encarta.msn.com/dictionary_1861738200/politically_correct.html

[13] Gentile, M. C. (1996). Ways of thinking about and across difference. In M. C. Gentile (Ed.), *Managerial excellence through diversity* (pp. 12–31). Long Grove, IL: Waveland Press.

[14] Burgoon, J., Berger, C., & Waldron, V. (2000). Mindfulness and Interpersonal Communication. *Journal of Social Issues, 56*(1), 105–127. Retrieved from Academic Search Premier database.

[15] Langer, E., & Moldoveanu, M. (2000). The Construct of Mindfulness. *Journal of Social Issues, 56*(1), 1–9.

[16] Mayfield, M. (2010). *Thinking for yourself: Developing critical thinking skills through reading and writing* (8th ed.). Boston: Wadsworth, p. 10.

[17] Langer & Moldoveanu.

[18] Berger, P., & Luckmann, T. (1966). *The social construction of reality: A treatise in the sociology of knowledge.* New York: Doubleday.

[19] Collier, M. J. (2000). Constituting cultural difference through discourse. *International and Intercultural Communication Annual, 23*(3). Thousand Oaks, CA: Sage.

[20] Putnam, L., & Fairhurst, G. (2001). Discourse analysis in organizations: Issues and concerns. In F. M. Jablin & L. L. Putnam (Eds.), *The new handbook of organizational communication: Advances in theory, research, and methods.* Thousand Oaks, CA: Sage, p. 109.

[21] Howard, J. A., & Alamilla, R. M. (2001). Gender and identity. In D. Vannoy (Ed.), *Gender mosaics: Social perspectives* (pp. 54–64). Los Angeles: Roxbury.
[22] Gentile, p. 14.
[23] Jenkins, p. 4.
[24] Scott, C. R., Corman, S., & Cheney, G. (1998). Development of a structurational model of identification in the organization. *Communication Theory, 8,* 298–336, p. 311.
[25] Other ways that humans construct their identities include "moments of personal reflection, or in transcendental experiences with natural environments, or in physiological mechanisms that are beyond participants' range of expressions" (Carbaugh, p. 30). Carbaugh, D. D. (1996). *Situating selves: The communication of social identities in American scenes.* Albany: State University of New York Press, p. 7; Hecht, M. L., Collier, M. J., & Ribeau, S. A. (1993). *African American communication: Ethnic identity and cultural interpretation.* Newbury Park, CA: Sage.
[26] Carbaugh, p. 7.
[27] Burr, V. (1995). *An introduction to social constructionism.* London: Routledge, p. 51.
[28] Jenkins, p. 59.
[29] Holtzman, L. (2000). *Media messages: What film, television, and popular music teach us about race, class, gender, and sexual orientation.* Armonk, NY: M. E. Sharpe.
[30] Blumenbach, J. F. (1973). *The anthropological treatises of Johann Fredrich Blumenbach.* Boston: Milford House. (Original work published 1865). Blumenbach based his work on other, similar classifications; however, his work became the foundation.
[31] Brah, A. (1992). Difference, diversity, and differentiation. In D. James & A. Rattansi (Eds.), *Race, culture, and difference* (pp. 126–145). London: Sage, p. 126.
[32] Orbe, M. P., & Harris, T. M. (2007). *Interracial communication: Theory into practice* (2nd ed.). Thousand Oaks, CA: Sage.
[33] Tajfel, H. (1982). *Social identity and intergroup relations.* Cambridge, UK: Cambridge University Press.
[34] Conrad, C., & Poole, M. S. (2002). *Strategic organizational communication: Toward the twenty-first century.* Fort Worth: Harcourt Brace, p. 351.
[35] McIntosh, P. (1998). White privilege and male privilege: A personal account of coming to see correspondence through work in women's studies. In M. L. Andersen & P. H. Collins (Eds.), *Race, class, and gender: An anthology.* Belmont, CA: Wadsworth.
[36] Gilbert, R. (2008). Raising awareness of class privilege among students. *Diversity & Democracy, 11*(3). Association of American Colleges and Universities.
[37] Rosenblum, K. E., & Travis, T. C. (2003). *The meaning of difference: American constructions of race, sex and gender, social class, and sexual orientation.* Boston: McGraw-Hill, p. 178.
[38] Rosenblum & Travis.
[39] Spradlin, A. L. (1998). The price of passing: A lesbian perspective on authenticity in organizations. *Management Communication Quarterly, 11*(4), 598–605.
[40] Padilla, L. M. (2001). "But you're not a dirty Mexican": Internalized oppression, Latinos & law. *Texas Hispanic Journal of Law & Policy, 7*(1), 58–113.
[41] United States Equal Employment Opportunity Commission (EEOC). (2007). EEOC takes new approach to fighting racism and colorism in the 21st century workplace. *United States Equal Employment Opportunity Commission.* http://eeoc.gov/press/2–28–07 (retrieved February 26, 2010).
[42] Findley, H., Garrott, S. C., & Wheatley, R. (2004). Color discrimination: Differentiate at your peril. *Journal of Individual Employment Rights, 11,* 31–38.

Chapter 2

[1] All names are fictitious.
[2] Conrad, C., & Poole, M. S. (2002). *Strategic organizational communication: Toward the twenty-first century* (5th ed.). Fort Worth: Harcourt Brace.
[3] McKinnon, S. L. (2009). Critical theory. In S. W. Littlejohn and K. A. Foss (Eds.), *Encyclopedia of communication theory* (pp. 237–242). Thousand Oaks, CA: Sage p. 237.

[4] Foucault, M. (1977). *Discipline and punish: The birth of the prison* (A. Sheridan, Trans.). New York: Pantheon Books.

[5] Deetz, S. A. (1992). *Democracy in an age of corporate colonization: Developments in communication and the politics of everyday life.* Albany: State University of New York, p. 252.

[6] Foss, S. K., Foss, K. A., & Trapp, R. (Eds.). (2002). *Contemporary perspectives on rhetoric* (3rd ed.). Long Grove, IL: Waveland Press, p. 325.

[7] Barker, J. (1999). *The discipline of teamwork: Participation and concertive control.* Thousand Oaks, CA: Sage, p. 43.

[8] Deetz, p. 253.

[9] Barker, J., & Cheney, G. (1994). The concept and practice of discipline in contemporary organizational life. *Communication Monographs, 61,* 20–43, p. 20.

[10] Barker, p. 45.

[11] Foucault, p. 52.

[12] Moon, D. G., & Rolison, G. L. (1998). Communication of classism. In M. L. Hecht (Ed.), *Communicating prejudice* (pp. 122–135). Thousand Oaks, CA: Sage, p. 130.

[13] Titsworth, B. S. (1999). An ideological basis for definition in public argument: A case study of the Individuals with Disabilities in Education Act. *Argumentation and Advocacy, 35,* 171–184.

[14] Barker & Cheney, p. 25.

[15] Barker, p. 44.

[16] Mumby, D. (2000). Power and politics. In F. M. Jablin & L. L. Putnam (Eds.), *The new handbook of organizational communication: Advances in theory, research, and methods.* Thousand Oaks, CA: Sage, p. 601.

[17] Barker & Cheney, p. 25.

[18] Edwards, R. (1979). *Contested terrain: The transformation of the workplace in the twentieth century.* New York: Basic Books.

[19] Tompkins, P. K., & Cheney, G. (1987). Communication and unobtrusive control in contemporary organizations. In R. McPhee and P. K. Tompkins (Eds.), *Organizational communication: Traditional themes and new directions* (pp. 179–210). Newbury Park, CA: Sage, p. 184. Barker (1999) notes that Elaine Tompkins coined the term "concertive control."

[20] Burke, K. A. (1950). *Rhetoric of motives.* New York: Prentice-Hall; Simon, H. A. (1976). *Administrative behavior: A study of decision-making processes in administrative organization.* New York: Free Press; Tompkins & Cheney.

[21] Media Awareness Network. (2009). *What is media literacy?* http://www.media-awareness.ca/English/teachers/media_literacy/what_is_media_literacy.cfm (retrieved January 5, 2010).

[22] Kellner, D., & Share, J. (2005). Toward critical media literacy: Core concepts, debates, organization, and policy. *Discourse: Studies in the Cultural Politics of Education, 26*(3), 369–386.

[23] Share, J. (2008). *Media literacy is elementary: Teaching youth to critically read and create media.* New York: Peter Lang Publishing.

[24] Kellner & Share.

[25] Conrad & Poole, 2002, p. 120.

[26] Tompkins & Cheney.

[27] Barker & Cheney, p. 21.

[28] Barker.

[29] Barker, p. 79.

[30] Vannoy, D. (Ed.). (2000). *Gender mosaics: Social perspectives.* Los Angeles: Roxbury, p. 6.

[31] Gramsci, A. (1971). *Selections from the prison notebooks of Antonio Gramsci.* Q. Hoare and G. N. Smith (Eds. & Trans.). New York: International Publishers, p. 12.

[32] Artz, L., & Murphy, B. O. (2000). *Cultural hegemony in the United States.* Thousand Oaks, CA: Sage, p. 3.

[33] Mumby, D. K. (1997). The problem of hegemony: Rereading Gramsci for organizational communication studies. *Western Journal of Communication, 61*(4), 343–375, p. 343.

[34] Deetz, p. 254.

[35] Mumby, 1997.

[36] Rosenblum, K. E., & Travis, T. (2003). *The meaning of difference: American constructions of race, sex and gender, social class, and sexual orientation.* New York: McGraw-Hill.

[37] Rosenblum & Travis.
[38] Terry, T. (1991). *Ideology: An introduction.* London: Verso; Mumby, 1997.
[39] Eisenberg, E., Goodall, H. L., Jr., & Trethewey, A. (2009). *Organizational communication: Balancing creativity and constraint* (6th ed.). New York: St. Martin's Press, p. 142.
[40] Macionis, J. (1999). *Sociology* (7th ed.). Upper Saddle River, NJ: Prentice-Hall, p. 244.
[41] Stark, R. (1994). *Sociology.* Belmont, CA: Wadsworth, p. 86.
[42] hooks, b. (1989). *Talking back: Thinking feminist, thinking black.* Boston, MA: South End Press.
[43] Vannoy, p. 2.
[44] Vannoy, p. 2.
[45] Brantlinger, E. (2001). Poverty, class, and disability: A historical, social and political perspective. *Focus on Exceptional Children, 33*(7), 1–24.
[46] Conrad & Poole, 1998, p. 18.
[47] Pearce, K. J. (2009). Media and mass communication theories. In Littlejohn & Foss (p. 625).
[48] Buzzanell, P. M. (1999). Tensions and burdens in employment interviewing processes: Perspectives of nondominant group applicants. *Business Communication, 36*(2), 134–162, p. 134.
[49] Orbe, M. P. (1998). *Constructing co-cultural theory: An explication of culture, power, and communication.* Thousand Oaks, CA: Sage.
[50] Ferguson, K. (1984). *The feminist case against bureaucracy.* Philadelphia: Temple University Press, p. 6.
[51] Mumby, D. K., & Clair, R. P. (1997). Organizational discourse. In T. A. van Dijk (Ed.), *Discourse studies: A multidisciplinary introduction* (pp. 181–205). London: Sage, p. 186.
[52] Lindsley, S. L. (1998). Communicating prejudice in organizations. In Hecht (pp. 187–205).
[53] Buzzanell.
[54] Jablin, F. M., cited in Miller, K. (2003). *Organizational communication: Approaches and processes* (3rd ed.). Belmont, CA: Wadsworth/Thomson, p. 146.
[55] Deetz, p. 28.
[56] Trethewey, A. (2000). Revisioning control: A feminist critique of disciplined bodies. In P. M. Buzzanell (Ed.), *Rethinking organizational & managerial communication from feminist perspectives* (pp. 107–127). Thousand Oaks, CA: Sage.
[57] Foucault, quoted in Foss, Foss, and Trapp, p. 354.
[58] Fowler-Hermes, J. (2001). The beauty and the beast in the workplace: Appearance-based discrimination claims under EEO laws. *Florida Bar Journal, 75*(4), 32–38.
[59] Fowler-Hermes.
[60] Mumby & Clair, p. 182.
[61] Deetz.

Chapter 3

[1] Lorber, J. (2009). Night to his day: The social construction of gender. In P. S. Rothenberg (Ed.), *Race, class, and gender in the United States* (8th ed., pp. 54–65). New York: Worth Publishers; West, C., & Fenstermaker, S. (1987). Doing difference. *Gender & Society, 9*(1), 8–37.
[2] Lorber, p. 54.
[3] A baby born with female and male biological characteristics is known as intersexed. Parents and health care providers often decide the child's sex, after which medical procedures and treatments are conducted to correct the condition. They treat the condition as an emergency situation, and they configure the child to the presumed natural sex. Some scholars believe that the dichotomy of female-male is an artificial one. They contend that sexual identity falls on a continuum. See: Carlton-Ford, S., & Houston, P. V. (2001). Children's experience of gender: Habitus and field. In D. Vannoy (Ed.), *Gender mosaics: Social perspectives* (pp. 65–74). Los Angeles: Roxbury.
[4] Rakow, L. F., & Wackwitz, L. A. (1998). Communication of sexism. In M. Hecht (Ed.), *Communicating prejudice* (pp. 99–111). Thousand Oaks, CA: Sage, p. 100.
[5] Rosenblum, K. E., & Travis, T. C. (Eds.). (2008). *The meaning of difference: American constructions of race, sex and gender, social class, and sexual orientation* (8th ed.). New York: McGraw-Hill.

[6] Rosenblum & Travis.
[7] Carlton-Ford & Houston, p. 73.
[8] Carlton-Ford & Houston, p. 68.
[9] Rosenblum & Travis.
[10] Rosenblum & Travis.
[11] Travis, C. (1996). The mismeasure of woman. In K. E. Rosenblum & T. C. Travis (Eds.), *The meaning of difference: American constructions of race, sex, and gender, social class, and sexual orientation.* (2nd ed., pp. 336–353). New York: McGraw-Hill.
[12] LeBon, G. Cited in Deaux, K., & Kite, M. E. (1987). Thinking about gender. In B. B. Hess & M. M. Feree (Eds.), *Analyzing gender: A handbook of social science research* (pp. 92–119). Newbury Park, CA: Sage, p. 93.
[13] Travis.
[14] Vannoy.
[15] Vannoy.
[16] Vannoy, p. 2.
[17] Vannoy, p. 4.
[18] Artz, L., & Murphy, B. O. (2000). *Cultural hegemony in the United States.* Thousand Oaks, CA: Sage.
[19] Nagy, A. R., & Rich, D. M. (2001). Constitutional law and public policy: Gender equity. In Vannoy (pp. 312–321).
[20] Godwin, S. E., & Risman, B. J. (2001). 20th-century changes in economics, work, and family. In Vannoy (pp. 134–144).
[21] Godwin & Risman.
[22] Artz & Murphy.
[23] Godwin & Risman, p. 137.
[24] Artz & Murphy.
[25] Godwin & Risman.
[26] Lips, H. (2007). *Sex and gender: An introduction* (6th ed.). New York: McGraw-Hill.
[27] Lorber.
[28] Wood, J. T. (2009). *Gendered lives: Communication, gender, and culture* (8th ed). Boston, MA: Wadsworth.
[29] Artz & Murphy; Whitaker, S. (2001). Gender politics in men's movements. In Vannoy (pp. 343–351).
[30] Wood.
[31] Barrett, F. J. (2001). Organizational construction of hegemonic masculinity: The case of the US Navy. In S. M. Whitehead & F. J. Barrett (Eds.), *The masculinities reader* (pp. 77–99). Malden, MA: Blackwell.
[32] Ferber, A. L. (2000). Racial warriors and weekend warriors. The construction of masculinity in mythopoetic and white supremacist discourse. *Men and Masculinities, 3*(1), 30–56.
[33] Wood, p. 104.
[34] Whitehead, S. M., & Barrett, F. J. (2001). The sociology of masculinity. In Whitehead & Barrett (pp. 1–26).
[35] Chua, P., & Fujino, D. C. (1999). Negotiating new Asian-American masculinities: Attitudes and gender expectations. *Journal of Men's Studies, 7*(3), 391–413, p. 408.
[36] Robins, G. (2010). A social network analysis of hegemonic and other masculinities. *Journal of Men's Studies, 18*(1), 22–44; Connell, R. W., & Messerschmidt, J. W. (2005). Hegemonic masculinity: Rethinking the concept. *Gender & Society, 19,* 829–859.
[37] Barrett, p. 79.
[38] Anderson, E. (2009). *Inclusive masculinity: The changing nature of masculinities.* New York: Routledge.
[39] Chesebro, J. W., & Fuse, K. (2001). The development of a perceived masculinity scale. *Communication Quarterly, 49,* 203–278.
[40] Kimmel, M. (1996). *Manhood in America: A cultural history.* New York: Free Press, pp. 124–125.
[41] Artz & Murphy, p. 163.
[42] Bureau of Labor Statistics. (2005) *Occupational Outlook Quarterly.* http://www.bls.gov/opub/ooq/2005/winter/art05.pdf (retrieved March 25, 2010).

[43] Bellas, M. L. (2001). The gendered nature of emotional labor in the workplace. In Vannoy (pp. 269–278).
[44] Lorber, J. (2001). Gender hierarchies in the health professions. In Vannoy (pp. 436–448).
[45] Barrett.
[46] Montecinos, C., & Nielsen, L. (1997). Gender and cohort differences in university students' decisions to become elementary teacher education majors. *Journal of Teacher Education, 48*(1), 47–55.
[47] Bose, C. E., & Whaley, R. B. (2001). Sex segregation in the U.S. labor force. In Vannoy (pp. 228–239).
[48] Bose & Whaley.
[49] U.S. Census Bureau. (2000). Money income in the United States: 1999. Current population reports. Series P60-209. Washington, DC: U.S. Government Printing Office.
[50] National Committee on Pay Equity. http://www.pay-equity.org/info-time.html (retrieved January 6, 2010).
[51] Bureau of Labor Statistics. News release. Friday October 16, 2009. USDL-09-1242.
[52] National Committee on Pay Equity.
[53] Reuther, C., & Fairhurst, G. T. (2000). Chaos theory and the glass ceiling. In P. Buzzanell (Ed.), *Rethinking organizational & managerial communication from feminist perspectives* (pp. 236–253). Thousand Oaks, CA: Sage.
[54] Duckworth, J. D., & Buzzanell, P. M. (2009). Constructing work-life balance and fatherhood: Men's framing of the meanings of *both* work and family. *Communication Studies, 60*(5), 558–573, p. 560.
[55] Duckworth & Buzzanell, p. 560.
[56] Flax, J. (1990). *Thinking fragments: Psychoanalysis, feminism, and postmodernism in the contemporary west.* Berkeley: University of California Press.
[57] Wood.
[58] Spade, J. Z. (2001). Gender and education in the United States. In Vannoy (pp. 85–93).
[59] Carlton-Ford & Houston.
[60] Spade.
[61] Spade.
[62] Polka, W., Litchka, P., & Davis, S. W. (2008). Female superintendents and the professional victim syndrome: Preparing current and aspiring superintendents to cope and succeed. *Journal of Women in Educational Leadership, 6*(4), 293–311.
[63] Institute of Education Sciences National Center for Education Statistics. Full-time instructional faculty in degree-granting institutions. *Digest of Education Statistics.* U.S. Department of Education. http://nces.ed.gov/programs/digest/d08/tables/dt08_249.asp (retrieved March 7, 2010).
[64] Artz & Murphy.
[65] Spade.
[66] The few, the beloved, the male elementary teachers. (August 21, 2008). *Missourian.* http://www.columbiamissourian.com/stories/2008/08/21/few-beloved-male-elementary-teachers/ (retrieved January 6, 2010).
[67] Riordan, C., Faddis, B. J., Beam, M., Seager, A., Tanney, A., DiBiase, R., Ruffin, M., & Valentine, J. (2008). Early implementation of public single-sex schools: Perceptions and characteristics. U.S. Department of Education. http://www.eric.ed.gov/ERICWebPortal/contentdelivery/servlet/ERICServlet?accno=ED504174 (retrieved March 5, 2010).
[68] Riordan et al.
[69] Cameron, D. (1998). Gender, language, and discourse: A review essay. *Signs, 23*(4), 945–975.
[70] Ivy, D. K., & Backlund, P. (1994). *Exploring genderspeak: Personal effectiveness in gender communication.* New York: McGraw-Hill, p. 73.
[71] Ivy & Backlund, p. 73.
[72] Jones, S., Johnson-Yale, C., Millermaier, S., & Perez, F. S. (2009). U.S. college students' internet use: Race, gender and digital divides. *Journal of Computer-Mediated Communication, 14,* 244–264.

[73] Hargittai, E., & Walejko, G. (2008). The participation divide: Content creation and sharing in the digital age. *Information, Communication & Society, 11*(2), 239–256.
[74] O'Barr, W. M. (2001). Language and patriarchy. In Vannoy (pp. 106–113).
[75] O'Barr.
[76] O'Barr.
[77] Ivy & Backlund, p. 152.
[78] Tannen, D. (2001). *You just don't understand: Women and men in conversation.* New York: Quill.
[79] Tannen.
[80] See, for example, Gray, J. (1993). *Men are from Mars, women are from Venus.* New York: HarperCollins.
[81] Conrad, C., & Poole, M. S. (2002). *Strategic organizational communication: In a global economy* (5th ed). Orlando, FL: Harcourt.
[82] Rakow & Wackwitz.
[83] Rakow & Wackwitz.
[84] Canary, D. J., & Hause K. S. (1993). Is there any reason to research sex differences in communication? *Communication Quarterly, 41*(2), 129–144.
[85] Canary & Hause, p. 140.
[86] Goldsmith, D. J. & Fulfs, P. A. (2010). "You just don't have the evidence": An analysis of claims and evidence in Deborah Tannen's *You just don't understand.* In M. E. Roloff (Ed.), *Communication yearbook 22* (pp. 1–49). New York: Routledge.
[87] See, for example, Ashcraft, K. L., & Mumby, D. K. (2004). *Reworking gender: A feminist communicology of organization.* Thousand Oaks, CA: Sage.
[88] Cameron, D. (2008). *The myth of Mars and Venus: Do men and women really speak different languages?* Cary, NC: Oxford University Press.
[89] Ashcraft & Mumby, p. 11.
[90] Buzzanell, P. (1995). Reframing the glass ceiling as a socially constructed process: Implications for understanding and change. *Communication Monographs, 62*(4), 327–354, p. 327.
[91] Ashcraft, K. L., & Pacanowsky, M. E. (1996). "A woman's worst enemy": Reflections on a narrative of organizational life and female identity. *Journal of Applied Communication Research, 24,* 217–239, p. 219.
[92] Acker, J. (1990). Hierarchies, jobs, bodies: A theory of gendered organizations. *Gender and Society, 4*(2), 139–158.
[93] Corsun, D. L., & Costen, W. M. (2001). Is the glass ceiling unbreakable? Habitus, fields, and the stalling of women and minorities in management. *Journal of Management Inquiry, 10*(1), 16–25.
[94] Wood; Allen, B. J. (2001). Gender, race, and communication in professional environments. In L. P. Arliss & D. Borisoff (Eds.), *Women and men communicating: Challenges and changes* (pp. 212–231). Long Grove, IL: Waveland Press.
[95] Ashcraft, K. L., & Allen, B. J. (2003). The racial foundation of organizational communication. *Communication Theory, 13,* 5–38, p. 27.
[96] Cheney, G., & Ashcraft, K. L. (2007). Considering "The Professional" in communication studies: Implications for theory and research within and beyond the boundaries of organizational communication. *Communication Theory, 17,* 146–175.
[97] Trethewey, A. (2000). A feminist critique of disciplined bodies. In Buzzanell, *Rethinking* (pp. 107–127).
[98] Pompper, D. (2007). The gender-ethnicity construct in public relations organizations: Using feminist standpoint theory to discover Latinas' realities. *Howard Journal of Communications, 18*(4), 291–311.
[99] Pompper, p. 299.
[100] Pompper, p. 299.
[101] Trethewey.
[102] Buzzanell, P. (2002). Employment interviewing research: Ways we can study underrepresented group members' experiences as applicants. *The Journal of Business Communication, 39*(2), 257–276.

103 Abel, K. Dads and paternity leave. *Family Education*. http://life.familyeducation.com/working-parents/fathers-day/36483.html (retrieved March 5, 2010).
104 Abel.
105 Nepomnyaschy, L., & Waldfogel, J. (2007). Paternity leave and fathers' involvements with their young children. *Community, Work & Family, 10*(4), 427–453.
106 Abel.
107 Hochschild, A. R. (2008). One thing I know. Feeling around the world. *Contexts.* http://contexts.org/articles/spring-2008/feeling-around-the-world/ (retrieved March 5, 2010).
108 Tracy, S. (2000). Becoming a character for commerce: Emotion labor, self-subordination, and discursive construction of identity in a total institution. *Management Communication Quarterly, 14*(1), 90–128, p. 91.
109 Miller, K. I., & Koesten, J. (2008). Financial feeling: An investigation of emotion and communication in the workplace. *Journal of Applied Communication Research, 36*(1), 8–32, p. 9.
110 Tracy.
111 See, for example, Meier, K. J., Mastracci, S. H., & Wilson, K. (2006). Gender and emotional labor in public organizations: An empirical examination of the link to performance. *Public Administration Review, 66*(6), 899–909.
112 Tracy.
113 Algoe, S. B., Buswell, B. N., & DeLamater, J. D. (2000). Gender and job status as contextual cues for the interpretation of facial expression of emotion. *Sex Roles, 42*(3–4), 183–208; Plant, E. A., Hyde, J. S., Keltner, D., & Devine, P. G. (2000) The gender stereotyping of emotions. *Psychology of Women Quarterly, 24*(1), 81–92.
114 Bellas, M. (2000). In Vannoy (pp. 269–278).
115 Bellas.
116 Tracy.
117 Tracy; Miller & Koesten.
118 Valentine, D. (2007). *Imagining transgender: An ethnography of a category.* Durham, NC: Duke University Press; Dunson, M., III. (2001). Sex, gender, and transgender: The present and future of employment discrimination law. *Berkeley Journal of Employment and Labor Law, 22*(2), 465–505.
119 Dunson.
120 Blair, Jennifer, personal correspondence.
121 American Civil Liberties Union. (2009). Know your rights. Transgender people and the law. http://www.aclu.org/hiv-aids_lgbt-rights/know-your-rights-transgender-people-and-law (retrieved March 5, 2010).
122 Transgender Law and Policy Institute. http://www.transgenderlaw.org (retrieved January 6, 2010).

Chapter 4

1 Omi, M., & Winant, H. (1994). *Racial formation in the United States: From the 1960s to the 1980s.* New York: Routledge & Kegan Paul.
2 Byerly, C. M., & Wilson, C. C. II. (2009). Journalism as Kerner turns 40: Its multicultural problems and possibilities. *The Howard Journal of Communications, 20*(3), 209–221; Dixon, T. H., & Linz, D. (2000). Overrepresentation and underrepresentation of African Americans and Latinos as lawbreakers on television news. *Journal of Communication, 50*(2), 131–154.
3 Omi & Winant, p. 3.
4 Rosenblum, K. E., & Travis, T. C. (Eds.). (2008). *The meaning of difference: American constructions of race, sex and gender, social class, and sexual orientation* (8th ed.). New York: McGraw-Hill.
5 Orbe, M. P., & Harris, T. M. (2007). *Interracial communication: Theory into practice* (2nd ed.). Thousand Oaks, CA: Sage.
6 Rosenblum & Travis, p. 18.
7 Omi & Winant, p. 13.
8 Omi & Winant, p. 138.

9 Holt, T. (2000). *The problem of race in the twenty-first century.* Cambridge, MA: Harvard University Press, p. 1.
10 Orbe & Harris, p. 38.
11 Omi & Winant, p. 60.
12 Stanfield, J. H. II, & Dennis, R. M. (1993). *Race and ethnicity in research methods.* Newbury Park, CA: Sage, p. 15.
13 The Center for Individual Rights. (2009). Ending racial double standards cases. http://www.usa.org/michican.htm (retrieved January 8, 2010).
14 Burnham, L. (2008). "A Black Scholar readers' forum on President Obama": Obama's candidacy: The advent of post-racial America and the end of black politics? *Black Scholar, 38*(4), 43–46.
15 Allen, B. J. (2009). Racial harassment in the workplace. In P. Lutgen-Sandvik & B. Davenport Sypher (Eds.), *The destructive side of organizational communication: Processes, consequences and constructive ways of organizing* (pp. 164–183). London and New York: Routledge.
16 U.S. Equal Employment Opportunity Commission. (February 28, 2007). *EEOC takes new approach to fighting racism and colorism in the 21st century workplace.* http://www.eeoc.gov/eeoc/newsroom/release/archive/2-28-07.html (retrieved January 8, 2010).
17 EEOC Charge statistics FY 1997 to FY 2009. http://www.eeoc.gov/eeoc/statistics/enforcement/charges.cfm (retrieved March 27, 2010).
18 Allen.
19 Kotkin, J. (2010). America in 2050: Strength in diversity. http://www.newgeography.com/content/001466-america-2050-strength-diversity (retrieved March 27, 2010).
20 Jones, J. (2005). Most Americans approve of interracial dating. http://www.gallup.com/poll/19033/most-americans-approve-interracial-dating.aspx (retrieved March 27, 2010).
21 Barker, V., & Giles, H. (2002). Who supports the English-only movement? Evidence for misconceptions about Latino group vitality. *Journal of Multilingual & Multicultural Development, 23*(5), 353–370, p. 353.
22 U.S. Census Bureau. (2008). Poverty 2008 Highlights. http://www.census.gov/hhes/www/poverty/poverty08/pov08hi.html (retrieved March 27, 2010).
23 Alfano, S. (2006). Report: Race gap in U.S. persists. CBS News. http://www.cbsnews.com/stories/2006/11/14/national/main2179601.shtml (retrieved March 27, 2010).
24 Moran, R. F. (2006). Whatever happened to racism? *St. John's Law Review, 79,* 899–927, p. 900.
25 Omi & Winant; Orbe & Harris.
26 Omi & Winant.
27 Omi & Winant.
28 Pulera, D. (2002). *Visible differences: Why race will matter to Americans in the twenty-first century.* New York: Continuum International.
29 Blumenbach, J. F. (1865). *The anthropological treatises of Johann Friedrich Blumenbach.* London: Published for the Anthropological Society by Longman, Green, Roberts, & Green, p. 264.
30 Omi & Winant, p. 64.
31 Orbe & Harris.
32 U.S. Census Bureau. (2002). *100 years ago the U.S. census reflected simpler times.* http://www.census.gov/dmd/www/dropin14.htm (retrieved January 8, 2010).
33 U.S. Census Bureau. www.census.gov; see also: Office of Management and Budget. (October 30, 1997). Revisions to the Standards for the Classification of Federal Data on Race and Ethnicity. www.whitehouse.gov/omb/fedreg_1997standards/?print=1 (retrieved January 11, 2010).
34 Pulera.
35 Census 2010. http://www.civilrights.org/census/ (retrieved January 11, 2010).
36 Census 2010.
37 Artz, L., & Murphy. B. O. (2000). *Cultural hegemony in the United States.* Thousand Oaks, CA: Sage.
38 Rosenblum & Travis.
39 Artz & Murphy.
40 Rosenblum & Travis.
41 Woo, D. (2000). *Glass ceilings and Asian Americans: The new face of workplace barriers.* Walnut Creek, CA: Altamira Press.

[42] Pulera.

[43] Stanfield & Dennis.

[44] Cerbone, D. (1997). Symbol of privilege, object of derision: Dissonance and contradictions. In B. Greene (Ed.), *Ethnic and cultural diversity among lesbians and gay men* (pp. 117–131). Thousand Oaks, CA: Sage.

[45] Streitmatter, R. (1999). The Nativist press: Demonizing the American immigrant. *Journalism & Mass Communication Quarterly, 76*(4), 673–683.

[46] Artz & Murphy.

[47] Styron, E. H. (2003). Native American education: Documents from the 19th century. http://www.duke.edu/%7Eehs1/education/ (retrieved December 16, 2003).

[48] Styron.

[49] Chamberlain, S. P. (2005). Recognizing and responding to cultural differences in the education of culturally and linguistically diverse learners. *Intervention in School & Clinic, 40*(4), 195–211, p. 197.

[50] Managing diversity at Duke: A toolkit for managers. http://www.duke.edu/web/equity/cultural_competency.pdf (retrieved January 12, 2010).

[51] Mercedes, M., & Vaughn, B. (2007). *Strategic Diversity & Inclusion Management Magazine.* San Francisco: DTUI, pp. 31–36.

[52] Cashmore, E. (2003). *Encyclopedia of race and ethnic studies.* New York: Routledge, p. 352.

[53] Pulera.

[54] Winant, H. (2005). Race and racism: Overview. In M. Horowitz (Ed.), *New dictionary of the history of ideas* (pp. 1987–1989). Detroit: Charles Scribner's Sons, p. 1988.

[55] Head, T. (2007). Institutional racism. http://civilliberty.about.com/od/raceequalopportunity/g/inst_racism.htm (retrieved January 12, 2010).

[56] Deitch, E. A., Barsky, A., Butz, R. M., Chan, S., Brief, A. P., & Bradley, J. C. (2003). Subtle yet significant: The existence and impact of everyday racial discrimination in the workplace. *Human Relations, 56*(11), 1299–1324, p. 1317.

[57] Project Implicit. Implicit Association Test. http://implicit.harvard.edu/implicit/research (retrieved January 12, 2010).

[58] Gladwell, M. (2005). *Blink: The power of thinking without thinking.* New York: Little, Brown, p. 85.

[59] Pulera, p. 110.

[60] Bates, T. (1998). Is the U.S. small business administration a racist institution? *The Review of Black Political Economy, 26*(1), 89.

[61] American Anthropological Association Statement on Race. (May 17, 1998). www.aaanet.org/stmts/racepp.htm (retrieved January 12, 2010).

[62] "Begun formally in 1990, the U.S. Human Genome Project was a 13-year effort coordinated by the U.S. Department of Energy and the National Institutes of Health. The project originally was planned to last years, but rapid technological advances accelerated the completion date to 2003. Project goals were to

- *identify* all the approximately 20,000–25,000 genes in human DNA,
- *determine* the sequences of the 3 billion chemical base pairs that make up human DNA,
- *store* this information in databases,
- *improve* tools for data analysis,
- *transfer* related technologies to the private sector, and
- *address* the ethical, legal, and social issues (ELSI) that may arise from the project. http://www.ornl.gov/sci/techresources/Human_Genome/project/about.shtml (retrieved January 12, 2010).

[63] Omi & Winant, p. 15.

[64] Omi & Winant, p. 55.

[65] Takaki R. T. (2008) *A different mirror: A history of multicultural America* (revised ed.). Boston: Back Bay Books/Little, Brown.

[66] Takaki.

[67] Omi & Winant.

68 Wander, P. C., Martin, J. N., & Nakayama, T. K. (1999). Whiteness and beyond: Sociohistorical foundations of whiteness and contemporary challenges. In T. K. Nakayama & J. N. Martin (Eds.), *Whiteness: The communication of social identity* (pp. 13–26). Thousand Oaks, CA: Sage.

69 Takaki.

70 Schugurensky, D. (July 7, 2002). Selected moments of the 20th century. http://fcis.oise.utoronto.ca/~daniel_schugurensky/assignment1/1978unger.html (retrieved January 12, 2010).

71 Woo.

72 Holtzman, L. (2000). *Media messages: What film, television, and popular music teach us about race class, gender, and sexual orientation.* Armonk, NY: M. E. Sharpe.

73 Harwood, J., & Anderson, K. (2002). The presence and portrayal of social groups on prime-time television. *Communication Reports, 15*(2), 81–98, p. 82.

74 Stanfield & Dennis, p. 17.

75 Mastro, D. E., & Greenberg, B. S. (2001). The portrayal of racial minorities on prime time television. *Communication Abstracts, 24*(4), 443–588; Harwood & Anderson.

76 Harwood & Anderson.

77 Mastro, D. E., Behm-Morawitz, E., & Kopacz, M. A. (2008). Exposure to television portrayals of Latinos: The implications of aversive racism and social identity theory. *Human Communication Research, 34*(1), 1–27.

78 Holtzman; Orbe & Harris.

79 Dixon, T. L., Azocar, C. L., & Casas, M. (2003). The portrayal of race and crime on television network news. *Journal of Broadcasting & Electronic Media, 47,* 498–523.

80 Owens, L. C. (2008). Network news: The role of race in source selection and story topic. *The Howard Journal of Communications, 19,* 355–370.

81 Smith-Shomade, B. E. (2008). *Pimpin' ain't easy: Selling Black Entertainment Television.* New York: Routledge.

82 MacNeil, R., & Cran, W. (2005). *Do you speak American? A companion to the PBS television series.* New York: Nan A. Talese/Doubleday

83 Cargile, A. C., & Giles, H. (1998). Language attitudes toward varieties of English: An American-Japanese context. *Journal of Applied Communication Research, 26*(3), 338–356.

84 Hotelier to Hispanic workers: Change names. (October 26, 2009). http://www.msnbc.msn.com/id/33479833/ns/us_news_race_and_ethnicity/ (retrieved January 12, 2010).

85 Perez, D. J., & Fortuna, L. (2008). Prevalence and correlates of everyday discrimination among U.S. Latinos. *Journal of Community Psychology, 36*(4), 421–433.

86 Perez & Fortuna, p. 430.

87 Orbe, M. P. (1998). *Constructing co-cultural theory: An explication of culture, power, and communication.* Thousand Oaks, CA: Sage

88 Orbe, p. 72.

89 Asian American and Pacific Islander work group report to the chair of the Equal Employment Opportunity Commission. (December 21, 2008). http://www.eeoc.gov.federal/reports/aapi.html (retrieved January 12, 2010).

90 Hyun, J. (2005). *Breaking the bamboo ceiling: Career strategies for Asians.* New York: HarperBusiness.

91 Galanti, G. (2008). *Caring for patients from different cultures,* (4th ed.). Philadelphia: University of Pennsylvania Press.

92 Covarrubias, P. O. (2008). Masked silence sequences: Hearing discrimination in the college classroom. *Communication, Culture & Critique, 1,* 227–252, p. 246.

93 Covarrubias, p. 247.

94 Sykes, B., & Brown, C. D. (1997). The implications of labeling white men: A diversity manager's perspective. In C. D. Brown, C. Snedeker, & B. Sykes (Eds.), *Conflict and diversity* (pp. 243–250). Cresskill, NJ: Hampton Press

95 Thomas, D., & Ely, R. J. (2001). Cultural diversity at work: The effects of diversity perspectives on work group processes and outcomes. *Administrative Science Quarterly, 46*(2), 229–273.

96 Martin, J. N., Krizek, R. G., Nakayama, T. L., & Bradford, L. (1999). What do white people want to be called? A study of self-labels for white Americans. In Nakayama & Martin (pp. 27–50), p. 28.

[97] Martin et al.; see also: Omi, M. (2001). The changing meaning of race. In N. J. Smelser, W. J. Wilson, & F. Mitchell (Eds.), *America becoming: Racial trends and their consequences*, vol. 1 (pp. 243–263). Washington, DC: National Academic Press.

[98] Rothenberg, P. (2007), *White privilege* (2nd ed.). New York: Worth Publishers, p. 1.

[99] McIntosh, P. (2003). White privilege and male privilege: A personal account of coming to see correspondence through work in women's studies. In M. S. Kimmel & A. L. Ferber (Eds.), *Privilege: A reader* (pp. 147–160). Boulder, CO: Westview, p. 154.

[100] McIntosh, pp. 150–152.

[101] Mouw, T. (2002). Are black workers missing the connection? The effect of spatial distance and employee referrals on interfirm racial segregation. *Demography, 39*(3), 507–528.

[102] Kmec. J. A. (2007). Ties that bind? Race and networks in job turnover. *Social Problems, 54*(4), 483–503.

[103] Young, I. P., & Fox, J. A. (2002). Asian, Hispanic, and Native American job candidates: Prescreened or screened within the selection process. *Educational Administration Quarterly, 38*(4), 530–554.

[104] Bussey, J., & Trasvina, J. (2003). Racial preferences: The treatment of white and African American job applicants by temporary job agencies in California. http://www.impactfund.org (retrieved August 17, 2007).

[105] Li, J., & Karakowsky, L. (2001). Do we see eye-to-eye? Implications of cultural differences for cross-cultural management research and practice. *The Journal of Psychology, 135*(5), 501–518.

[106] U.S. Dept. of Labor (1995). Good for business: Making full use of the nation's human capital. The environmental scan. A fact-finding report of the Federal Glass Ceiling Commission. http://www.dol.gov/oasam/programs/history/reich/reports/ceiling.pdf (retrieved April 5, 2010).

[107] Editors of DiversityInc (2010). 2010 DiversityInc Top 50 Companies for Diversity. http://www.diversityinc.com/article/7313/ (retrieved April 7, 2010).

[108] Essandoh, V. G. (2008). Why law firm affinity groups are a valuable resource. *The National Law Journal*. http://www.law.com/jsp/nlj/PubArticleNLJ.jsp?id=1202425493943&hbxlogin=1 (retrieved April 7, 2010).

[109] Editors of DiversityInc.

Chapter 5

[1] Moon, D. G., & Rolison, G. L. (1998). Communication of classism. In M. L. Hecht (Ed.), *Communicating prejudice* (pp. 122–135). Thousand Oaks, CA: Sage.

[2] Holtzman, L. (2000). *Media messages: What film, television, and popular music teach us about race, class, gender, and sexual orientation*. Armonk, NY: M. E. Sharpe.

[3] Holtzman, p. 99.

[4] Stark, R. (2001). *Sociology*. Belmont, CA: Wadsworth.

[5] Ellis, D. G. (1999). *Crafting society: Ethnicity, class, and communication theory*. Mahwah, NJ: Lawrence Erlbaum, p. 176.

[6] Artz, L., & Murphy, B. O. (2000). *Cultural hegemony in the United States*. Thousand Oaks, CA: Sage.

[7] Weber's original categories are class, status, and party. However, according to Stark, most social scientists use the synonymous three Ps to avoid confusion regarding distinctions between Weber's terms.

[8] Weber, M. (1947). *The theory of social and economic organizations*. (T. Parsons, Ed., A. M. Henderson & T. Parsons, Trans.). New York: The Free Press.

[9] Artz & Murphy.

[10] Bourdieu, P. (1987). What makes a social class? On the theoretical and practical existence of groups. *Berkeley Journal of Sociology, 22*, 1–18. Bourdieu also cited *symbolic capitol*, "the form the different types of capital take once they are perceived and recognized as legitimate," p. 4.

[11] Eakin, E. (2001, January 6). The intellectual class struggle. *New York Times*, p. A15.

[12] Dworkin, A. G., & Dworkin, R. J. (Eds.). (1999). *The minority report: An introduction to racial, ethnic, and gender relations* (3rd ed.). Fort Worth: Harcourt Brace.

[13] Ellis, p. 195.
[14] Holtzman.
[15] Holtzman.
[16] Rosner, B., & Campbell, S. How to build a career network. http://www.payscale.com/how-to-build-a-career-network-recession (retrieved January 14, 2010).
[17] Rosner, B., & Campbell, S. How to make social networking work for you—4 tips. http://www.payscale.com/social-networking-tips (retrieved January 14, 2010).
[18] Bolles, R. (2009). What color is your parachute 2009: A practical manual for job-hunters and career-changers. Berkeley, CA: Ten Speed Press.
[19] Domhoff, W. G. (September 2005, updated October 2009). Wealth, income and power. http://sociology.ucsc.edu/whorulesamerica/power/wealth.htm (retrieved January 15, 2010). See also, Gilbert, D. (2008). *The American class structure in an age of growing inequality* (7th ed.). Thousand Oaks, CA: Pine Forge Press.
[20] Henry, P. (2001). An examination of the pathways through which social class impacts health outcomes. *Academy of Marketing Science Review,* vol. 2001, no. 3, p. 1. http://www.amsreview.org/articles/henry03-2001.pdf (retrieved January 14, 2010).
[21] Reay, D. (1996). Dealing with difficult differences: Reflexivity and social class in feminist research. *Feminism & Psychology, 6*(3), 443–456, p. 450.
[22] Levine, R. F. (Ed.). (2006). *Social class and stratification: Classic statements and theoretical debates* (2nd ed, p. 70). Lanham, MD: Rowman & Littlefield.
[23] Holtzman.
[24] Henry.
[25] Spade, J. Z. (2001). Gender and education in the United States. In D. Vannoy (Ed.), *Gender mosaics: Social perspectives* (pp. 85–93). Los Angeles: Roxbury, p. 89.
[26] Brantlinger, E. (2001). Poverty, class, and disability: A historical, social and political perspective. *Focus on Exceptional Children, 33*(7), 1–19.
[27] Magnus, S. A., & Mick, S. S. (2000). Medical schools, affirmative action, and the neglected role of social class. *American Journal of Public Health, 90*(8), 1197–1202.
[28] Henry.
[29] Markson, E. W., & Hollis-Sawyer, L. A. (Eds.). (2000). *Intersections of aging.* Los Angeles: Roxbury.
[30] Borrego, S. E. (2008). Class on campus: Breaking the silence surrounding socioeconomics. *Diversity & Democracy, 11*(3). Association of American Colleges and Universities, p. 2.
[31] Lott, B., & Bullock, H. E. (2001). Who are the poor? *Journal of Social Issues, 57*(2), 189–206.
[32] U.S. Department of Health and Human Services. Estimated state median income, by family size and by state for FY 2009. http://www.acf.hhs.gov/programs/ocs/liheap/guidance/SMI75FY09.pdf (retrieved January 14, 2010).
[33] Catholic Campaign for Human Development. Poverty U.S.A.: The state of poverty in America. http://www.usccb.org/cchd/povback/povfacts.htm (retrieved January 14, 2010).
[34] Catholic Campaign for Human Development. Poverty U.S.A.: The working poor. http://www.usccb.org/cchd/povback/povfact3.htm (retrieved January 14, 2010).
[35] Corporate Ethics International. Issue: CEO pay. http://businessethicsnetwork.org/section.php?id=275 (retrieved January 14, 2010).
[36] Ellis.
[37] Artz & Murphy.
[38] Lott & Bullock.
[39] Holtzman, p. 112.
[40] Holtzman.
[41] Artz & Murphy.
[42] Holtzman, p. 112
[43] Artz & Murphy.
[44] Artz & Murphy.
[45] Morgen, S., & Maskovsky, J. (2003). The Anthropology of welfare "reform": New perspectives on U.S. urban poverty in the post-welfare era. *Annual Review of Anthropology, 32,* 315–338.
[46] Sammon, P. J. (2000). The living wage movement. *America, 183*(5), 16.

[47] See: I Have A Dream Foundation. http://www.ihaveadreamfoundation.org/html/.

[48] U.S. Department of Education. Gaining early awareness and readiness for undergraduate programs (GEAR UP). http://www.ed.gov/programs/gearup/funding.html (retrieved January 14, 2010).

[49] Holtzman, p. 98. Some of these perspectives have been critiqued as racist (e.g., the Moynihan report claimed that the matriarchal structure of the black family contributed to black poverty).

[50] hooks, b. (2000). *Where we stand: Class matters.* New York: Routledge, p. 5.

[51] *Merriam-Webster's Collegiate Dictionary.* http://www.merriam-webster.com/dictionary/american%20dream (retrieved February 4, 2010).

[52] Allen, R. L., & Kuo, C. (1991). Communication and beliefs about racial equality. *Discourse & Society, 2*(3), 259–279, p. 263.

[53] Brantlinger, E. (2001). Poverty, class, and disability: A historical, social and political perspective. *Focus on Exceptional Children, 33*(7), 1–24.

[54] Ehrenreich, B. (2008). *Nickel and dimed: On (not) getting by in America.* New York: Henry Holt, p. 220.

[55] Holtzman, p. 107.

[56] Holtzman.

[57] Stark, R. (1996). *Sociology* (6th ed.). Belmont, CA: Wadsworth, p. 301.

[58] Artz & Murphy.

[59] Clawson, D., & Clawson, M. (1999). What has happened to the U.S. labor movement? Union decline and renewal. *Annual Review of Sociology, Annual 25,* 95–119.

[60] Artz & Murphy.

[61] Sorokin, E., & Wetstein, C. (May 6, 2002). Activists lobby for Chavez holiday (California Journal: News from thee golden state). *Insight on the News, 18*(16), p. 31.

[62] Ellis, p. 185.

[63] Ellis, p. 190.

[64] Magnus & Mick.

[65] Dworkin & Dworkin.

[66] Cunningham, B. (May 1, 2004). Across the great divide class. *Columbia Journalism Review,* 31–38.

[67] Cunningham, p. 32.

[68] Cunningham, p. 34.

[69] Cunningham, p. 32.

[70] *New York Times.* (2005). http://www.nytimes.com/pages/national/class/ (retrieved January 15, 2010).

[71] Cunningham, p. 35.

[72] Clawson, R. A. & Trice, R. (2000). Poverty as we know it. (media portrayals of the poor). *Public Opinion Quarterly, 64*(1), 53–64, p. 53.

[73] Haberman, M. (1991). The pedagogy of poverty versus good teaching. *Phi Delta Kappan, 73*(4), 290–294.

[74] Dworkin & Dworkin.

[75] Lott, B. (2001). Low-income parents and the public schools. *Journal of Social Issues, 57*(2), 247–259, p. 249.

[76] Lott.

[77] Soto, R. (2008). Race and class: Taking action at the intersections. *Diversity & Democracy, 11*(3). Association of American Colleges and Universities, p. 13.

[78] Aronson, P. (2008). Breaking barriers or locked out? Class-based perceptions and experiences of postsecondary education In J. T. Mortimer (Ed.), *Social class and transitions to adulthood. New directions for child and adolescent development*, Vol. 119, 41–54, p. 42.

[79] Soto.

[80] Baldry, C. (1999). Space—The final frontier. (Critical Essay). *Sociology, 33*(3), 535–553, p. 539.

[81] Catanzarite, L. (2000). Brown-collar jobs: Occupational segregation and earnings of recent-immigrant Latinos. *Sociological Perspectives, 43*(1), 45–76.

[82] Joseph, N., & Alex, N. (1972). The uniform: A sociological perspective. *American Journal of Sociology, 77*(4), 719–730.

[83] Joseph & Alex, p. 720.
[84] Joseph & Alex, p. 722.
[85] Boo, K. Excerpt from Pride, prejudice and the not-so-subtle politics of the working class, originally published in *The Washington Post*, March 14, 1993. www.pbs.org/peoplelikeus/resources/essays1/index.html (retrieved January 14, 2010).
[86] Gorman, T. J. (2000). Cross-class perceptions of social class. *Sociological Spectrum, 20*, 93–120, p. 107.
[87] Boo.

Chapter 6

[1] Hearn, J., & Parkin, W. (1995). *Sex at work: The power and paradox of organisation sexuality.* New York: St. Martin's Press, p. 176.
[2] Kinsey, A. C. et al. (1999). The heterosexual-homosexual balance. In R. A. Nye (Ed.), *Sexuality* (pp. 345–347). New York: Oxford University Press.
[3] Davidson, J. K., Sr., & Moore, N. B. (Eds.). (2001). *Speaking of sexuality.* Los Angeles: Roxbury.
[4] Crooks, R., & Baur, K. (2008). *Our sexuality* (10th ed.). Belmont, CA: Thomson Learning, p. 257.
[5] Manisses Communications Group. (2003). Anti-gay bullying widespread among teens. *Mental Health Weekly, 13*(4), 6.
[6] Girl Scouts and discrimination. http://www.bas-discrimination.org/html/gsusa.html (retrieved January 18, 2010).
[7] Crooks & Baur, p. 337.
[8] Nye, R. A. (Ed.). (1999). *Sexuality.* New York: Oxford University Press, p. 15.
[9] Katz, J. N. (1995). *The invention of heterosexuality.* New York: Dutton.
[10] History Channel (2000). The history of sex [videorecording]/the History Channel; Arts and Entertainment Network. [South Burlington, VT]: A&E Home Video: History Channel; New York, NY: Distributed by New Video Group. Produced by MPH Entertainment, Inc. Originally broadcast as a television series in 1999.
[11] History Channel.
[12] Nagel, J. (2000). Ethnicity and sexuality. *Annual Review of Sociology, 26*, 107–133.
[13] Davidson & Moore.
[14] Rosario, V. A. (2002). *Homosexuality and science.* Santa Barbara, CA: ABC-CLIO.
[15] Katz.
[16] Nye.
[17] Koch, P. B. (2001). Sexual knowledge and education. In Davidson & Moore (Eds.) (pp. 378–386).
[18] Rosario.
[19] History Channel.
[20] History Channel.
[21] History Channel.
[22] Nye.
[23] Katz, p. 21.
[24] Katz.
[25] Katz, p. 58.
[26] Katz, p. 86.
[27] Reiss, I. L., & Reiss, H. M. (2001). The stalled sexual revolutions of this century. In Davidson & Moore (pp. 3–15), p. 4.
[28] Koch.
[29] White, K. (1999). The deconstruction of Victorian sexuality. In Nye (pp. 314–317), p. 316.
[30] White, p. 316–317.
[31] Koch, p. 381.
[32] Katz p. 92.
[33] See: http://www.aasect.org
[34] Koch.
[35] Koch, p. 383.

[36] Rosario.
[37] Nye.
[38] Abelove, H., Barale, M. A., & Halperin, D. M. (Eds.). (1993). *The lesbian and gay studies reader.* New York: Routledge, p. 176.
[39] Abelove et al., p. 176.
[40] Crooks & Baur, p. 240.
[41] Abelove et al., p. 176.
[42] Slagle, R. A. (1995). In defense of Queer Nation: From identity politics to a politics of difference. *Western Journal of Communication, 59,* 85–102, p. 86.
[43] Slagle, p. 98.
[44] Pillard, R. C., & Bailey, J. M. (2001). Human sexual orientation has a heritable component. In Davidson & Moore (pp. 279–294).
[45] Pillard & Bailey.
[46] Byne, W. M. (2001). Why we cannot conclude sexual orientation is a biological phenomenon. In Davidson & Moore (pp. 290–294), p. 294.
[47] Rubin, G. (1993). Thinking sex: Notes for a radical theory of the politics of sexuality. In Abelove et al. (pp. 3–44), p. 34.
[48] Szymanski, D. M., & Gupta, A. (2009). Examining the relationships between multiple oppressions and Asian American sexuality minority persons' psychological distress. *Journal of Gay & Lesbian Social Services, 21*(2), 267–281.
[49] Haber, D. (2009). Gay aging. *Gerontology & Geriatrics Education, 30,* 267–280, p. 277.
[50] Crooks & Baur, p. 18.
[51] Kim, J. L., Sorsoli, C. L., Collins, K., Zylbergold, B. A., Schholer, D., & Tolman, D. L. (2007). From sex to sexuality: Exposing the heterosexual script on primetime network television. *Journal of Sex Research, 44*(2), 145–157.
[52] Kim, et al., p. 154.
[53] Sprecher, S., Harris, G., & Meyers, A. (2008). Perceptions of sources of sex education and targets of sex communication: Sociodemographic and cohort effects. *Journal of Sex Research, 45*(1), 17–26.
[54] Hust, S. J. T., Brown, J. D., & L'Engle, K. (2008). Boys will be boys and girls better be prepared: An analysis of the rare sexual health messages in young adolescents' media. *Mass Communication and Society, 11*(1), 3–23.
[55] Wire, S. D. (April 24, 2008). U.S. funding of abstinence-only programs debated. *LA Times.* http://articles.latimes.com/2008/apr/24/nation/na-abstinence24 (retrieved January 18, 2010); see also: Vesely, R. (October 23, 2006). Some states abstain from abstinence-only funding. *Reproductive Health.* http://www.womensnews.org/story/reproductive-health/061023/some-states-abstain-abstinence-only-funding (retrieved January 18, 2010).
[56] Bond, B. J., Hefner, V., & Drogos, K. L. (2008). Information-seeking practices during the sexual development of lesbian, gay, and bisexual individuals: The influence and effects of coming out in a mediated environment. *Sexuality & Culture, 13,* 32–50.
[57] Hearn & Parkin.
[58] Hearn & Parkin.
[59] Runblad, G. (2001). Gender, power, and sexual harassment. In D. Vannoy (Ed.), *Gender mosaics: Social perspectives* (pp. 352–362). Los Angeles: Roxbury, p. 352; See, also, the U.S. Equal Employment Opportunity Commission. *Facts about sexual harassment.* http://www.eeoc.gov/facts/fs-sex.html (retrieved June 9, 2003).
[60] Dellinger and Williams.
[61] Spradlin, A. L. (1998). The price of passing: A lesbian perspective on authenticity in organizations. *Management Communication Quarterly, 11*(4), 598–605.
[62] Spradlin, p. 600.
[63] Spradlin, p. 603.
[64] Spradlin, p. 603.
[65] Ward, J., & Winstanley, D. (2005). Coming out at work: Performativity and the recognition and renegotiation of identity. The Editorial Board of *The Sociological Review,* 447–475.

[66] Horan, S. M., & Chory, R. M. (2009). When work and love mix: Perceptions of peers in workplace romances. *Western Journal of Communication, 73*(4), 346–369.
[67] Powell, G. N., & Foley, S. (1998). Something to talk about: Romantic relationships in organizational settings. *Journal of Management, 24*(3), 421–449.
[68] Paul, R. J., & Townsend, J. B. (1998). Managing the workplace romance: Protecting employee and employer rights. *Review of Business, 19*(2), 25–31.
[69] Paul and Townsend.
[70] Horan and Chory.
[71] Overman, S. (1998). When labor leads to love. *HR Focus, 75*(11), 1–4.
[72] Reiss and Reiss.
[73] Wood, J. T. (2011). *Communication mosaics: An introduction to the field of communication* (6th ed.). Belmont, CA: Wadsworth.
[74] Clair, R. (1993). The use of framing devices to sequester organizational narratives: Hegemony and harassment. *Communication Monographs, 60,* 113–136.
[75] Dellinger, K., & Williams, C. (1997). Makeup at work: Negotiating appearance rules in the workplace. *Gender & Society, 11*(2), 151–177.
[76] Richardson, B. K., & Taylor, J. (2009). Sexual harassment at the intersection of race and gender: A theoretical model of the sexual harassment experiences of women of color. *Western Journal of Communication, 73*(3), 248–272, p. 252.
[77] Richardson and Taylor.
[78] Richardson and Taylor, p. 267.
[79] Sexual harassment support in the workplace. http://www.sexualharassmentsupport.org/SHworkplace.html (retrieved January 18, 2010).
[80] U.S. Equal Employment Opportunity Commission. (March 11, 2009). Sexual harassment. http://archive.eeoc.gov/types/sexual_harassment.html (retrieved January 18, 2010).
[81] Reiss and Reiss, p. 14.
[82] Campanile, C. (28 July 2003). School's out. *New York Post.* http://www.nypost.com/p/news/school_out_city_is_launching_first_QKeRisd8Le1wv5OMEUcfSO (retrieved February 24, 2010).

Chapter 7

[1] Smith, C. P. (2007). Support services for students with Asperger's Syndrome in higher education. *College Student Journal, 14*(3), 513–531.
[2] I am extremely grateful to disability studies scholar Amy Vidali for providing invaluable insights and information.
[3] Greenwell, A., & Hough, S. (2008). Culture and disability in sexuality studies: A methodological and content review of literature. *Sex Disability, 26,* 189–196.
[4] United States Government Accountability Office. (October 2009). Higher education and disability. GAO-10-33. http://www.gao.gov/new/items/d1033.pdf (retrieved January 21, 2010).
[5] United States Government Accountability Office.
[6] Waldrop, J., & Stern, S. M. (2003). Disability status: 2000. Census 2000 brief. Washington, DC: U.S. Department of Commerce.
[7] Longmore, P. K., & Umansky, L. (Eds.). (2001). *The new disability history: American perspectives.* New York: New York University Press, p. 12.
[8] Longmore & Umansky, p. 4.
[9] Campbell, F. A. (2008). Exploring internalized ableism using critical race theory. *Disability & Society,* 151–162, p. 155.
[10] Potok, A. (2002). *A matter of dignity: Changing the lives of the disabled.* New York: Bantam Books, p. 12.
[11] Hunt, P. (1998). A critical condition. In T. Shakespeare (Ed.), *The disability reader: Social science perspectives* (pp. 7–19). London: Cassell, p. 16.
[12] Baynton, D. C. (2001). Disability and the justification of inequality in American history. In Longmore & Umansky (pp. 33–57), p. 33.
[13] Baynton, p. 52.

[14] Baynton, pp. 33–34.

[15] U.S. Department of Justice. (September 2005). A guide to disability rights laws. http://www.ada.gov/cguide.htm#anchor62335 (retrieved January 19, 2010).

[16] Barbotte, E., Guillemin, F., Chau, N., & the Lorhandicap Group. (2001). Prevalence of impairments, disabilities, handicaps and quality of life in the general population: A review of the literature. *Bulletin of the World Health Organization, 79*(11), 1047–1055, p. 1047. http://www.who.int/bulletin/archives/79(11)1047.pdf (retrieved January 19, 2010).

[17] Braithwaite, D. O., & Braithwaite, C. A. (2003). "Which is my good leg?": Cultural communication of persons with disabilities. In L. A. Samovar & R. Porter (Eds.), *Intercultural communication: A reader* (10th ed., pp. 165–176). Belmont, CA: Wadsworth., p. 167.

[18] Braithwaite & Braithwaite, p. 167.

[19] Longmore & Umansky.

[20] Longmore & Umansky, p. 19.

[21] Thompson, R. G. (1997). *Extraordinary bodies: Figuring disability in American culture.* New York: Columbia University Press.

[22] Campbell, F. A. (2000). Inciting legal fictions: Disability's date with ontology and the ableist body of the law. *Griffith Law Review, 10,* 42-62., p.151.

[23] Campbell, p. 44.

[24] Longmore & Umansky, p. 2.

[25] Davis, L. J. (1995). *Enforcing normalcy: Disability, deafness, and the body.* London: Verso.

[26] Harlan, S., & Roberts, P. M. (1998). The social construction of disability in organizations. *Work & Occupations, 25*(4), 397–437.

[27] Potok, p. 90.

[28] Barton. L. (1998). Sociology, disability studies and education: Some observations. In Shakespeare (pp. 53–64), p. 55.

[29] Byrom, B. (2001). A pupil and a patient: Hospital schools in progressive America. In Longmore & Umansky (pp. 133–156).

[30] Scotch, R. K. (2001). American disability policy in the twentieth century. In Longmore & Umansky (pp. 375–392), p. 377.

[31] Baroff, G. S. (2000). Eugenics, baby Doe, and Peter Singer: Toward a more perfect society. *Mental Retardation, 38*(1), 73–77.

[32] Allen, G. E. Social origins of eugenics. http://www.eugenicsarchive.org/html/eugenics/essay/1text.html (retrieved January 19, 2010)

[33] Allen.

[34] Topic: Fitter family contests. http://www.eugenicsarchive.org/eugenics/topics_fs.pl?theme=8&Search=&matches= (retrieved January 19, 2010).

[35] Micklos, D. None without hope: *Buck v. Bell* at 75. http://www.karmak.org/archive/2001/06/buckvbell.html (retrieved January 19, 2010).

[36] Beckwith, J. (1993). A historical view of social responsibility in genetics. *Bioscience 43*(5), 327–333, p. 327).

[37] The eugenics movement in the U.S. http://www.notdeadyet.org/eughis.html (retrieved January 20, 2010).

[38] Longmore & Umansky, p. 9.

[39] Fawcett, B. (2000). *Feminist perspectives on disability.* Harlow Essex, England: Pearson, p. 22.

[40] Baynton.

[41] Baynton, p. 36.

[42] Scotch, p. 385.

[43] Corker, M. (1998). Disability discourse in a postmodern world. In Shakespeare (pp. 221–233), p. 221.

[44] Scotch, p. 378.

[45] Center for Independent Living. (2005). History of CIL. http://www.cilberkeley.org/history.htm (retrieved January 20, 2010).

[46] Heumann, J. E. (2003). Foreword to Independent living movement. *International Experiences,* by J. Alonso and V. Garcia. http://www.independent/living.org/docs6/heumann2003.html (retrieved January 20, 2010).

47 Potok, p. 35; Bennett, L. (2001). Wheels of justice. In M. Fleming (Ed.), *A place at the table* (pp. 108–117). New York: Oxford University Press.
48 People First History. http://www.people1.org/about_us_history.htm (retrieved January 20, 2010).
49 Potok, p. 51.
50 U.S. Equal Employment Opportunity Commission. U.S. Department of Justice Civil Rights Division. (October 9, 2008). Americans with Disabilities Act: Questions and Answers. http://www.ada.gov/qandaeng.htm (retrieved January 20, 2010).
51 U.S. Equal Employment Opportunity Commission. (August 1, 2008). The ADA: Your responsibilities as an employer. http://www.eeoc.gov/facts/ada17.html (retrieved January 20, 2010).
52 Harlan & Roberts.
53 Crawford, C. H. (February 2003). Disability power: Do we have the will? *The Braille Forum 41*(6). http://www.acb.org/magazine/2003/bf022003.html#bf02 (retrieved January 20, 2010).
54 Longmore & Umansky, p. 11.
55 Branson, J., & Miller, D. (2002). *Damned for their difference: The social construction of deaf people as disabled.* Washington, DC: Gallaudet University Press.
56 Solomon, A. (May 25, 2008). The autism rights movement. New York News and Features. http://nymag.com/news/features/47225/ (retrieved January 20, 2010).
57 Potok, p. 49.
58 Lanham, S. (March 23, 2009). Disability 101—People First Language. http://www.summitdaily.com/article/20090329/NEWS/903299993/1057&title=Disability%20101%20%People-First%20Language (retrieved January 20, 2010); see also, Snow, K. (2009) People first language. http://disabilityisnatural.com/images/PDF/pfl09.pdf (retrieved January 20, 2010).
59 Fox, S. A., & Giles, H. (1996). Interability communication: Evaluating patronizing encounters. *Journal of Language and Social Psychology, 15*(3), 265–290. For a review of theories about interability communication, see Fox, S. A., Giles, H., Orbe, M. P., & Boorhis, R. Y. (2000). Interability communication: Theoretical perspectives. In D. O. Braithwaite & T. L. Thompson (Eds.), *Handbook of communication and people with disabilities: Research and application* (pp. 193–222). Mahwah, NJ: Lawrence Erlbaum.
60 Wolfson, K., & Norden, M. F. (2000). Film images of people with disabilities. In Braithwaite & Thompson (pp. 289–305).
61 Farnall, O., & Smith, K. A. (1999). Reactions to people with disabilities: Personal contact versus viewing of specific media portrayals. *Journalism & Mass Communication Quarterly, 76*(4), 659–672; Harlan & Roberts.
62 Canter, M., & Hurd, G. A. (Producers) & Jimenez, N., & Steinberg, M. (Directors). (1992). *The Waterdance.* Columbia TriStar.
63 Black, R. S., & Pretes, L. (2007). Victims and victors: Representation of physical disability on the silver screen. *Research & Practice for Persons with Severe Disabilities, 32*(1), 66–83.
64 Black & Pretes, p. 80.
65 Farnall & Smith.
66 Potok, pp. 90–91.
67 Graf, N. M., Blankenship, C. J., & Marini, I. (2009). One hundred words about disability. *Journal of Rehabilitation, 75*(2), 25–34.
68 Graf et al., p. 31.
69 Graf et al., p. 31.
70 Braithwaite, D. O. (1996). "I am a person first": Different perspectives on the communication of persons with disabilities. In E. B. Ray (Ed.), *Communication and disenfranchisement: Social health issues and implications* (pp. 257–272). Mahwah, NJ: Lawrence Erlbaum.
71 Braithwaite.
72 Braithwaite & Braithwaite, p. 169.
73 Braithwaite, p. 270.
74 Potok, p. 4.

[75] Braithwaite.
[76] Braithwaite, p. 268.
[77] Potok.
[78] Stone, D. L., & Collela, A. (1996). A model of factors affecting the treatment of disabled individuals in organizations. *Academy of Management Review, 21*(2), 352–402.
[79] Stone & Collela.
[80] Texas Council for Developmental Disabilities. (February 2007). Describing people with disabilities. http://www.txddc.state.tx.us/resources/publications/pfanguage.asp (retrieved January 21, 2010).
[81] Snow, K. Disability is natural. http://www.disabilityisnatural.com/ (retrieved January 21, 2010).
[82] Lanham.
[83] Lanham.
[84] Lanham.
[85] Thompson.
[86] Braithwaite & Braithwaite.
[87] Fox & Giles, p. 269.
[88] Braithwaite, p. 260.
[89] Gill, C. J. (2001). Divided understandings: The social experiences of disability. In G. L. Albrecht, K. D. Seelman, & M. Bury (Eds.), *Handbook of disability studies* (pp. 351–372). Thousand Oaks, CA: Sage, p. 353.
[90] Gill, p. 353.
[91] Gill, p. 362.
[92] Gill, p. 364.
[93] Braithwaite.
[94] Overboe, J. (1999). Difference in itself: Validating disabled people's lived experience. *Body & Society, 5,* 17–29, p. 24.
[95] United Cerebral Palsy Web site. http://www.ucp.org
[96] Office of Disability Employment Policy. (February 2009). The job accommodation network. http://www.dol.gov/odep/pubs/fact/jan.htm (retrieved January 20, 2010).
[97] Schartz, H. A., Hendricks, D. J., & Blanck, P. (2006). Workplace accommodations: Evidence-based outcomes. *Work 27,* 345–354.
[98] Kreps, G. L. (2000). Disability and culture: Effects on multicultural relations in modern organizations. In Braithwaite & Thompson (pp. 177–192).
[99] Herold, K. (2000). Communication strategies in interviews for applicants with disabilities. In Braithwaite & Thompson (pp. 160–175), p. 164.
[100] Harlan & Roberts.
[101] Stefan, S. (2002). *Hollow promises: Employment discrimination against people with mental disabilities.* Washington, DC: American Psychological Association.
[102] Farnall & Smith; Harlan & Roberts.
[103] Leotta, J. (2002). *IBM's disability initiative raises the standard.* The Solutions Marketing Business Group. http://www.disability-marketing.com/profiles/ibm.php4 (retrieved January 20, 2010).
[104] http://www.passionworks.org/about/index.html (retrieved January 20, 2010).
[105] Harter, L. M., Scott, J. A., Novak, D. R., Leeman, M., & Morris, J. F. (2006). Freedom through flight: Performing a counter-narrative of disability. *Journal of Applied Communication Research, 34*(1), 3–29, pp. 25–26
[106] United States Government Accountability Office. (October 2009). Education needs a coordinated approach to improve its assistance to schools in supporting students. http://www.gao.gov/new/items/d1033.pdf (retrieved January 21, 2010).

Chapter 8

[1] *Merriam-Webster's Collegiate Dictionary.* http://www.merriam-webster.com/dictionary/age (retrieved January 27, 2010).

[2] Barker, V., Giles, H., & Harwood, J. (2004). Inter- and intragroup perspectives on intergenerational communication. In J. F. Nussbaum & J. Coupland (Eds.), *Handbook of communication and aging research* (2nd ed., pp. 139–166). Mahwah, NJ: Lawrence Erlbaum.

[3] Coupland, N., & Coupland, J. (1995). Discourse, identity, and aging. In Nussbaum & Coupland (pp. 78–104).

[4] Dychtwald, K. (1999). "Age Power": How the new-old will transform medicine in the twenty-first century. *Geriatrics, 54*(12), 22–27; Dychtwald, K. (1999). *Age power: How the 21st century will be ruled by the new old.* New York: Jeremy P. Tarcher/Putnam.

[5] U.S. Census Bureau (March 3, 2009). Facts for features. Older Americans month: May 2009. http://www.census.gov/Press-Release/www/releases/archives/facts_for_features_special_editions/013384.html (retrieved April 9, 2010).

[6] Administration on Aging. (August 27, 2003). Fact sheet. Older Americans Act: A layman's guide. http://www.co.pierce.wa.us/xml/abtus/ourorg/humsvcs/altc/pierceseniorinfoolderamericansactguide.pdf (retrieved January 25, 2010).

[7] Haber, D. (2009). Gay aging. *Gerontology & Geriatrics Education, 30,* 267–280, p. 270.

[8] Department of Health and Human Services Administration on Aging. (2003). Facts and figures: Statistics on minority aging in the U.S. http://www.aoa.gov/AoAroot/Aging_Statistics/minority_ aging/Index.aspx (retrieved April 9, 2010).

[9] Mather, M. (May 2007). The new generation gap. Population Reference Bureau. http://www.prb.org/Articles/2007/NewGenerationGap.aspx?p=1 (retrieved January 25, 2010).

[10] Takamura, J. (1999). Getting ready for the twenty-first century: The aging of America and the Older Americans Act. *Health and Social Work, 24*(3), 232–238, p. 232.

[11] Calasanti, T. (2000). Incorporating diversity. In E. W. Markson and L. A. Hollis-Sawyer (Eds.), *Intersections of aging: Readings in social gerontology* (pp. 188–202). Los Angeles: Roxbury, p. 192.

[12] Markson, E. W., & Hollis-Sawyer, L. A. (Eds.). (2000). *Intersections of aging: Readings in social gerontology.* Los Angeles: Roxbury, p. 1.

[13] Vogel, S. (July 16, 2009). Age discrimination claims jump, worrying EEOC, worker advocates. *Washington Post.* http://www.washingtonpost.com/wp_dyn/content/article/2009/07/15/AR2009071503760.html (retrieved April 9, 2010).

[14] AARP Web site. About AARP. http://www.AARP.org/aarp/About_AARP (retrieved January 25, 2010).

[15] Couper, D., & Pratt, F. (2005/2006). Aging education for the future. *Continuance Magazine,* p. 3. http://www.iii.siuc.edu.pdf/AgingEducation.pdf (retrieved January 23, 2010).

[16] Couper & Pratt, p. 3.

[17] Markson & Hollis-Sawyer, p. xxix.

[18] Haber, C. (2000). Old age as time of decay. In Markson & Hollis-Sawyer (pp. 39–51).

[19] Barusch, A. (2006). Native American elders: Unique issues and special needs. In B. Berkman (Ed.), *Handbook of social work in health and aging* (pp. 293–300). Cary, NC: Oxford University Press.

[20] Takamura.

[21] Vesperie, M. (2001). Introduction: Media, marketing, and images of the older person in the information age. *Generations, 25*(3), 4–77.

[22] Hutchison, E. D., & Charlesworth, L. W. (2000). Securing the welfare of children: Policies past, present and future. *Families in Society: The Journal of Contemporary Human Services, 81*(6), 576–585.

[23] Fass, P. S., & Mason, M. A. (2000). Introduction. Childhood in America: Past and present. In P. S. Fass & M. A. Mason (Eds.), *Childhood in America* (pp. 1–7). New York: New York University Press, p. 1.

[24] Fass and Mason, p. 3.

[25] Baldwin, P. C. (2002). "Nocturnal habits and dark wisdom": The American response to children in the streets at night, 1880–1930. *Journal of Social History, 35*(3), 593–611

[26] Markson & Hollis–Sawyer.

[27] U.S. Department of Health and Human Services. Administration for Children and Families. http://www.acf.hhs.gov/programs/cb/aboutcb/about_cb.htm (retrieved January 27, 2010).

[28] See: Grossman, J. Fair Labor Standards Act of 1938: Maximum struggle for a minimum wage, Originally in *Monthly Labor Review* (June 1978). http://www.dol.gov/asp/programs/history/flsa1938.htm#* (retrieved September 9, 2003).

[29] Regulating teen labor. (2001). *Federal Bank of Boston Review, 11*(2), p. 22.

[30] West, E. (1996). *Growing up in twentieth century America*. Westport, CT: Greenwood Press.

[31] Dychtwald.

[32] Raines, C. (1997). *Beyond generation X: A practical guide for managers*. Menlo Park, CA: Crisp.

[33] Zemke, R., Raines, C., & Filipczak, B. (2000). *Generations at work: Managing the clash of veterans, boomers, xers, and nexters in your workplace*. New York: AMACOM, pp. 13–14.

[34] O'Neil, E. (2002). Shaping America's health care professions: How the health sector will respond to "generation X." *The Western Journal of Medicine, 176*(12), 39–42.

[35] Markson & Hollis-Sawyer.

[36] Sellers, J. B. (2000). Rural Navajo and Anglo elders aging well. In Markson & Hollis-Sawyer (pp. 368–374), p. 372.

[37] Johnson, C. L. (2000). Adaptation of old black Americans. In Markson & Hollis-Sawyer (pp. 133–141).

[38] Reio, T. G., & Sanders-Reio, J. (1999). Combating workplace ageism. *Adult Learning, 11*(1), 10–13.

[39] Trethewey, A. (2001). Reproducing and resisting the master narrative of decline: Midlife professional women's experiences of aging. *Management Communication Quarterly, 15*(2), 183–226, p. 186.

[40] McGuire, S. L. (2005/2006). Finding positive books about aging for young readers. *Continuance Magazine*, p. 5. http://www.iii.siuc.edu.pdf/AgingEducation.pdf (retrieved January 25, 2010).

[41] Pratt, F., & Cooper, D. (2005/2006). A word about the future. *Continuance Magazine*, p. 6. http://www.iii.siuc.edu.pdf/AgingEducation.pdf (retrieved January 25, 2010).

[42] O'Neil.

[44] Ng, S. H., Liu, J. H., Weatherall, A., & Loong, C. F. (1997). Younger adults' communication experiences and contact with elders and peers. *Human Communication Research, 24*(1), 82–109, p. 82.

[44] Williams, A., & Giles, H. (1996). Intergenerational conversations: Young adults' retrospective accounts. *Human Communication Research, 23*(2), 220–250, p. 224.

[45] Williams & Giles.

[46] Williams & Giles, p. 224.

[47] Williams & Giles.

[48] Hummert, M. L., Shaner, J. L., Garstka, T. A., & Henry, C. (1998). Communication with older adults: The influence of age stereotypes, context, and communicator age. *Human Communication Research, 25*(1), 124–152.

[49] Raman, P., Harwood, J., Weis, D., Anderson, J. L., & Miller, G. (2008). Portrayals of older adults in U.S. and Indian magazine advertisements: A cross-cultural comparison. *Howard Journal of Communications, 19,* 221–240, p. 221.

[50] One magazine subscription site on the Internet site lists 68 magazines for teens! http://www.magazines.com/category/teen (retrieved January 25, 2010).

[51] Wainwright, D. K., Nagler, R., & Serazio, M. J. (2007). Buy me, be me: Gender, sexuality, and thin-ideal messages in teen magazine advertisements. Paper presented at the annual meeting of the NCA 93rd Annual Convention, Chicago, IL.

[52] Wainwright et al.

[53] Ng et al.

[54] Ng et al.; Williams & Giles.

[55] Ryan, E. B., Giles, H., Bartolucci, G., & Henwood, K. (1986). Psycholinguistic and social psychological components of communication by and with the elderly. *Language and Communication, 6,* 1–24; Harwood, J., Giles, H., Fox, S., Ryan, E. B., & Williams, A. (1993). Patronizing young and elderly adults: Response strategies in a community setting. *Journal of Applied Communication Research, 21,* 211–226.

[56] Williams & Giles; Ng et al.

[57] Thimm, C., Rademacher, U., & Kruse, L. (1998). Age stereotypes and patronizing messages: Features of age-adapted speech in technical instructions to the elderly. *Journal of Applied Communication Research, 26*(1), 66–82, p. 66.

[58] Hummert, M. L., Shaner, J. L., & Garstka, T. A. (1995). Cognitive processes affecting communication with older adults: The case for stereotypes, attitudes, and beliefs about communication. In Nussbaum & Coupland (pp. 105–131).

[59] Williams & Giles.

[60] Ota, H., Giles, H., & Somera, L. P. (2007). Beliefs about intergenerational communication in Japan, the Philippines, and the United States: Implication for older adults' subjective well-being. *Communication Studies, 58*(2), 173–188.

[61] Williams & Giles.

[62] Williams & Giles.

[63] Ota et al.

[64] Ota et al.

[65] Ota et al., p. 185.

[66] Williams & Giles, p. 233.

[67] Williams & Giles.

[68] Williams & Giles, p. 238.

[69] Williams & Giles, p. 240.

[70] Williams & Giles, p. 243.

[71] Edwards, H., & Giles, H. (1998). Across the ages: Why generational communication matters. *Communication World, 15*(7), 21–25.

[72] Zemke et al., p. 11.

[73] Zemke et al., p. 13–14.

[74] Zemke et al., p. 17.

[75] Zemke et al., p. 2.

[76] Wilson, S. (2009). Does OLD mean UNEMPLOYABLE: Beware of ageism by euphemism. http://www.barrymaher.com/ageism.htm (retrieved April 9, 2010).

[77] Wilson.

[78] Capowski, G., & Peak, M. H. (1994). Ageism: The new diversity issue. *Management Review, 83*(10), 10–16.

[79] Age Discrimination in Employment Act Charges FY 1997–FY 2008. U.S. Equal Employment Opportunity Commission. http://www1.eeoc.gov//eeoc/statistics/enforcement/adea.cfm? (retrieved January 25, 2010).

[80] Steinhauser, S. (January 1999). Successfully managing an age diverse workforce. *Managing Diversity, 8*(4). http://clem.mscd.edu/~steinhas/managing_diversity.htm (retrieved January 25, 2010).

[81] AARP.

[82] Freeman, N. K., & King, S. (2001). Service learning in preschool: An intergenerational project involving five-year-olds, fifth graders, and senior citizens. *Early Childhood Education Journal, 28*(4), 211–217, p. 213.

Chapter 9

[1] Gallos, J. V., & Ramsey, V. J. (1997). *Teaching diversity: Listening to the soul, speaking from the heart.* San Francisco, CA: Jossey-Bass, p. 220.

[2] Rosenblum, K. E., & Travis, T. C. (2003). *The meaning of difference: American constructions of race, sex and gender, social class, and sexual orientation*. Boston: McGraw-Hill.

[3] Yep, G. A. (2002). My three cultures. Navigating the multicultural identity landscape. In J. N. Martin, T. K. Nakayama, & L. A. Flores (Eds.), *Readings in intercultural communication: Experiences and contexts* (pp. 60–66). Boston: McGraw-Hill, p. 63; Also see: Freire, P. (1970). *Pedagogy of the oppressed.* New York: Continuum.

[4] Yep, p. 60.

[5] Johnson, A. (2006). *Privilege, power, and difference* (2nd ed.). New York: McGraw-Hill.

[6] Thanks to Sonja Foss for this idea.
[7] Covey, S. R. (1989). *The 7 habits of highly effective people. Powerful lessons in personal change.* New York: Simon and Schuster, p. 72.
[8] *Merriam Webster's On-Line Dictionary.* http://www.m-w.com/cgi-bin/dictionary?book=Dictionary&va=proactive
[9] Covey.
[10] Johnson, A. G. (2010). Excerpt from privilege, power, and difference. http://www.agjohnson.us/books/privilege/excerpt-from-privilege-power-and-difference/ (retrieved April 14, 2010).
[11] Johnson (2010).
[12] Spradlin, A. (1998). The price of "passing": A lesbian perspective on authenticity in organizations. *Management Communication Quarterly, 11,* 598–605.
[13] See, for example, Multicultural Pavilion. (1995–2009). http://www.edchange.org/multicultural/index.html (retrieved February 3, 2010).
[14] Fassett, D., & Warren, J. (2007). *Critical communication pedagogy.* Thousand Oaks, CA: Sage.
[15] Allen, B. J. (In Press). Critical communication pedagogy as a framework for teaching difference. In D. Mumby (Ed.), *Organizing difference: Pedagogy, research, and practice.* Thousand Oaks, CA: Sage.
[16] Johnson (2006), pp. 133–134.
[17] Johnson (2006), p. 135.
[18] See: Lahiri, I. & Jensen, K. (2002). *Uncovering classism: A checklist for organizations.* Available on-line from the GilDeane Group. http://www.workforcedevelopmentgroup.com/popu/articles_uncovering-classism.html (retrieved February 3, 2010).
[19] University of Wisconsin Madison Office for Equity and Diversity. http://www.oed.wisc.edu/p_i.html#seed (retrieved April 15, 2010).
[20] Covey, p. 72.
[21] Anti-Defamation League.(2005). *Positive impact: Tools for respecting differences.* Denver, CO: ADL.
[22] Orbe, M. P. (1998). *Constructing co-cultural theory: An explication of culture, power, and communication.* Thousand Oaks, CA: Sage.
[23] Williams, A., & Giles, H. (1996). Intergenerational conversations: Young adults' retrospective accounts. *Human Communication Research, 23*(2), 220–250, p. 224.
[24] Ryan, E. B., Meredith, S. D., MacLean, M. J., & Orange, J. B. (1995). Changing the way we talk with elders: Promoting health using the Communication Enhancement model. *The International Journal of Aging & Human Development, 41*(2), 89–108.
[25] Gibb, J. (1961). Defensive communication. *The Journal of Communication, 11,* 141–148.
[26] Jennifer Simpson, private correspondence, April 11, 2003. She elaborates: "As a concept, it seems to have its roots in early iterations of sexual harassment training." BNA Communications produced video-based training programs on sexual harassment, including *Intent vs. Impact*, created by Stephen Anderson, a nationally known harassment expert. (see: http://www.andersondavis.com).
[27] Simpson.
[28] Foss, S. A., & Foss, K. A. (2003). *Inviting transformation: Presentational speaking for a changing world.* Long Grove, IL: Waveland Press.
[29] Barrett, F., & Fry, R. E. (2005). *Appreciative inquiry: A positive approach to building cooperative capacity.* Chagrin Falls, OH: Taos Institute.
[30] Arnett, R. D., Harden Fritz, J. C., & Bell, L. M. (2009). *Communication ethics literacy: Dialogue and difference.* Thousand Oaks, CA: Sage.
[31] Wolvin, A. D. (2010). *Listening and human communication in the 21st century.* Malden, MA: Blackwell.
[32] Johnson (2006), pp. 142–143.
[33] Southern Poverty Law Center. *Speak up.* http://www.splcenter.org/sites/default/files/downloads/publication/SPLCspeak_up_handbook_0.pdf (retrieved April 15, 2010).
[34] Bates-Ballard, D., & Smith, G. (2008). *Navigating diversity: An advocate's guide through the maze of race, gender, religion and more.* © Patty-Bates Ballard and Gregory Smith.
[35] Mayfield, M. (2010). *Thinking for yourself: Developing critical thinking skills* (8th ed.). Boston: Wadsworth.

Index